The Language of Cricket

Also from Carcanet

Fly-fishing: a book of words
C. B. McCully

Horse Racing: a book of words
Gerald Hammond

Theatre: a book of words
Martin Harrison

Whisky: a book of words
Gavin D. Smith

John Eddowes

The Language of Cricket

CARCANET

No later ed. 03/12

First published in Great Britain in 1997 by
Carcanet Press Limited
4th Floor, Conavon Court
12–16 Blackfriars Street
Manchester M3 5BQ

A CIP catalogue record for this book
is available from the British Library.
ISBN 1 85754 270 3

The publisher acknowledges financial assistance
from the Arts Council of England.

Set in 10pt Plantin by CentraCet, Cambridge.
Printed and bound in England by SRP Ltd, Exeter.

General Editors' Preface

This series offers a new conception and analysis of the vocabularies used in our sports, pursuits, vocations and pastimes. While each book contains an essential lexicon of words and phrases – explored historically and in depth – each also contains generous quotation, practical reference, anecdote and conjecture. The result is more than a dictionary: specific, inclusive, thought-provoking, each volume offers the past and present through a weave of words, in all their curiosity and delight.

Those intrigued by the language particular to their area of interest will find the relevant book a coherent and challenging treatment of the topic; those interested in the English language itself will find the series yielding significant material on semantic scope and change; and general readers who wish to understand the vocabularies of human endeavour will find the series tracing the necessary but implacable relationships between words and world.

Editors, chosen because of their intimate enthusiasm for their subjects, have been encouraged to be comprehensive in their coverage: vocabularies typically range from the demotic to the esoteric, from slang to the technical and specialised. Within that range, emphasis is also placed on *how* each lexicon developed, and *why* its terms acquired their peculiar descriptive power. These are books to read with pleasure as well as keep on the reference shelf.

Gerald Hammond
C. B. McCully

Acknowledgements

Thanks for their help to David Terry, of the British Society of Sports Historians, and to Tony Brown of the Test and County Cricket Board. The book would have been impossible without H. S. Altham's *A History of Cricket*, the assistance of the staff of the British Library, E. W. Swanton, Dr Heiner Gillmeister of the University of Bonn, and of Stephen Green, Curator MCC (in particular his monograph on early mentions of the game. and his saving me from one egregious error) and his assistants. MCC is also thanked for permission to quote selectively from the Laws. Thanks must also be given to the Curator at the Melbourne Cricket Club. With great generosity, Peter Wynne-Thomas of the Association of Cricket Statisticians gave me full access to his collection of historical material, and checked the MS. Stephen Griffiths and T. J. McCann of the West Sussex Record Office furnished much material, both from previous writings and from their research and local knowledges, as did the Sussex Archaeological Society. John Goulstone gave valuable help, as did Angus Prain and M. S. C. Harding of the Gentlemen of Hampstead and the Non-Conformists CC. Thanks also to the Cricket Society, and to Patricia Hughes for her research.

Thanks are given to: BBC Radio and Television, BSB Sky TV, ABC TV; *Daily Telegraph, Sunday Telegraph, The Times, Sunday Times, Observer, Evening Standard, Independent, Independent on Sunday, Daily Mail, Mail on Sunday, The Advertiser, The Cricketer International, The Third Man, Wisden Cricket Monthly.*

Thanks are given to all the writers who generously gave permission for their work to be used. Valuable insights came from C. J. Wright's *Guide to the Pilgrims' Way and North Downs Way*, and from Dom John Bolton of the Benedictines of Worth Abbey. The section on 'swing' is an all-too-brief account of a complex set of phenomena, but owes much of the work of Dr Brian Wilkins, E. Palfrey FIS, and Dr Rabi Mehta, now of NASA. Not all these authorities are in agreement. Oxford University Press and the staff of the Oxford English Dictionary were unstinting with their time and permission to quote, in particular from W. J. Lewis's *The Language of Cricket* (1934), the prime source for many of the words and their journey into the language of today.

Copyright quotations from books by C. L. R. James, Richie Benaud OBE, and Simon Raven, are reproduced by kind permission of the Curtis Brown Group Ltd, London. The extract from *Fred Now and Then* by Don Mosey is reprinted by kind permission of Reed Consumer Books; the extracts from *Boycott on Cricket* are reprinted by kind permission of Partridge Press and Transworld Publishing. The extracts from P. G. Wodehouse's work are reproduced courtesy of A. P. Watt on behalf of the Trustees of the Wodehouse Trust.

Many writers are undeservingly neglected in these pages: the literature of cricket is so vast that one Vandal can make but a feeble attempt at sacking it.

Abbreviations

Du: Dutch
Fr: French
Gk: Greek
OE: Old English
OF: Old French
OG: Old German
ON: Old Norse

OED: Oxford English Dictionary
ODEtym: Oxford Dictionary of Etymology

BLC: Badminton Library of Sports and Pastimes: *Cricket*, first
edition 1888 and subsequent editions
H. P.–T.: Percy Francis Thomas, who wrote six pamphlets
collectively entitled *Old English Cricket* under these initials
(translated variously as HyPoTheticas, Hippo Pot Thomas)
P. W.–T.: refers to the private collection of Peter Wynne-
Thomas
WCM: *Wisden Cricket Monthly*

Introduction

'Cricket is an art. Like all arts it has a technical foundation. To enjoy it does not require technical knowledge, but analysis that is not technically based is mere impressionism.' Thus the West Indian writer, C.L.R. James, in *Beyond a Boundary*. One of the purposes of this book is to increase that enjoyment, to help remove the puzzlement caused by such mentions as 'bowlers hitting the deck'. To take another example, today millions would know immediately the identity of a young man were he described merely as 'an eccentric purveyor of spitting googlies and bouncing Chinamen', but might not know what exactly was his stock in trade (the answer is under *action*). The words have been chosen as being where possible the most expressive. I thought it wrong to restrict myself to first-class cricket, or to reject archaic usage where it is picturesque, forceful, or shows how the game developed. And of all the words in the game, 'cricket' fills that bill the fullest.

At the end of the seventeenth century, rather suddenly, a game seemed to be widespread in the south of England. It was well enough known to be mentioned in two dictionaries, and common enough to be mentioned in law-court records without explanation of what it was. At the end of the eighteenth century, it was played by all classes, played by a gallery of figures as colourful as any we see today. In the nineteenth, with its connotations of fair play, and some danger, it became one of the adjutants of Empire. The origins were mysterious. The word 'cricket' has a sprightly onomatopoeia, yet it seemed chimerical; the game itself had unique qualities: unpredictable, unfair, beautiful above all others, yet a social, even political cement as no other has ever been.

   For long it was thought that 'cricket' was from *crycc*, the Old English term for 'a shepherd's staff'. This contributed to the idea that the game had come to the Saxon shore, becoming the product of the shepherds and villages in the Weald, then a trackless forest between the North and South Downs, avoided by Romans and Normans alike, who built their roads around it.

   But the *Oxford English Dictionary* says 'cricket' cannot come from the Anglo-Saxon, for the 'cc' indicates a palatal consonant. Dr John Considine, an Assistant Editor, says 'Old English *crycc* is certainly the same word as early Middle English *crucche* and late Middle English *crutche*, so it cannot be the etymon of "cricket": if it had been, the form would necessarily have been **crutchet*.[1] I think that Flemish *krik* is therefore the likeliest etymon.' Dr Heiner Gillmeister, of the University of Bonn, also rules out 'the possibility of an Old English/Middle English root of *cricket*, i.e. OE *crycc*, from Germanic **krukjo–* – present English *crutch* – because the final velar stop underwent palatization in Old English.' The assumption of a local variation would be highly speculative, and it would be very unusual to form a diminutive with a foreign suffix, in this case -*et*, from the French. 'On the other hand, it is very likely that the Germanic root **krukjo-*, meaning "curved stick", formed the basis of the word all the same.'

There might seem little difference in this difference: there is after all a proto-Indo-European root *ger-*, to bend or hook, which with the *g* changing by Grimm's law of devoicing to *k*, leads to a number of words throughout European languages such as *krucka*, a stick. Dr Considine considers there is no reason to postulate an unattested Old English -*et* suffix in the case of 'cricket', and does not, in this case, personally find it convincing. There is, moreover, no -*et* suffix as such in Dutch, which is almost indistinguishable from Flemish. What, then, is the ancestry of the game?

Before looking at the roots of the word and the game, some of the earliest assumed mentions must be cleared up, starting with the most famous. In 1300 the chaplain John de Leck and the chamberlain Hugo to Prince Edward, the son of Edward I, were reimbursed for the money laid out by them for the prince, specifically 'ad ludendum ad *creag* et alios ludos. . . . apud newenton mense martii 20s. – summa 6.0.0.' – playing at 'creag' and other games, at Newenton in March, 20 shillings, total six pounds: a lot of money. At first sight there seems to be no other word but something similar to cricket that 'creag' can mean, and it has long been taken as that.

But Dr Considine says 'creag' must be the same as the medieval Latin *greachia* (the letters 'c' and 'g' were often transliterated, both in Latin and English). The dissolute young prince is found again in 1305, again with his chaplain: 'Domino

---

1. Asterisks in front of a word denote a reconstructed form not instanced in a written text. 'Velar' refers to a sound formed by contact with the soft palate.

Johanni de Leck, capellanos Domino Edwardi fil' ad creag et
alios ludos per manus proprias 100s. Apud Westm. 10 die
Aprilis.' Again, a large sum of money, paid out by the chaplain's
own hands, and the probability of a game of chance. The entries
support the *Anglo-Norman Dictionary*, which suggests that 'creag'
or 'greachia' was a dicing game. A manuscript of 1306 in the
Public Record Office refers to an innkeeper 'indictatus . . . quod
noctantur . . . receptat ludentes ad greachiam'. *Indicare* is to
inform against, betray, so the publican was running a late night
game. 'Creag' does not appear to mean cricket.

The next recorded mention of cricket is said to be in 1487
when, in the Archives de France, 'un cannonier' left the Chateau
of Liettes (close to St Omer in the Pas de Calais) and then 'arriva
en ung lieu ou on jouoit a la boule pres d'une atache ou criquet
. . .' The reason the incident is preserved is that the gunner gave
an opinion on the state of the game, a player said to him 'Why
do you speak about our bowls? Do not speak further about them,
any more than I do when you are playing . . .'(or words to that
effect). The player received a javelin wound in his arm, from
which he died the following day.

'Criquet' was supposed to be a clarifying synonym for 'atache',
which had a number of meanings, such as 'vine-stake'. And it
passed into Huguet's *Dictionnaire de la Langue Francaise de la
XVIme Siecle*, and is repeated in Godefroy's *Dictionnaire de
l'Anciene Langue Francais* of 1881–1902. However, the philolo-
gist Leonard Hector examined the text, and found that the word
taken as 'criquet' was in fact 'etiquet', which already had the
meaning 'petit pieu qui sert de but a certains jeux'. He pointed
out in the *Journal of the Society of Archivists* (Vol. 4, 1970-3,
pp. 579–80) that 'criquet' in the 'sense required is found
nowhere else in the French literature of any date.' He observed,
somewhat tartly, that 'it must be rare indeed that a *hapax
legomenon* interprets, instead of being interpreted by, a relatively
commonplace word.'

Also misleading is the translation of one of Gargantua's games
as cricket *c.* 1550, the French reading that he played 'a la crosse',
more probably referring to early hockey or golf than to cricket,
the word 'crosse' today being applied to the stick and club, but
not the bat, and having the primary meaning of a bishop's crook
or crozier.

The last of the pretenders is the earliest. It takes us back to the
gates of Troy. Joseph of Exeter, the Swan of Iscanus, cleric and
crusader (fl. *c.* 1200) wrote his own Iliad in Latin, and a couplet
has always been translated thus: 'Throughout the livelong day /

The youth at cricks did play'. This is Teuthras the dead Trojan, meditating from the shades on the ages of man. However, A.K. Bate of the Classics Department of the University of Reading translates it thus: 'The next age, the little boy, incessantly occupied, / Tires himself, now with a rolling ball, now the spinning top, now the bow . . .' Not cricket at all.

The removal of all the above mean that the earliest date for cricket is given at the Court Leet held in Guildford on 'Monday after the feast of St Hilary in the fortieth year of our lady Elizabeth', or 1598. A coroner of the town, John Derrick, gave a statement relating to an enclosure, including the words: 'And also this deponent saith that hee being a scholler in the free Schole of Guildford, hee and diverse of his fellowes did runne and plaie there at Creckett and other plaies'.[2] Derrick was then fifty-nine, so he would be playing *c.* 1550 onwards. This date is important, and we shall come back to it later. It is also worth noting that Derrick is derived from the Flemish 'Hendrik'.

Meanwhile, from the gates of Troy another thread reaches, first to chivalry in Northern France and Flanders, now northern Belgium, bordering the Channel then as far as Dunkirk, and then to the shores of Kent.

The *Roman de Troie* by Benoit de Saint-Maure, from the second half of the twelfth century, at the date Joseph was writing, recounts from the *Iliad* the defence of the Trojan gate by Deiphobos against the Greeks. The Trojans then sally, and under Hector break through the surrounding Greek ramparts, Hector himself battering in the Greek gate, driving them back to their black ships.

Dr Gillmeister sees modern ball games as based on the first romantic revival of the age of chivalry. The tournaments of the day often included 'the passage of arms', in which a narrow passage was defended by a group of knights against an equal number. One of these was the re-enactment of the Pas de Saladin, the defence of a narrow defile, by Christian knights against Saladin. This was frequently depicted on the walls of the halls of medieval castles. Another was the more common assault on the gate of a walled city, the weak point of the wall, as at Troy, or later. Gillmeister argues that 'competitive ball games could be viewed as adaptations by the lower classes of medieval society of the chivalric tournament.' And he sees the early French game of 'soule' as the ancestor of most competitive European

2. Ref. BR/OC/1/2, reproduced by kind permission of the Surrey Record Office, Guildford Muniment Room.

ball games, including 'Soule a la crosse', which seems to be a form of hockey, with the goal the town gate. The Northern French version is 'choule', and 'chulle' is found in a Yorkshire dialect poem of about 1400, implying, as we shall see later, a earlier wave of ball games not going under the name of cricket, however similar.

The early term of cricket goes back to a Flemish phrase *met dekrik ketsen*, literally 'to chase with a curved stick'. This was shortened to *krikets*, which finally became *cricket*. A parallel development resulted in *rackets* from an underlying **raketsen*, 'to chase back'. In both cases use was made of the Flemish verb *ketsen*, a loan from the Northern French *cachier*, a variant of Parisian French *chasser*, 'to chase'. In either case, too, the final *s* was dropped, because it was considered as a marker of an English plural. That is why Chaucer as early as 1385 could mention a game of *raket* which, he said, was played to and fro . . . from the 13th century onwards, ball games, if not invented altogether new, at least began to be brought into conformity with the rules and terminology observed in the passage of arms.[3]

Far-fetched? Certainly wide-ranging, but Dr Considine sees fewer problems with this derivation than any other.

This all went on over a period of centuries, when languages were developing, without fully standardised conventions of orthography. Loan-words are often altered to look like words in the receiving language. *Krik*, or *krek*, was used over a wide area in Northern France and Flanders. *Caet bal* is translated as 'esteuf àla main' (handball) in Meunier's 1562 *Vocabulaire Francois-Flameng*, and the 1592 edition of Mellema's *Dictionaire Francoys-Flameng* has *De Kaetse int Kaetspel* for 'Chasse de Jeu de paulme'. Spellings based on Dutch or Flemish, two extremely similar languages, are often used in the very early mentions of cricket.

The basic words of the game are best explained by Flemish derivation.

Sometimes a seemingly obviously English word has an equivalent not in Dutch but in Flemish, for example 'ball'. A casual observer might think it comes from French *bal*, but the OED derives it from Middle English *bal* and Old Norse *bo'llr*, and gives OTeut. **ballu-z* whence probably MHG *bal, balles* and

---

3. Dr Heiner Gillmeister 'The Flemish Ancestry of Early English Ball Games: the Cumulative Evidence' in N. Müller and J.K. Rühl (eds), *Olympic Scientific Congress: Sport History . . . Official Report* (Niedernhausen: Schors-Verlag, 1985). Dr Gillmeister also derives 'hockey' from the French diminutive 'hoquet' of the Flemish 'hok' or 'hoek', a curved stick.

Middle Dutch *bal*. Not from the French: 'the later ME spelling
balle coincided graphically with Fr. *balle* and *bale*, which has
hence been erroneously assumed to be the same.' The Dutch
form is *bal*, pronounced not unlike the English 'ball'. Meunier
translates 'bale a jouer' as *bal*, Sasbout in his *Dictionaire Flamen-
Francoys*, published in Antwerp in 1576 has *bal* for 'pile' (which
goes back to the Latin), and the 1682 *Dictionnaire Francois-
Flamen* of D'Arsy and Mellema gives 'boule' as *een bol*, and
'bouler' as *bollen*.

'Bat' could come, says the OED, from either OFr *batte*, or OE
bat, (see entry under ***bat***), perhaps from the Celtic. And the first
bats we know of were not unlike a shepherd's crook or hockey
stick. Again, we do not know whether this was to cope with the
trundling style or because they were indeed pastoral implements,
crooked so the shepherd could catch the hind leg of his charges.

A 'Famous Old Cricketer', quoted by the Revd James Pycroft,
one of the early historians of the game, was born in 1675, and he
said that 'when I was a boy every cottage in the cricket playing
districts in Kent had a well-greased bat either kept in the bacon-
rack or hung up behind the kitchen door.' And *his* grandfather
before him had been a famous player. What those districts were
we don't know: it was, says H. P.-T., 'a peculiarity of the jargon
of that county (Kent) that almost any handleable piece of wood
there got called a bat', such as the washing beetle or 'copper-
stick': bands of smugglers were known as Batsmen 'from their
carrying stout ashen poles, five or six feet long, called bats'.

But 'bat' does not appear to have been the original word
applied to the implement, so it does not detract from the Flanders
derivation. 'Bat' has its apparently first dictionary mention ('A
club to strike the ball with, at the play called Cricket') in N.
Bailey's *An Universal Etymological Dictionary* (1721), long after
'stave'.

Two medieval illustrations show a straight stick. A manuscript
in the Bodleian library shows an early Flemish version, where a
nun seems to be offering, or about to throw, a ball at a monk
holding a straight piece of wood. It is also possible that she has
just caught him, to judge by the slightly self-satisfied expression
on her face. Two monks and two nuns in the background seem
to be either fielding or applauding. There is no wicket in the
picture, nor in any other of the illustrations of this time. The
illumination was completed by a Flemish workshop between
1338 and 1344, as can be inferred from two dated colophons at
the end, and this constitutes proof that some sort of bat and ball
game was played, and recognisable, in Flanders at that time. The

other, in the British Library, shows a piece of wood (by pure coincidence uncannily like a stump) being brandished at a ball; again, no wicket. From this evidence, 'bat' does not necessarily imply the shepherd's crook. The word is not found in the Flemish dictionaries of the sixteenth century except meaning 'bath'. Even that early, there seem to be two separate games, one with the straight stick on its way to becoming stoolball and one already like hockey. There are three depictions of players with curved sticks, one on a vessel in the Danish National Museum, from 1333 (Labouchere, Provis, and Hargreaves, *The Story of Continental Cricket*), and another from a fourteenth-century book of prayers, copied in the Great East Window of Gloucester Cathedral, which was made about 1350, and shows two boys with hockey sticks and a ball, very possibly at the ancient Franco-Flemish game of *soule*. But the most detailed and striking is in the British Library, in the illuminated manuscript known as *Queen Mary's Psalter*, probably from the second decade of the fourteenth century, and in which biblical stories are depicted. In the panel before Cain kills Abel with a jawbone, they both brandish crooks curved for the hinder leg of sheep and remarkably similar to hockey sticks today: Abel holds a ball about 4 inches in diameter. A flock of what are probably small sheep rather than disconsolate armadillos is in the background. The inscription tells us they guard 'leurs bestes' and play at 'festes' with 'crozces' and 'pelottes', a ball: this comes from *pelotter*, meaning *frapper* or hit, so the ball has a sense of being one which is hit. It may be merely a coincidence caused by finding only some of the available mentions, but their close grouping might suggest an early craze – or that returning soldiers had brought the game with them. There were frequently English armies on the Continent, defending the possessions of the Crown: at the time the first references to games are known to appear, *c.* 1150, the county of Boulogne, which then ran up into the area of Flanders, belonged to King Stephen through marriage. And in Ghent in 1340 Edward III, at the head of his impoverished army, assumed the title and the arms of the King of France. So at these early dates there were opportunities for games to be exported into England.[4]

---

4. All this has to be seen *sub specie* H.S. Altham's opening of the first volume of *A History of Cricket*, which has the Egyptians at ninepins five thousand years ago, Nausicaa at ivory-wristed fielding practice with her maidens when Odysseus was discovered, Athenian boys at hockey, while 'only pinkeye stayed Horace and indigestion Virgil from joining Maecenas in a ball game on the famous journey to Brundisium and in A.D. 150 Fronto could write to Marcus Aurelius, with

Of the core words associated with the game, 'Innings' was also notably Kentish, referring to land recovered from the sea in Romney Marsh and enclosed against reinundation (H.P.-T.). The first attested use is given in the OED as 1530, in the singular, fitting reasonably well into the time frame.

'Pitch' is a more basic term, in the sense that a pitch would have to be found and described early on as the game was formed. The OED derivation helps us here, first by giving the meaning '1. To thrust in, fix in; make fast, settle; set, place.' The example given is '*To pitch the wickets* (Cricket) to stick or fix the stumps in the ground and place the bails.' The derivation is given as ME. *piche, picche*. This is not from the French, and also shows, to those who might well doubt it, a confirmation by comparison of the transference of *cryc, crycce*, to 'crutch'. Thus Wyclif has for Numbers 2: 3: 'at the east Judah schal picche his tentis.'

The land measurements involved use eleven as a base, as in the twenty-two yards of the pitch. As Altham points out in his *History of Cricket* (p. 25), the Anglo-Saxon measure of the 'gad' or 'goad', five and a half yards, is a quarter of the chain, 22 yards, the pitch, and is the width of an acre-strip. Long and thin to avoid turning. And 22 yards by a furlong is an acre, the amount of land man and ox could plough in a day. This also has a Flemish equivalent. Rowland Bowen, whose *Cricket: A History of its Growth and Development throughout the World* contains valuable references to early cricket in Kent and Surrey, also found in Doursther's 1840 *Dictionnaire Universel des Poids et Mesures Anciens et Modernes* that measurements based on eleven were not unique to the Saxon: 'dans plusieurs villes de Belgique et de Hollande telles qu'Anvers, Bruxelles, Malines, Amsterdam etc., le pied se divise en 11 pouces de 8 ou 11 lignes chacun.' 'Ligne' was a measurement of length, the 'Ligne de Paris' being a twelfth of an inch. 'Eleven' in English is the first number which has a wholly Germanic derivation.

Two cricketing words are not apparently Germanic. 'Bail' has an equivalent in OFr *bail*, a cross-beam, but none apparently in Flemish. This may be because the early game did not have the bail, but simply two stones or sticks through which the ball had to be bowled. The illustration in *Les Jeux des Jeunes Garçons, avec une explication et une devise morale*, reprinted in Paris in 1807, shows the wicket as being merely two stones on the

---

reference to an argument between them, "Malitosam pilam mihi dedisti" – you have bowled me a pretty dirty ball!'

ground, two or three feet apart, and the batsman with something like a hockey-stick. The game is called *criquet* and described as 'peu connu en France, mais très-fréquent en Suisse'. Franco-Flemish dictionaries do not have an entry for 'bail'.

'Umpire' is from *impair*, a third party called in to resolve a dispute, the first OED mention being from 1440, in a translation from *Aesop's Fables*: 'Among those owmperis was werre non, ne stryf .' Its derivation from the French means little, as there seems no equivalent in Flemish, and the game would be established before umpires were brought in. The first mention we have, in the Latin poem of 1709 by James Goldwin, refers to 'bini moderatores'. But it is fair to say that these two words probably apply to a later stage of the game, and it is when we come to the aiming-point that the derivation from Flemish is clearest.

The word for 'wicket' was widely known in Northern France and Flanders, and goes further back, to an Old Norse word *vik* with a meaning of hiding place, or small door, appearing as Anglo-Norman *wicket* in the twelfth century. Its use to mean a small door appears in the fifteenth century, with spellings of *wicket, viquet,* and also *guichet,* which is the modern French (von Wartburg, *Französisches Etymologischen Wörterbuch*). *Wicket* meaning 'passage' is found *c.* 1190: a later citation gives it as Belgian Dialect. *Wiket* is found in *Piers Plowman*: Littré has Walloon *wichet,* and Norman *viquet.* As Gillmeister points out, one of the features of northern French is the preservation of 'w' where Central French substituted 'g' (as Guillaume and William). If it did make the voyage as 'v', it may have changed in Kent, as one of the Kentish dialect peculiarities is the substitution of 'w' for 'v' (Pegge's *Alphabet of Kentishisms*, 12): it's how Dickens shows Sam Weller as coming from Kent. So thus we have 'vik', 'viket', becoming 'wicket'. The 1592 edition of Mellema has *winquet* for 'guichet'.

But that is not all. All the other games with aims, and which resemble cricket, derive the word for the target from that area: stoolball, or, less frequently found, stumpball, stoball or stowball. These, particularly stoolball, seem to be earlier arrivals, which travelled further west and north, with very much the kinds of modifications we might expect. With the help of Dr J. Harskamp, head of the Dutch section of the British Library, we found that 'stob' is sometimes used for 'stump', which in turn is *stobbe* in Old Dutch. *Stoel* is Dutch for 'stool', and also a rare and archaic word for 'stump'. 'Stool' in English is a old word for tree-stump, especially in Sussex dialect, 'the roots of copse or hedgewood', says Halliwell, in his *Dictionary of Archaic Words*. Halliwell also has 'stob' as 'a small post'. Stoolball is still played in Hampshire today, and the aim of the game has for long been a target fixed on a post about four feet above ground, possibly so the ball did not have to bounce.

Most telling, 'stump' is in Dutch *stomp*, but is not found in Anglo-Saxon, according to Skeat's *Etymological Dictionary*, which also does not list 'stob'. Neither are found in Bosworth's *Dictionary of the Anglo-Saxon Language*. However the University of Michigan's *Middle English Dictionary* has 'stump' as cognate with MDu *stompe* and MLG *stump* and gives a first reference in 1440: 'Stumpe, of a tree hewyn don'. So it looks rather as if the word came over after the Saxons, from Flanders or Holland. 'Stob' has the following reference from 1324: 'Iche Edward Kynge have yeoven of my forest the keeping . . . To Randolph Peperking . . . With hart and hynd, do and booke. . . With grene and wilde, stob and stokke.' *Stomp* is given as 'soest' in Sasbout, so it seems there was no French word signifying any of the aiming-points of the game.

That all refer to the target strengthens the Franco-Flemish theory, and leads back in turn to the tournament. Gillmeister's thesis has the merit of explaining targets, and for a variety of games apart from cricket, such as football and hockey.

Stoolball appears to have pre-dated cricket. It may well be simply an earlier wave of a bat, ball and target game known in roughly the same way in Flanders. The first mention so far known is in 1450, when Myre forbade its being played in churchyards in his instructions to parish priests. The game does not need level ground, and the number of churchyard complaints of both cricket and stoolball indicate little difference then between the games. Altham has it as a game for both sexes, as it is today, with the milking-stool of the country maidens as a target, and says (1926) it has 'recently enjoyed a welcome resurrection', part of which was because W.W. Grantham realised after the Great War that it could be played with one arm. It is still widely played in Kent, Sussex and Hampshire. Robert Herrick in his *Hesperides* of 1648:

> At stool-ball, Lucia, let us play,
> For sugar-cakes and wine . . .

> If thou, my deere, a winner be
> At trundling of the ball
> The wager shalt thou have, and me,
> And my misfortunes all.

The game had already moved further afield: 'Petrus Frankeleyne posuit iiiixx oves [put 24 sheep] in stoball field contra ordinacionem.' This was in one of the two Kirklingtons, one in north Yorkshire and the other in Nottinghamshire, in 1523. So there was already a degree of organisation – to the extent of having a field set aside to play on – and this form of ball-game had spread much further than the Weald.

Then, in the reign of Elizabeth I, the Earl of Leicester passed through Stratford-upon-Avon in 1587 with his company, the Earl of Leicester's Men. These seem to have included Thomas Pope, George Bryan and William Kemp, later fellow-players of Shakespeare's. It may have been now that Shakespeare joined the troupe. They visited Wotton (Underwood) 'and thence went to Wotton Hill where he plaid a match at stoball.'

In the 1564 Midsummer Quarter Sessions at Malden in Surrey complaints were made that the constables suffered 'stoleball' to be played on Sundays, and there too, in 1583, men were indicted for playing on the Sabbath. In 1592 in Canterbury, Bottolph Wappoll was so enraged at being told to stop playing and go to Divine Service by one of the sidesmen that he 'beat him that the blood ran about his ears'. These are some of the early notices from Grantham's *Stoolball and How to Play It* (1931). There are more of them than of cricket, and more in the literature: Donne, Beaumont and Fletcher, Chapman's translation of the *Odyssey*. It seems there was an earlier and wider diffusion of an almost identical game. Cricket, with its more interesting type of wicket, may have largely supplanted its rivals, and in this intervening process Florio (see below), to make sure people knew what he was talking about, defined it closely, using perhaps the term by which it was then known. The games were seemingly fairly entwined: R.S. Holmes in *A History of Yorkshire County Cricket Club*, (1904), says that fomerly, 'A stool was laid on its side, and a parti-coloured leather ball stuffed with saw dust was bowled at the seat of the stool. The wooden stools . . . were called crickets.' They were indeed, but as Edmund Weiner has pointed out, the word, with that meaning, appeared too late in England to be the source of the game.[5]

5. The Flemish *krickstoel* has also been put forward as a root word: the meaning is a low stool before the hearth, and it seems to fit both the OED's view on 'cricket' as not coming from the palatalised forebear of 'crutch', and 'stool' as an origin of the aiming-point of the game. But 'cricket' as a low stool 'is unlikely to be connected', according to Edmund Weiner, Deputy Chief Editor of the OED: 'It appeared only in the mid-seventeenth century, whereas the name of the game

Two references show the diffusion of the perhaps earlier game of stoolball or stoball, the first from *c.* 1640 in the Vale of Berkeley in Gloucestershire: 'witness to the inbred delight that both gentry, yeomanry, rascallity, boys and children to take in a game called stoball . . . (the boy) at seven was furnished with his double staves and a gamester thereafter'. Then Aubrey, the historian of Wiltshire, in 1667 informs us that 'stoball is peculiar to North Wiltshire, west Gloucestershire and a little part of Somerset near Bath.' The bat was of willow, three and a half feet high, and the leather-covered ball was stuffed with quills and hard as stone. Further on in the same passage the ball has a stone centre wrapped with twine, to make it bounce. This looks very like early cricket, in the area the Grace family lived in two hundred years later. But where, when and how the games separated or merged is probably unknowable now.

Stoolball seems to have migrated: Bowen records it mentioned in Massachusetts on Thanksgiving Day 1621, several cricket matches being played in Virginia almost a hundred years later, in 1709, and an extremely wide and low wicket is pictured in an illustration which seems from the dress of the players to be about 1850, from *100 Years of Philadelphia Cricket* by J.A. Lester (1951), so the old wicket must have lasted there much longer.

Cricket appears, then, on the evidence available, to be one of a series of similar games which crossed the Channel. It is even possible that the name helped it to become the most popular. After all, the Marylebone Stoolball Club in solemn conclave is not as tremulogenic as MCC, and 'Stoolball, lovely stoolball' not the catchiest of tunes. Why did it come to Kent, generally accepted as the cradle of cricket, and do the early spellings of the game reflect its ancestry? We might expect different spellings anyway, but 'k' at the start, 'e' in the middle, and 's' on the end might suggest Flanders.

The cricket historian John Goulstone found the plural form frequently used in East Kent. In 1708 Thomas Minter writes 'Wee beat Ash Street at crekits', Ash Street being near Canterbury, where the *Kentish Post* was published, in which in 1762 and 1763 there are mentions of 'a match at crickets' no less than seven times in June and July, as against one 'cricket match', where 'cricket' is used in a more adjectival sense. White Kennett's

---

was already established in England by 1600' (correspondence with the author). It does, though, show the presence of the word 'krik' in England, and it was evidently in ordinary use.

Parochial Antiquities of 1695 gives 'crickets' – the author though writing of Oxford, was a native of Dover. Kentish dialects are reported from the Bishopbourne area in *Bell's Life*, which covered the game in some depth, in its issue of 8 May 1842: 'they don't give no couragement to crickets now-a-days' and 'crickets is born and bred in us Kent folk.'

At this time the singular was used in London. It is not unreasonable to suppose that the earlier form, coming from *krik, ketsen*, took deepest root where it came earliest.

Does the spread of the game support the theory it came over the narrowest part of the channel?

'The coming of the Flemings is the great industrial romance of Kent. In no direction is the foreign influence to be more productive of far-reaching benefit than with regard to the manufacture of cloth' *(The Victoria History of the County of Kent)*. In 1270 Henry III issued a welcome to 'all workers of woolen cloth'. Behind this was the English remark about the Order of the Golden Fleece of Burgundy (the duchy had considerable possessions in Northern France), that the fleece was ours, but the gold theirs. Edward III sought to have Netherland clothmakers, enticing them with 'unsuspected emissaries' who would approach journeymen and apprentices, telling them they could set up on their own in England and be much better off. English cloth was thick and stiff, like frieze, but the Flemish weavers could produce a cloth woven so fine it was impermeable.

Cranbrook in Kent became the centre of weaving trade after John Kemp, a Flemish clothworker, settled there by royal invitation in 1331. Nearby Tenterden is named after the 'tenters' on which the cloth was stretched. 'The frequent forms of the type *tainter, teinteri* from the 14th to 17th c. suggest assoc. with Fr *teindre*, dye' *(ODEtym)*. 'Tenterhooks' is the survival today. There were, according to W. Cunningham in *The Growth of English Industry and Commerce in Modern Times* (1905), small settlements in Hythe, Cranbrook, Chatham, and Bromley in Kent, Winchester and South Stoneham in Hampshire, Dorking and Esher in Surrey. None are mentioned in Sussex, apart from the extreme west of the county.

When put on a map, the very early mentions of the game show up in clusters. Moving from east to west, the first is around Maidstone, where weaving had been established since 1227, and where in 1640 men were prosecuted for playing cricket on Sunday in the churchyard. The vicar of neighbouring Otham, the Reverend Thomas Wilson, said in 1635 that it 'had been said to be a very prophane town ... insomuch as I have seen ... stool-ball, crickets ... and many other sports openly and publicly on the Lord's day'. 'Crickets', he said, was 'undesirable at all times, but damnable on the Sabbath.' Note the plural. His biographer said 'The vain and sinful custom of sports was reformed before his coming', for Wilson moved to Maidstone. If this shows the hold of the Puritan on the country at that time, the men of Maidstone were not so easily subdued. The game seems developed enough to be distinct from stool-ball.

Only five miles south, in 1646 the first recorded cricket match with players 'of some social standing' took place at Coxheath in Kent: this is inferred because a bet was that one shilling and fourpence halfpenny would be made up to three whole shillings if Thomas Harlackenden and Samuel Filmer lost to four men of Boughton Monchalsey, now Boughton Monchelsea, a neighbouring village.

And a few miles further south again, in Marden, a village halfway between Maidstone and Cranbrook, a handwritten rhyme was found in a Bible:

> All you that do delight in cricket
> Come to Marden, pitch your wicket.
> Marden boys I am sure they like it
> To play with might and valyer ...

That was c. 1680, according to Waghorn's *Dawn of Cricket*, and in 1640 'three clothiers of Goudhurst and Marden, Thomas Goude, Matthew Waldren, and Francis Blocke', had invented a process for dying wool.

And in Cranbrook itself in 1652 there was a positive irruption of the game. Fortunately for us, the authorities found it seemly to prosecute: 'John Rabson esquire, Thomas Basden clothier, and John Reade husbandman, all of Cranbrook, together with divers other persons unknown to the jurors unlawfully and unjustly did play at crickett in the close and field in Cranbrook called Bullfield which was in the possession of Jehosaphat Starr of Cranbrook, yeoman.' That was between 17 May and 6 July 1652, and later it was deemed necessary to bring a 'Presentment against Stephen Osburne clothier, Thomas Ward barber, Thomas Basden clothier, John Reade husbandman and Isaac Walter the younger, labourer, all of Cranbrook for playing cricket (but not with others) in the same field on 20 May, and between 20 May and 6 July 1652.' Both indictments were rejected as 'not true bills'. Perhaps the tide was turning against Puritanism and the Major-Generals. It is eerie to see clothiers involved some three hundred and twenty years after the first settlement there.

The old Roman road from Hastings ran close by all three places on its way to Rochester and Watling Street, used by Chaucer's pilgrims, which also runs by Rochester on the way from London to Canterbury and Dover. The towns and villages on the route were well-placed for transport in either direction. But a far more important route becomes apparent when we resume our search westwards, for just twelve miles on, around Sevenoaks, there is another group of very early mentions. The village of Chevening saw a match in 1610 between Weald and Upland, and saw more cricket played there in the eighteenth century (Thomas Lennard, 15th Lord Dacre, was buried there in 1714 having lost his estates, probably through gaming. These estates were at Dicker, outside Hailsham, where he played in 1677, taking £3 for 'match money'). Just north of Sevenoaks, Shoreham is mentioned in 1668: the case came to Maidstone Quarter Sessions where Sir Roger Twysden resisted the attempts of the Excise to levy on beer: 'Nor was ever complayned of to the Justices of the Peace for selling unlicensed, but at an Horsrace or kriceting sold a bushell or two of Malt made into drinks.' Though the game was well enough attended to draw crowds, the 'k' was still in general use. (Cricket on The Vine at Sevenoaks goes back to at least 1737.)

The next cluster is forty miles further west, in Surrey, at Guildford, with the first written mention, that of John Derrick above. The cloth industry was important, as it was in Godalming, six miles south: for both towns the River Wey provided the water-power for the mills, and the North Downs and flatlands the grazing for sheep (centuries later, the first factory for producing cricket sweaters was in Godalming).

By 1636, just ten miles east of Guildford, cricket was established at East Horsley; it was played at nearby Shere in 1671, 'in contempt of the laws of England, in evil example', and is mentioned at the tiny hamlet of Wanborough, on the Hog's Back, just west of Guildford, in 1613, when Nicholas Hockley 'made an assault and affray on a certain Robert Hewett and by and with a certain stick called "a cricket staffe" value one penny drew blood therefore he is in mercy 3s 4d.' – a substantial fine.

The chalk uplands run further west along the narrow sliver of the Hog's Back to its end where, five miles further on, stands the town of Farnham. 'It is quite evident that Farnham was the cradle of cricketers. "Surrey", in the old scores, means nothing more than the Farnham parishes. This corner of Surrey, in every match against All England, was reckoned as part of Hampshire,' notes the Revd Pycroft in 1837, compiling *The Hambledon Club*

and the Old Players. And: 'The Holt, near Farnham, and Moulsey
Hurst, both adjoining Hants, were the Surrey grounds; they were
aided occasionally by the men of Alton, where the ale was brew-
ed.' John Aubrey, in his *History of Surrey*, Volume III (1718),
says Farnham was 'heretofore a clothing town', a reference to
the coming of the hops which were to supplant weaving. The
association of the area with wool goes back further, to the great
monastery of Waverley a few miles east of the town, the first of
the Cistercian monasteries to be founded in England, in 1128.
They ran enormous quantities of sheep, which they kept on the
high ground. The outlying Granges were sheep farms run by
monks, and the Bishop of Winchester had great numbers himself
and built a castle at Farnham for his overnight stop on his way
to London. Wanborough itself was a Waverley grange, and had
a large fish pond for the monks who were otherwise vegetarian.
Whether the field marked on the Tithe map as the 'Pleasure
Ground' was a cradle of cricket we cannot know, but there is a
connection, it seems, between bat and ball games and monastic,
even conventual, orders if we remember the Flemish illustration.

More importantly, the three towns which are the centre of the
clusters, Maidstone, Sevenoaks, and Guildford, are all along the
Pilgrims' Way.

This had claim to be the most important road in the kingdom.
It connects Dover and Folkestone with Canterbury and Winchester. It runs along the edge of the North Downs, and is sometimes
the same as the North Downs Way. It runs above the clay and
the forests of the Weald, but far enough from the crest to provide
protection against the wind. The sheep would be run on the
North Downs, the towns and villages were well sited for the
shearing and working of the wool (the abbey in Farnham rented
the Bishop's Fulling Mill for ten years), and the finished product
could be transported along the Way to the Channel ports.

In those days, and for centuries before, Winchester was not
only far more important than today (it was the treasury of the
Saxon and Norman kings, and the bishop of Winchester was
sometimes the chancellor), but also a major cloth-working town
where a small settlement of Flemings dated from at least the
twelfth century. The town is seen by H. P.-T. as a centre of early
cricket, before the future Bishop Ken was 'attempting to wield a
cricket bat' at the school around 1650. But it would be likely that
the game went from town to gown.

As early as the twelfth century, St Giles's fair exported raw
wool to Flanders and imported cloth, probably from Southampton. Both ends of the Way, Winchester and Canterbury,

were also strategically placed to defend a number of Channel ports. The high ground of Salisbury Plain was not far, allowing easy access (for those days) to the west and its ores, easily accessible, too, from Portsmouth and Southampton,

Flemish clothworkers might well move inland along the Way, where they knew they would find established weaving industries, and fellow countrymen. They had the opportunity to become graziers as well. The sheep would furnish leather for balls; casings of two, mid- to late tenth century, and early to possibly mid-eleventh century have been found in Winchester, and wool identified as the fine thread. In the case of Cranbrook and the neighbouring sites, the old Roman road would be used.

The high ground runs on to Salisbury Plain. Even the very first mention of a bat-and-ball game supports the theory of grazing lands. It comes from Bemerton, near Salisbury: 'this bit of country lies amid the same chalk downs that stretch away easterly to the sea, to Dover and Beachy Head, while its folk were akin to those of Hants, and spoke the same dialect, so they might be expected to share the same amusements with only local modifications' (H. P.-T., *Cricket in the Weald*, 105).

John Combe (not Shakespeare's), or his relatives, made an offering at the tomb of Bishop Osmund, a cast of his head and shoulders in wax, showing the injuries he had sustained while peacemaking among his neighbours, who were playing a bat and ball game with great clubs (*ludentes ad pilam cum baculis magnis*). As is so often the case, he was clobbered and he lay unable to see or hear for three months, until cured by the fact of his offering. (He said so to a papal commission; the bishop was later canonised.) This happened *c.* 1420, so even then we have ur-cricket, maybe ur-stoball, maybe proto-hockey. It looks as if some earlier form spread further West, along the high ground which radiates from Salisbury Plain. This is not to say cricket itself was not widely diffused, because as early as 1562 at Maldon in Essex, the county archivist recently found: 'Item they do present John Porter alias Browne . . . and Robert servant unto Rychard Roberts . . . playing at unlawful game named clyckett and for that they were both in fault . . .'. Maldon is at the mouth of the Blackwater River, close to the old Roman Road which runs from London to Ipswich, not an unreasonable destination for Flemish immigrants.

Close to the other end of the Way, in 1629, the curate of Ruckinge in Kent, Henry Cuffen, retorting to criticism of his playing 'cricketts' (again the final 's') after Evensong because it was played by 'very mean and base persons', said that on the

contrary it was played by 'persons of repute and fashion'. That
he felt this necessary shows the game came up from under.
Ruckinge is on the edge of the Weald, on the flat grazing land of
Romney Marsh, only some five miles from the Pilgrim's Way,
and twenty from Folkestone,

The early grounds were high and dry, rather than the mud of
the Weald. This is shown by Hambledon, after abandoning
Broad-Halfpenny Down, pitching on Windmill or Stoke
Downs, cricket being played on the hills above Lewes, and
Winchester playing on St Catherine's Hill. In the case of
Hambledon and Winchester at least, there seems an association
with fairs, Broad-Halfpenny Down meaning the down where the
toll for setting up the booth was exacted. This might support the
exchange of weavers' and others' finished goods.[6]

This is only a possible best fit to the available evidence, but it
has some kind of corroboration from highly reprehensible
goings-on to the east and south of Chichester in Sussex, close to
the South Downs.

In 1611, on the flat lands of Selsey Bill, in the village of
Sidlesham, Bartholomew Wyatt and Richard Latter played
cricket instead of attending divine service and were fined 12d.
and made to do penance. In 1647, only three miles away, in the
neighbouring parish on the coast, at Selsey, Henry Brand was
killed with a 'cricket batt' – a blow on the head from another
Latter, Thomas.

In 1622 at Boxgrove, just inland, the vicar's servant and others
played cricket in the churchyard, aided and abetted by the two
churchwardens, on two consecutive Sundays, so no wonder the
Revd Earle presented a Bill: the miscreants were forced to read a
penance, fined, and admonished by the Bishop himself. The 'two
old churchwardens' were mentioned as defending and 'mayn-
teyning them in it', not surprisingly as two of the players were
their sons. Cricket is spelt variously creket, crekett, kreket. The
Boxgrove Incident implies that the bat was probably straighter
than a crook, the ball was hard and frequently hit in the air,

6. An even more tenuous connection of weavers with cricket was brought to light
in 1912, when Neville Cardus answered the advertisement for a junior cricket
coach at Shrewsbury. William Attewell, the old pro from Notts, was his senior,
and told him that he would work his loom in his cottage even at night, after a
day's cricket. 'In Yorkshire, the same freedom to exercise his craft or trade,
though different in procedure and method, was prevalent. Consequently it was
possible to play cricket on mid-week afternoons. So gradually, the County
championship was evolved . . .' (Cardus and Arlott, *The Noblest Game*).

because 'they use to break the Church-windowes with the ball', and 'a little childe had like to have her braynes beaten out with a cricket bat.'

(It seems that before 1744, the date of the first Laws, a batsman could hinder a fielder if the ball was in the air, perhaps even have a second shot at it. Edward Tye killed Jasper Vinall accidentally in 1624 at Horsted Green: he hit it in the air, tried to hit it again as it came down, but 'Jasper arrived suddenly behind his back' and was hit with someting called a 'bacillus' – a small stick rather than a great staff or crook. Horsted Green is the odd man out among the early mentions, some distance from the others, and near the source of the River Ouse that flows down to the port of Newhaven. See *catch*).

In both the Selsey and Boxgrove incidents the churches were next door to Priories, even part of them. The splendid church of the Virgin Mary and St Blaise had Cistercians next door, and St Blaise is the patron saint of woolcombers, having being tortured with wool-combs. This seems far from coincidence: Boxgrove was a rich parish, and its inhabitants might well have had occasion to name their church in gratitude for their major source of income.

The well-known painting *c.* 1220 on a window-splay of Cocking church, on the way through the Downs from Chichester to Midhurst, is hardly evidence at all, because although the man and boy in the picture seem to have crooks (or possibly large billhooks), there's no ball. But there was a monastery right next door, with about six Cluniac monks, administered from Seez in Normandy soon after the Conquest. In Midhurst, a mile or two from the northern edge of the South Downs, on the old road to London, eight men were found cricketing on the Sabbath in 1637: there too was a priory, Easebourne, where the church now stands.

The association with wool, with the monastic orders, craft, animal spirits, and education, always emerges: *Queen Mary's Psalter* is one of a group of works, dating from about the second decade of the fourteenth century, which is 'stylistically similar in depiction and exhibits provenance and patronage from southern Benedictine establishments in Canterbury Hyde and Chertsey' (Lucy Sandler, *Gothic Manuscripts 1285–1385* I, 31). And Cain and Abel are not specified as shepherds in the Bible, so it is an invention that the Master who was the chief artist found suitable and interesting. And the illustrator responsible for the Flemish colophon must have thought his picture needed no explanation.

A line of reasoning might be that the monasteries and priories

ran vast flocks of sheep which were never broken up by inherit-
ance, and monks wove their own habits, so must have been to
some extent weavers: Selsey Bill is particularly dry, so suited to
wool spinning. The monks also often ran schools and played
Roman games with a ball or 'pilam' in their leisure hours.
Cistercians in particular reclaimed marginal lands of no interest
to the barons, made them productive, and built their abbeys
where it was suitable for wool spinning. All of these Sussex
villages, and particularly Selsey and Sidlesham, are close to the
harbour of Dell Quay, just south of Chichester, so a suitable
shipping point for the Continent for sheep and wool. The land
around the old church of Selsey is damp and sedgy, on the edge
of the water, just the sort of land the monks might have
reclaimed. A few miles east lies Slindon, four and five centuries
later one of the centres of early cricket, and close by is Goodwood, home of the Dukes of Richmond, the second duke being
a notable patron of the game.

We might conjecture further, and suppose that the dissolution
of the monasteries, from 1536, led to a lack of weavers, while
greater events were happening on the other side of the Channel.
The Low Countries, and this included Flanders, were starting
the first attempt to free themselves, first from Charles V, and
then from the 'unparalleled tyranny' of Philip II. The struggle of
the Dutch lasted over a century, from long before 1566, when
the revolt was widespread, to 1648, when the Peace of Munster
was signed. An English army was frequently on the Continent in
these years, and refugees came in some number to England. By
either a version of the general game could have been brought
over and popularised. Even by 1561 the inhabitants of Sandwich
were empowered to permit the foreign craftsmen, 'very skilful',
wrote Elizabeth, to carry on their manufacture of cloth articles in
the town: 'The year of this third Flemish commercial invasion
has been called the great era of the woollen trade. Kent was the
centre of its activities' (*Victoria History of Kent*). They may have
brought with them at this time the name of a particular game.

Some corroboration comes from the timing of the early
mentions of the game. The earliest date yet found after Maldon
in 1562 comes from Hendrick Nicklaes, a Dutch fulminator:
'They make there, divers-sort of of Puppet Works or Babyes, for
to bring up children in vanitee. There are made likewyse, many
kyndds of Bales, Cut-Staves or Kricket-staves, Rackets, and
Dyce, for that the foolish People should waste or spend their
tyme ther-with, in foolishness.' This is a translation, *c.* 1580, by
Christopher Vitell(s) from 'Bas-Almayne', of Niklaes's *Terra*

Pacis of 1575. The original does not mention 'kricket-staves' :
'Men maeckt dahr velerleye Poppen-werckes, um de Kinderen,
in de Ydelzeit upp tho voeden. Men maeckter velerleye Ballen,
Kolven, Raketten under Teilingen up dath idt dohrische Volck,
eren Tydt to Dohrheit, daer-mede oever edder thoe bringen
solde.' 'Kolven', meaning clubs, is the root of golf. Yet Vitell – a
native of Delft in Holland – translated it without qualification as
'Kricket-Staves' – and spelt it with a 'k'.

Some light is shed by the entry in John Florio's dictionary of
1598, under *sgrillare*: 'to make a noise like a cricket, be merry, to
play cricket-a-wicket.' The noise obviously refers to *grillo*, current Italian for the insect (*sgrillare* has disappeared; in some
references it is mis-written as *sgrittare*), but it is improbable that
the game was much to the Borgias or Gonzagas, although some
aspects might have been to their taste. We now have 'cricket'
and 'wicket' together, and it is possible Florio put it like this to
define the game clearly, perhaps to separate it from similar games
also with an aim. Florio had already published other lexicograph-
ical work, and his reputation was high: 'wise beyond either his
fortune or his education,' said Sir William Cornwallis.

Florio was brought up largely in England, with an interval on
the Continent, for reasons of religion, in the reign of Mary. If he
returned to the Continent he might have used the road through
Kent, maybe Stane Street, maybe picking up the Pilgrims' Way
around Rochester, on his way to Dover or Folkestone. He was in
the pay and patronage of the Earl of Southampton towards the
end of the century. If he compiled his work in 1596 and 1597 he
must have known Shakespeare, whose acquaintance with Southampton went back to at least 1591, the start of the Sonnets.
Florio may have told him much about Italy for the plays, but it
is no more than fanciful to think that he turned to him for this
definition.

There is one possible hint at a ball game similar to cricket in
Shakespeare, in *King Lear*, IV. 6.241, when Edgar says to
Osward, in the Folio: 'I'se try whether your costard or my ballow
be the harder . . .' This is corrected to 'bat' in Q1 and Q2. It
seems certain that when Shakespeare wrote, the game would be
as understandable to us as an afternoon at the Globe.

In 1616 the fifth edition of John Bullokar's *English Expositor*
defines cricket as 'a kind of game with a ball' (the date of the first
edition is uncertain). In 1611, Cotgrave's French-English
dictionary has 'crosse': 'a cricket staffe, or the crooked staffe
wherewith boys play at cricket.' However exact or otherwise the
definition may be, both involve bats – and 'crosse' is the episcopal

crozier, so we can see the shape of the bat already, of which we have adequate illustrations later – curved like a hockey-stick, not just the straight stick of the medieval illustrations.

Rather like the old bats of Stonyhurst College, founded by Jesuits in 1593 for the children of the then-persecuted English Catholics at St Omer, 25 miles south-east from Calais, towards Flanders. When they returned to England, at the time of the French Revolution, they brought with them a game which had a stone for target, about a foot and a half high and a foot wide, and bats half-way between hockey-sticks and clubs. The school may have picked up the game from local influences: it is also possible, although not as likely, that the game was rather well formed in England at the end of the sixteenth century, and was brought over from Kent.

The game had of course already reached London, where, naturally, the immigrants also went. The first mention there is by a Royalist writer saying Oliver Cromwell went up to London in 1617 and excelled at football, wrestling and cricket, 'gaining for himself the name of royster.' The pamphlet was written at the time of the civil wars, possibly to discredit Cromwell. And in 1656 Cromwell's Commissioners had banned 'Krickett' ('k' again) throughout Ireland, and burned the bats and balls in Dublin.

John Stow's *Survey of London* in 1633 mentions places where 'the more common sort divert themselves at Football, Wrestling, Cudgels, Ninepins, Shovel-board, Cricket.' There is a mention at Eltham in 1654, Richmond in 1666, and Croydon in 1707. It had arrived at Clapham Common by 1700. The first recorded county match seems to be that between Kent and Surrey in 1709. Another 'county' match was London vs Kent in 1719. The game, in Lamb's Conduit Fields, was stopped by a dispute in Kent's second innings, and the Kent men sued the Londoners for the stake of £60, before Lord Chief Justice Pratt. Because His Lordship did not understand the game, he ordered them to replay it and London won by 22 runs (H. P.-T.). His Lordship's failure to understand, and the dispute in the first place, may refer to the Laws not being codified until 1744. The costs were £200.

'Krickett', according to the diary of the Revd Henry Teonge, chaplain on the *Assistance* 1675–9, was being played by English merchants in Aleppo on 6 May 1676. Again Flemish-style, and Teonge, a Cambridge man, presumably knew the orthodox spelling. By now, the origins of the game were obscured by its diffusion. Prime Minister Harley, though, in 1723 spoke of the 'renown' of Kent and Dartford for the game.

The etymology, geography, and history of 'cricket' suggest that it did not emerge with the mild and ruddy Anglo-Saxon, armed with bat and fair play, from the fastness of his muddy Weald, but that it is a step-child of high spirits, high skills, and international trade: even the search of a nation and individuals for liberty.

Cricket slowly decrepitated and disappeared on the other side of the Channel, perhaps stultified by the lubber-lipped Hapsburgs (see *lob*). But in England the game developed, and codified, so that rival teams followed the same understanding of the game. The English nobility were less removed from the people than in France, perhaps because of the *novi homines* of Tudor times, and the dispersal of Royalists to their estates after their defeat in 1648. The Sackvilles of Knole, the Gages, and the Dukes of Richmond and Dorset, were certainly eminent in the rise of the game.

Then, as the country grew richer, different villages started to play each other. Men would travel two days on horseback for a game: Hambledon had its own charabanc. This meant that the differing local rules would be discussed, as in the Articles of Agreement drawn up between the second Duke of Richmond and Mr Brodrick before a match in 1727, and the reference to old 'Nestor' the adjudicator, found among the spectators in Goldwin's 1709 Latin poem, the first description of a cricket match. This, and a more equitable and free country, let alone the rampant betting, probably led to fair play as a necessity as much as a concept. And, of course, helped it to develop. Middlesex met Surrey thrice in 1730, and in 1744 the match between Kent and All England was celebrated by James Love's *Cricket An Heroick Poem*. In the same year, the first Laws that have come down to us were codified, and printed around the borders of a silk scarf.[7] In 1745 Kent and Sussex are reported to have played three games in one month.

John Nyren said that he had seen the lads in remote villages in the latter part of the eighteenth century playing a game with a single stick for a wicket, 'ditto for a bat, and the same repeated, of about three inches in length, for a ball.' Animal spirits and twiggen makeshifts provide the most satisfactory explanation of the spread through the country of the game.

7. The Laws were in printed form, in Latin, in *The New Universal Magazine* of 1752 and the earliest in booklet form are those of 1755, which are in the MCC Library at Lord's.

This was just after the time of the Hambledon supremacy. The first mention of this cradle of the true game is in 1756, although the club was formed around 1750, and in 1768 they beat Kent easily. In 1775 five of Hambledon played five of Kent, and scraped home, although the best bowler in England, 'Lumpy' Stevens, was the '*given man*' for Kent, and got the ball through the stumps so often without dislodging the bail that the third stump was introduced. Probably this was influenced by the new-fangled 'length bowling' which came in about this time, and the changing of the whole aspect of the stumps to 22" by a mere 6". It was about now, too, that white began to be worn for the game, the men of Hambledon no doubt shedding their sky-blue jackets with black collars to play.

The growing popularity of the game meant a shift of the centre of interest away from Hampshire to London, and in 1787 the Marylebone Cricket Club was founded, moving to its present premises in 1814. It derived from the White Conduit Club, which in turn came from the Je-ne-sais-quoi. In 1790 round-arm bowling began to appear.

In 1796 Eton played Harrow, in defiance of Dr Heath, the Eton Head Master, and beat them by 66 runs, a most unfortunate margin. The entire eleven was then beaten by the minute philopolyflagellant, who no doubt made many a merry jest on the virtues of long division and the use of *averages* as he rolled up his sleeves: loyally, he probably wished the winning total to be even greater, 132 or 198.

The establishment of the game was complete, and its history fairly clear, but what of the men? There seems little to fill the great gap except the companion to Nyren's *Young Cricketer's Tutor: The Cricketers of my Time*, also of 1833. Both were edited by the first encourager, even awakener, of Keats, Charles Cowden Clarke: 'Nyren came to the glorious parties at the house of Vincent Novello, and Novello's son-in-law, Clarke, took the opportunity of jotting down his lusty talks in remembrance of the cricketers of his time. Apparently they could do this in spite of the seas of harmony rolling over them from Novello at the organ.' How far did the editing go? Was it ghost-editing? The language seems to be too plain for Clarke. Leigh Hunt reviewed it thus: 'Mr Nyren remembers, and Mr Clarke records, everything with a right taste; masculine as the game and pleasant as the punch after it' (from Edmund Blunden's *Cricket Country*; see under *cricketer* for some of the portraits).

The first generally accepted County Championship was won by Gloucestershire in 1870, the year of their formation, and the

era of the Graces (there had been a reckoning of the standing of
the first counties for some years before). After a team had gone
to North America in 1859, and to Australia in 1861, the first
victory over a representative England XI was recorded in 1877,
followed by the first Australian tour of 1878, when they beat an
MCC side. The first Test on English soil in 1880 ended in a
draw in England's favour, but in 1882 the Australians at last beat
England in England for the first time, and the legend of The
Ashes was born. From there the game has spread so that now
the International Cricket Council has 9 full members, 21 associated members, and 11 affiliates.

A brief comparison with tennis is illuminating: the fastest
bowlers, at about 90 m.p.h. over a little more than nineteen
yards, get the ball to the batsman in 0.46 of a second. By chance,
the fastest tennis serve measured, at 132 m.p.h., travels the 86
feet of the court diagonal and another two feet, which is about
the closest you would stand, in 0.45 sec. But the batsman has a
far more difficult job. Apart from protecting himself and his
wicket against a hard ball, he has more decisions to make, the
ball bounces closer to him and may move after bouncing. His
bat has a hitting width of about three inches out of the four-and-
a-quarter, since anything outside that will be unproductive and
dangerous, as opposed to over six inches for a racquet. He also
has the fielders to consider, and has only one chance. The game
is so demanding of intelligence that you have to be a fool to try.

Accept   of a fieldsman, to accept, or take, a catch, often in slips or gully. Often the context is when a batsman gives a *chance*: 'Pollard got Hassett . . . it propped quickly . . . it was a nasty one to get so early, and Hassett nicked it to Crapp, who accepted it' (Fingleton, *Don*, 149, referring to the Leeds Test of 1948).

account   the batsman's score. 'Speight took 35 minutes to open his account but settled in to play with great authority and went on to hammer five sixes and 16 fours off 147 balls in nearly three-and-a-half hours' (*Brighton Evening Argus*, 14 May 1994). See also *score, tally, tins*.

across the line   is when the bat does not come down to meet the ball down the line of the approaching ball, but across it. This means the bat has less time to connect, so the batsman is liable to be dismissed. Thus Angus Fraser pinned Fleming of New Zealand down with a spell 'which culminated in the young left-hander aiming fatally across the line . . .' (Richard Hutton, *The Cricketer*, August 1994). 'Mr Rooke played all across at one of Clarke's' – *Bell's Life* 1855. Also of a *delivery* moving away from a batsman, across his body.

action   the way in which a bowler physically delivers the ball. The classic action is side-on, with the bowling arm vertical, but many great bowlers, e.g. Clarrie Grimmett, have a round-arm action. It is difficult for a wrist-spinner to have a really high arm while retaining the spin. Roger Harper, taking three quick wickets for West Indies at the Oval Test on 4 August 1988, was described in the *Daily Telegraph* as looking like a very old aeroplane whose wings were about to fall off. First mentioned when John Nyren (Lucas, 75), speaking of the bowler David Harris, says *c.* 1833: 'He would bring it from under the arm with a twist and nearly as high as his armpit, and with this action *push* it, as it were, from him.' 'Frog in a blender', attributed to South African journalist Andy Capastagno, describes the way in which Paul Adams of South Africa (1995) bowls his *chinamen* and *googlies*. See also *straight-arm*.

action break   obsolete, replaced by *cut* as in *leg-cutter*. 'At the moment of "release" his finger swept across the ball and the body was flung towards the left' is how Cardus, in his essay on Surrey's Tom Richardson (fl. 1900), describes his action break: 'he could pitch outside the wicket on the hardest turf, and hit the leg stump' (*on Cricket*, 42) – this as a fast bowler.

age   as the first cricketers emerge from the mists of Broad-Halfpenny Down, the Reverend John Mitford in 1833 remembers the player Fennex at 76 'providentially preserved to show

27

us what the ante-Homeric heroes were.' The *Homeric Age*, or *Middle Ages*, ran from about 1760 to 1832, when the death of Thomas Lord and the Great Reform Bill coincided. The next thirty years go unnamed, until we reach the *Age of Grace* from about 1864, and the final development of the game.

Then came the *Golden Age of Batting*, or the Augustan Age, from about 1890 to the Great War. The ante-Homerics are as visible as those of today – and in John Nyren they had a pen which etched deeper their exuberant individuality.

The *Second Golden Age* was written by Gerald Howarth to portray the period 1919–39. Like the first, it was a golden age for batting, personified by Walter Hammond and Don Bradman. E.W. Swanton CBE suggests the present day may be the *Brazen Age*.

aggregate   the root is Latin *grex*, flock or herd, plus *ad-*, and the meaning the total number of runs or wickets taken in a given time: thus the series aggregate of Salim Malik, captain of Pakistan, who was able to **read** Shane Warne, was 557 runs in three Tests for an average of 92.83, 1994–5.

agricultural   a heavy, clumsy swipe at a ball. *The Times*, 25 July 1955: 'Keith . . . took an agricultural swing at Wardle and was bowled' (OED). From Greek *agros*, a field, Sanskrit *a'jras*: probably originally pasture land. The same root produces 'acre'. Implies a stroke as if with a farming implement – see *Stogumber mow, bucolic*.

aim   in batting, to aim a stroke: in bowling, to direct a ball: Lewis (p. 1) quotes *The World*, 25 August 1788: 'And . . . somebody said, rather neatly, there were a few other trulls than those aimed at Lord Winchelsea' (referring to some of the women spectators).

air   the bowler 'gives the ball air' by imparting a higher trajectory. This 'flights' it, so the batsman does not know where it will bounce. 'I like watching him bowl [Roly Jenkins of Worcestershire and England], because he is never afraid to give the ball air, tossing it higher than most leg-break bowlers . . .' (Hammond, *Secret History*, 74). It means daring to attack: 'Wardle, giving the ball more air and attacking the batsmen most of the time, played the lead role in having Australia out for 221 and then 6 for 118' (Whitington, 242). Of the same bowler, E.W. Swanton remarked, 'The better the wicket the more the necessity of using the air. This Bloemfontein wicket was a beauty – and Wardle, exploiting all the arts of flight and spin, had 14 for 96 in 25 overs. I wonder when any bowler on a

plumb surface last had 14 wickets in a day' (*Report*, 42). Johnny
Wardle, of Yorkshire and England, could bowl either *orthodox*
spin or *chinamen* and *googlies*.

Through the air: applies to all forms of bowling, not only
slow: 'There are certain variations necessary to a bowling attack
in Australia . . . and the first thing an Englishman has to learn is
to try to beat the Australian batsman through the air' (Hammond, p. 28).

air-break   obsolete and previously rare: Lewis (p.1) gives the
word in 1902, with last mention 1920, '"Swerve" or "airbreak",
whether "in-swerve" or "out-swerve" . . . is valuable to fast and
medium-paced bowlers if combined with length.'

air-shot   when a batsman makes a shot and meets with
nothing but air.

alley   is a few inches wide running from the bowler's hand to
on or just outside the off stump: see *corridor*.

all out   something of a misnomer, as a side is said to be *all out*
when all the players capable of batting have been given out –
except one, who is not out. This seems to apply even when, as
in the Kingston Test of 1976 between India and Jamaica, five
Indian batsmen were absent injured in the second innings, and
the Indian total was 97 all out although only five wickets had
fallen (no declaration was made by Bishen Bedi, the Indian
captain).

all-rounder   an *all-rounder* is a player who would get into a
side on either his batting or bowling, according to the generally
accepted definition by Neville Cardus, but this is not always
true, some rather *bits-and-pieces players* being included in
teams as all-rounders. Fielding appears to be always excluded.
The fielding of, say, Phil Sharpe of Yorkshire, a superlative slip
fielder, who averaged 53.40 against Hall, Griffith, Sobers and
Gibbs of the 1963 West Indians, and Colin Bland, who spent
hours practising on his South African farm, brought another
dimension to the game but did not qualify them to be described
as all-rounders. W.G. Grace, George Giffen, Bosanquet,
Wilfred Rhodes, Walter Hammond, Keith Miller, Ian Botham,
Kapil Dev, and Gary Sobers unquestionably were all-rounders.
The last had a batting average in the 1966 series against England
of 103.14 and a bowling average of 27.25. In 1955 in the West
Indies, Keith Miller averaged 73.16 with the bat and 32 with
the ball, and in the 1905 Ashes Tests Sir Stanley Jackson, as he
became, headed batting and bowling with 70.28 and 15.46.
Pakistan's Mushtaq Mohammad uniquely headed both in two
series. Hammond was often too preoccupied with batting to do

much bowling, but his overall batting average of 58.45 in Tests compared with a bowling average of 37.80 speaks for itself. Sobers in Tests overall averaged 57.78 with the bat and 34.03 with the ball, Botham 33.54 and 28.40, Imran Khan 37 and 22.81. Tour averages sometimes throw up an unexpected all-rounder: Ken Barrington of Surrey and England had averages of 112 and 18.71 (7 wickets) in India 1963–4 and 86.76 and 7.25 (24 wickets) in South Africa in 1964–5. A curious feature is that over the last fifty years or more the great all-rounders have almost always had a quality of exuberance: fast or fast-medium bowlers, hard-hitting batsmen, strokeplayers like Kapil Dev who could illustrate a coaching manual in half an hour, and brilliant close fielders (Hammond, Miller, Sobers, Botham) who might have had even more exceptional records had they batted or bowled only. The finest all-round performance in a single game probably belongs to George Giffen, who for South Australia against Victoria made 271 out of 562, and took 16 for 166. First use seems to be the team: 'A stronger Eleven "all round" . . .' in *Baily's Magazine* (which carried copious sports reporting) of July 1861 (p. 140), followed by 'those rarities . . . a genuine all-round cricketer' in the December issue (p. 154).

amateur   one who plays without pay, but usually with expenses. They could, if exceptional, profit handsomely: W.G. Grace was paid £3,000 for one Australian tour. Later, amateur tourists were given 'broken time' payments: the perception that these might be tax-free made Jim Laker think of reverting to amateur status, as recorded in his book *Over to Me*. Also a Gentleman, as opposed to a Player, e.g. the Gentlemen v. Players match. Gentlemen had their initials before their name, players after, or were called Mr while the plain name sufficed for the professionals, which led to the absurd announcement that the Warwickshire eleven before the Great War was to be drawn from B.W. Quaife and Quaife (W.), his father player, or Mr B.W. Quaife and Quaife W. The XI might also have included Jeeves, P. (for Percy), a medium-fast bowler, killed in the First World War. (See *shamateur, gentlemen*.)

analysis   the record of a bowler's performance, with first the number of *overs* and balls bowled, then the number of *maiden overs*, *runs* scored off the bowler, now including *wides* and *no-balls* bowled, and finally *wickets* taken. 'The analysis of the Bowling is given of all those matches possessing the most interest', *F. Lillywhite's Guide to Cricketers*, 1854 (Lewis, 22). R. Holden Esq., took all 20 in 1818 for Gentlemen of England vs. MCC, but as he was the only bowler (it not being unknown for the Gents to be short of bowling) and bowled from both ends, the status of his record is uncertain. Altham (135) prints the following analysis for H.F. Boyle of Australia v. Marylebone Cricket Club in 1878 (four-ball overs): 1.ww .... .1.1 .... .w.. w... ..w. w', which translates into 8.1 overs, 6 maidens, 3 runs, and 6 wickets.

The most remarkable County *analysis* must be that of Hedley Verity, the Yorkshire left-armer who, in 1932, finished with 19.4–16–10–10 against Northamptonshire. Richie Benaud's father took 10–30 and 10–35 in a match played over two successive weeks in the 1923–4 Australian season – all 20. Spofforth is said to have done the same in December 1881.The record in Tests may belong for all time to Jim Laker of Surrey and England. On a rain-affected pitch he finished with 19–90 in the Old Trafford Test of 1956. The Australians write it as 90–19. No-balls were sometimes recorded. Thus Jim Sims had the following analysis for Middlesex against the 1948 Australians: 24–2–65–6 (1nb). Sometimes the average is tacked on: 'Chapman was merciful enough to declare at eight for 342. Even Grimmett 84.1/10/298/9/33.1 was happy to desist' (Hele, 39).

The world's best analysis is apparently held by Alex Kelly, who on 23 June 1994 when 17 took all ten for nought for Bishop Auckland against Newton Aycliffe in only 27 balls: 10 for 0 had been done before, but in a full five overs.

The first known usage in English is by Ben Jonson in *The Phoenix Analysde* of 1601. The Greek prefix *ana*, meaning 'up', or 'back, again, renew', precedes the stem from the verb *luein* 'to loose', so painfully familiar to generations of schoolboys: *Analyses* is the title of Aristotle's treatise on logic.

anchor man   the batsman who holds up one end while his partner gets the runs at the other: 'General Frothbury . . . would make remarks like "Get on with it, will you, and stop finicking about" – regardless of Kenyon's clear duty as anchor man, which was not to "get on with it" but to stay put . . .' (Raven, 14). The General was umpiring at the time.

angle   a bowler will *angle* the ball's trajectory, either by firing it into the batsman or using the width of the bowling crease. Seeing the ball coming to him at an angle, the batsman may step across and angle it down through the slips or to *fine* leg, or try to: '[Peter Kirsten] was made to hop about before Malcolm took out his leg stump with an angled yorker' (*WCM*, October 1994).

ankler   a ball hit by the batsman skimming low to a fielder:

'Kieran . . . took a fizzing ankler to dismiss Morrell' (*Wandsworth Borough News*, 3 September 1993).

anti-batsman behaviour   so far, only found with reference to the ball, and not to the fielders, bowler, or *sledging*: 'cut, lift, and every other type of anti-batsman behaviour the ball may display . . .' (Wilkins, 41).

appeal   a player cries 'How was that?' and the umpire adjudicates. The Laws of 1744 and 1755 state that umpires 'are not to order any man out, unless appealed to by one of the Players.' W.E.W. Collins, *Country Cricketer's Diary*, 1908: '"How's that?" came the second appeal, as the wicket-keeper, ball in hand, pulled up a stump' (OED). This was because the *bails* were already off. Note that the early Laws state 'unless appealed to by one of the Players'. This can be one of the batsmen, and Brodribb (p.107) relates that in the third MCC–Argentina match H.W. Marshal trod on his wicket and had almost reached the pavilion when he turned back and made an appeal to the bowler's umpire: he had been unsighted, but the *square*-leg umpire gave him 'not out' as he had completed his stroke before the wicket was broken. See also *run out*, and *how's that*.

Indiscriminate over-appealing ('bad form' according to Prince Ranjitsinji) to try to pressurise an umpire was one of the factors leading to the installation of a *third umpire*.

Body language is sometimes used: Dennis Lillee, the great Australian fast bowler, and many others, sometimes turned towards the umpire with both index fingers raised as if to induce a mimetic gesture. Appeals can also be made by either the fielding or batting side against the light – see *bad light*.

approach shot   see *over the top*.

arm   of a ball, to go with the arm: see *arm ball*. Also of a bowler, 'Bowes was a pure arm bowler' (Larwood, 101), meaning that he did not put his body into the action. Of a fielder, a *good arm* means that he has a powerful throw.

arm ball   a ball that continues its line after pitching. Particularly used by bowlers from round the wicket. Thus a left-armer might come a little wide of the stumps, and have a ball pitching on or just outside the off stump which goes *with the arm*, i.e. carries on towards the leg stump. The master of this art was Jim Laker, the right-hand Surrey and England off-spinner, who was able to produce both this and a *drifter*, or *floater*, which would move away in the air, with what appeared to be an off-spinner's action. This confusion might be amplified by his ability to spin his *stock ball*, the off-break, a great deal so that the *Robins* *effect* also made it drift out – but then bite back savagely. John Emburey of Middlesex and England points out he rarely sees an arm-ball these days, except from Tim May, Robert Croft and Graeme Hick, and 'one reason for the arm-ball not being bowled as often as it once was is because batsmen don't sweep as much as they used to . . . the batsman, thinking he could sweep the ball away to leg, would often get out lbw, bowled, or get a top edge . . .' (*The Cricketer,* August 1994).

around the wicket   see *round the wicket.*

Ashes   the ashes of English cricket, referring to the first defeat of an English team on her own soil. On 28 August 1882, Australia batted first and made only 63, to which England replied by scoring 101. The Australians only managed 122 in their 2nd innings, leaving England with 85 to win. W.G. Grace and A.N. Hornby opened and 50 was up for the loss of only 2 wickets. Frederick Spofforth, the original *demon bowler,* got to work, and the scoreboard showed 75 for 9. The last man in was Peate and by this time the scorer's hand had become so agitated that this reads in the original more like Geese. Peate made 2 from his first ball and was then clean-bowled. The 'demon bowler' had immortal figures of 14 for 90, and was carried shoulder-high to the pavilion. England was stunned and on the 2nd September a mock obituary notice was published in *The Sporting Times*:

   In affectionate remembrance of English cricket which died at The Oval on 29th August, 1882. Deeply lamented by a large circle of sorrowing friends and acquaintances.

R.I.P.

NB – The body will be cremated and the ashes taken to Australia.

On 14 September, the Hon. Ivo Bligh's team set sail for Australia with the manifest intention of regaining these 'Ashes'. Their ship, the *Peshawur,* was involved in a collision leaing Colombo, and had to spend five days in repair. The ship arrived in Adelaide on 10 November, where the English team disembarked. It was during this eventful voyage that the romance of the Ashes probably began, for on board ship were also the Hon. William John Clarke, at that time the President of the Melbourne Cricket Club, his wife Janet, and her companion and music teacher to the Clarkes' children, Florence Rose Morphy.

It seems that Cupid's bow was as highly strung as ever, and no wonder, for Florence was a beauty: her eyes gaze out from her portrait with unusual *douceur,* even considering the rather chocolate-box fashion of that time. She and Ivo were next to

meet at Rupertswood, the Clarkes' more than baronial mansion
some thirty miles outside Melbourne, when the English amateurs came to stay at the end of November. Clarke was one of
the most important men in the whole of Australia at that time: he
had received his baronetcy from Queen Victoria just two weeks
earlier. The whole team stayed at Rupertswood for Christmas.

And it was here that the Ashes were transubstantiated from
myth to reality. On Christmas Eve, all attended the local church
of St Mary's at Sunbury, and in the afternoon a social cricket
match was arranged between the team and the guests at
Rupertswood. Pat Lyons, one of the general hands on the
estate, and Tom Patterson, the dairyman, both were there, and
both told the Hon. Michael Clarke the story of the match.
Lyons in particular might have remembered it well for the
frantic chasing of sixes and fours: he related that after the
match, Lady Clarke burnt a bail, placed it in a wooden (not
pottery) urn, and, according to Florence fifty years later, she
'and the other ladies, presented it to the Hon. Ivo'. So the Ashes
came into being before they were won back.

Australia won the first match by 9 wickets, England won the
next two. On 1 of February, after the England XI had won their
third Test and thus regained the Ashes for the first time, the
Melbourne *Punch* published a number of poems.

> O'er cricket's tomb the British Lion wept,
> The Kangaroo the cherished ashes kept;
> But Bligh's escutcheon never can be stained,
> Since he those sacred ashes has regained . . .

started one. Another longer poem, had the fourth of its six
stanzas cut out and pasted to the (now pottery) urn, it is said
by Lady Clarke.

> When Ivo goes back with the urn, with the urn;
> Studds, Steel, Read and Tylecote return, return;
> The welkin will ring loud,
> The great crowd will feel proud,
> Seing Barlow and Bates with the urn, the urn;
> And the rest coming home with the urn.

There is also a story that the Ashes were first presented *after*
the Third Test, but Joy Munns in *Beyond Reasonable Doubt*
points out there is no evidence to support this. Had the original
presentation been after victory, we would, almost certainly,
have heard more of it. Yet no eyewitness accounts have
survived.

Meanwhile Mrs Anne Fletcher, the wife of J.W. Fletcher,
secretary of the Paddington Cricket Club, who had stayed in

the same hotel as the teams, made a small crimson velvet bag, with a victor's bays on the front surrounding '1883', all in yellow silk. We don't know when or how the bag was presented, or even if it was sent, but Ivo Bligh's note of thanks is dated 16 February: 'Many thanks for the pretty little bag you have so kindly sent me. The ashes shall be consigned to it forthwith and always kept there in memory of the great match.'

Why was the giving of the Ashes for so long a mystery? Firstly, cremation was then a controversial issue still to be resolved, and the father of the journalist who obituarised the Ashes in 1882 was a supporter of cremation, which was not legalised in England until 1902. But more importantly, the urn and the bag were considered personal gifts – and of what memory! – by Ivo Bligh, who lodged them at Cobham Hall in Kent. Upon his death in 1927, Lady Darnley (Ivo Bligh succeeded to the title of Earl of Darnley and had, of course, married Florence Murphy) forwarded the Ashes to the MCC for safe keeping and they lie in the Memorial Gallery at Lords.

asking rate   when a captain declares his innings closed, he can set the other side a total number of runs to get. This can also be expressed in runs per hour or per over, as an *average* of either unit, and is the *asking rate.*

asterisk*   not out, of a batsman. Also denotes the captain on the scorecard. The dagger denotes the wicket-keeper.

Atlas   George Headley of Jamaica, so called because he carried the West Indies batting, in a Test career lasting from 1929 to 1954. See also *Hercules.*

attack   the array of bowlers possessed by the fielding side. Implies, but does not necessarily mean, vehemence. Lewis gives Denison's *Sketches*, 52: '...not to diminish the means of defence, but to add to the powers of attack.' More rarely referring to batting: 'Usually the bowler appears to attack, and the batsman to defend; but Lambert seemed always on the attack, and the bowler at his mercy' – E.H. Budd, referring to the start of the 18th century (Lucas, 224).

attacking bowler   a bowler who devotes his energies to capturing wickets, rather than saving runs in the hope a batsman will get himself out: prime examples being the Australians Bill O'Reilly and Dennis Lillee, and Ian Botham.

attacking field   an *attacking field* for a fast bowler might be four slips, a gully, two short legs, and two men out. Or it might be, as sometimes in the 'Bodyline' Tests of 1932–3, six short legs spread in an arc between silly mid-on and leg slip. Derek Underwood's field on a poor pitch at the Oval in 1968 was an extreme for a slow bowler, with a slip and two gullies, silly point, silly cover, silly extra-cover, and four short legs: no fielder was more than four or five yards from the bat.

Attacking fields can also tempt: the slow left-armer Archdale of the Battersea Bohemians will leave a gulf between mid-wicket and a straight mid-on, and angle the ball into the leg stump from round the wicket on a full length, encouraging a drive to that area.

aunt, aunt Sally   obsolete for wicket keeper. 'Practice may improve an "Aunt Sally" . . . but unless he has natural genius . . . a lad is not likely to become a star wicket-keeper' (Giffen, 239).

Auld Enemy   The *Ashe*s are fought between the *Auld Enemies*. Why a Scots derivation is not certain.

average   in batting, the number of runs a batsman has made divided by the number of times he has been out (retired counts as out, retired hurt does not). First use appears to be, 'In looking over carefully the list of matches for twenty years, we shall find no scores on the average at all approaching those of Walker and Beldham; thus clearly evincing their superiority' (Revd John Mitford, reviewing Nyren in the *Gentleman's Magazine*, 1833). The only men to have averaged over 100 in an English first-class season are Sir Donald Bradman and Geoffrey Boycott OBE (twice).

In bowling, the number of runs conceded, thus including *no-balls* and *wides*, divided by the number of wickets taken. In 1958 H.L. Jackson of Derbyshire took 143 wickets at 10.99, the lowest of any bowler in the century who had taken 100 wickets in County games.

The word may have a maritime origin, from the Arabic *awariya*, goods damaged by sea, itself from *awar*, damage at sea, from *ara*, to mutilate. Not unnaturally, as a trading word, it is first known in Europe from the ports of Genoa and Pisa in the Italian *avaria*, and thence spread through Europe, even to Swedish and Russian. The meaning came to be the apportionment of the loss, e.g. to the members of a syndicate engaged in that venture.

away[1]   to *move away* of a ball, either in the air or off the pitch, is from leg to off – away from the batsman.

away[2]   an *away game* is to play not on one's home ground. Formerly also an '*out* match': *Baily's Magazine* of June 1875 points to a recurring problem: 'First-rate M.C.C. elevens are not to be got together, especially for out-matches, as easily as he supposes.'

away³   a batsman's call for a run: 'Away!' (1845, P.W.-T.).

away-swing   the movement of a ball away from the batsman in the air, i.e. from leg to off, whether he is right- or left-handed.

away-swinger   the ball which moves in the direction described above: synonymous with out-swing. See also *swing*, *posthumous swing*.

B short for *bowled*, including also *played on*. First reference has Harris B by Hadswell (Nyren, *Tutor*, 111), and by 1769, the first complete scorecard has the Duke of Dorset b 14.

back-cut a late cut, or cut behind square. Obsolete in England, in common Australian use. 'Then Hutton crashed Miller through the covers for four to make him 50 in 110 minutes, and then in this same over, with Miller bowling faster, he back-cut one like Kippax' (Fingleton, *Don*, 95). See also *mix them*.

back foot, back foot player a batsman who plays or is playing off the *back foot*: 'Yardley ... looked perfectly at ease ... he was playing pace off the back foot ... an object lesson to those innumerable Englishmen who are obsessed with the conviction that the way to play pace is to push up the pitch ...' (Fingleton, *Don*, 124).

backlift the lift of the bat to make the stroke at the ball by swinging the bat through an arc. Sobers' and Lara's are both referred to as wristy, meaning the wrists are cocked, turned up, at the end of the backlift: Tony Lewis in the *Sunday Telegraph* on New Year's Day 1995 said that Lara's was the highest in the world.

A straight *backlift* towards the stumps is preferred, though some, including Bradman, took the ball towards second slip. Over the last ten or fifteen years, a certain indignation has been forthcoming from those who regard the premature backlift as being in some way a sign of the decadence of the game. But it is a return to the Golden *Age*, when C. B. Fry had not only lifted his bat but had started on the downstroke when the ball left the bowler's hand, even if the bowling was fast: this allowed him to hit the ball with great power. W.G. Grace and Archie Maclaren also stood with lifted bat.

See also *pickup*, which can also mean the bat lifts easily in the hands.

back spin the rotation of the ball in an opposite direction to its line of flight. This makes it skid off the pitch, trapping batsmen lbw. It seems to 'come off' the pitch faster, but this is an illusion, perhaps because it is usually bowled a little quicker, and with a much flatter trajectory. See also *flipper*. Considering how easy it is to impart it to underarm bowling, it is surprising the first mention is by E.R. Wilson in 1920: 'Back spin is undercut applied to the back half of the ball, and is more easily put on with a low action' (BLC, 1920, 84).

back up to *back up* 'esp. in Cricket (of a fielder): to run behind another fielder in readiness to stop the ball if he should fail to do it' (OED). Of the batsman at the bowler's end to start in readiness for a run; and similarly in other games (the opposite of *sit on the handle*). The first adjuration not to commit this cardinal sin comes from R. Cotton in 1767: 'Ye Fieldsman look sharp . . . When the ball is return'd back it sure' (Ashley-Cooper, ix). The other meaning is that the non-striker walks or runs down the pitch, the first mention being the cryptic 'By backing up too far, he ran himself out', from the *New Sporting Magazine*, October 1836. The start which can be gained by good backing up is several yards, valuable in one-day cricket, the art being to have just the bat stretched behind, grounded at the crease as the bowler delivers; then when the ball is in the air some yards can be gained. The bowler may knock down the wicket if the batsman is out of his ground when he delivers, but it is usual to give a warning (see *mankadded*). There is also an obsolete meaning, the last mention in Lewis being in Collins's *Country Cricketer's Diary* i. 13: 'Two other men . . . trotted off to back up the captain . . . They ran seven for that hit.'

backward 'of a fieldsman or his position; farther from the line of the wicket than is standard practice, as *backward point*' (OED), gully, or square leg, when standing a little behind the line of the wicket.

bad light the umpire may *offer the light* if the visibility is too poor for the batsmen to continue to play, or, more rarely, for the fielders to see the ball in the opinion of the umpires. Or, as happened in the Third Test at Sydney in 1994, the quicker bowlers may be banned and the slower allowed. This caused some comment at the time, but there was a precedent from the Leeds Test in 1947, when no less umpires than Frank Chester and J.J. Hills 'informed the captains that if the pace bowlers were not used, play could continue. The captains agreed and there was no interruption of play. Whether the umpires have the power to offer such a compromise is another matter' (Brodribb, 116). And a fielding captain can cause play to be called off by bringing back his *quicks*.

First-class umpires carry a *light meter*, which is only calibrated in numbers, not lumens. Thus when the batsman is offered the light, the umpire takes a reading. If the batsman declines, his later plea will be rejected if the light has improved. Questions start to be asked when the reading is around five. On first-class grounds, there is a row of five lights beside the score-box, and when three are lit play usually discontinues.

The acronym *BLSP* means 'bad light stopped play'.

bag (see also *coffin*) the long bag in which a player's gear is carried. Also a haul of wickets (to bag five wickets), to take a catch, or bag a brace (*pair*).

baggage-master   looks after the baggage on tour: it may be up to a hundred pieces. The famous 'Fergie', Bill Ferguson, probably made more tours with England than anyone else, except perhaps George Duckworth.

bail   each of the two pieces of wood laid across the tops of the three stumps which form the wicket. Originally the wicket consisted of a single *bail*, about two feet long, laid across two stumps. By 1744, though, the length was fixed at six inches. Thus we see, in 1770 in James Love's poem *Cricket*, l. 19: 'The bail, and mangled Stumps bestrew the Field.' This was before the introduction of the middle stump. 'The first match with three stumps and two bails took place on the Burway Ground, at Chertsey, in the match Chertsey v. Coulsden, played September 6th, 1776', said Haygarth, one of the earliest historians of cricket, in his *Scores and Biographies* (I, 23 fn.). The bails are at present made four inches long, turned and shaped on the lathe; heavy bails are used when conditions are exceptionally windy, made from the Guaiacum, or lignum vitae, a tropical tree, reputedly the heaviest wood, from which a medicinal resin is distilled, thus 'tree of life'. Iron bails were briefly tried, unsuccessfully, in Yorkshire.

OED has bail as a cross-bar, and the first mention available is in *Turberville's Booke of Falconrie* of 1575, although there was probably much earlier usage: 'Set them upon some pearche or bayle of wood that they by that means may ... eschue the dragging of their traines upon the ground.' It seems clear from this that the bail may have been in use from early times – from the time of the hurdle as wicket. Derivation is probably from the same French word, maybe going back to the L. *bajulus*, bearer of a burden: it might be more likely if we considered a yoke, or a burden carried by two men on a long stave. H. P.-T. has another derivation, less likely, from the L. *bacillus*, a small stick, with the meaning of a stick put up to separate two animals in a pen.

bail ball, bail trimmer   'Tom Walker laid down a bail-ball in a style peculiarly his own ...' (Mitford, 235/2). It is a ball that removes the bails without disturbing the stumps, or hardly at all. Walker fl. *c.* 1780 and was banned from *round-arm* at that time by a meeting of the council of the Hambledon club. Also *bailer*: 'and Conover losing his wicket to a bailer from Charley' (*American Cricketer*, 1878).

Balista   see *bowling machine*.

ball[1]   the OED derivation is from the Saxon line: from Old
Norse *bollr*, through ME *bal*, and has 'perhaps the earliest
English sense' as a globular body with which to play tennis,
hockey, cricket, foot-ball. Derivation through the French line
balle for 'ball' and 'bale' is said to be erroneous.

In 1995 the oldest known cricket ball was found in a house in
Lewes. The lady's shoe it was found with helped to date it to
about the same time, 1780. There are only four main seams,
and the leather is too rough to have been buffed and polished
at any stage. The stuffing has gone, probably perished, but the
stitching is well preserved, flattened but intact. The quarter
seams are at right angles to each other, and have a single row of
exterior stitching. The ball is brownish in colour, probably too
brown to have ever been dyed any kind of bright red, although
there are references to the crimson before this.

It may be older. 'Mr Duke informed me that his old firm
made a treble seam ball for George IV, then Prince of Wales,
when still a boy' – Fred Gale (*Game of Cricket*, 129). According
to Farington's Diary of 21 October 1811, he visited Mr Duke's
cricket-ball factory at Penshurst: 'He told me that his family
had been famous for this art for 250 years past.' It is noteworthy
that this is about the same period as the very first mentions of
the game, and that Penshurst is not far from the North Downs,
only a few miles south of Sevenoaks.

The first mention we have of a ball specifically for cricket is
from the nephew of Milton, Edward Phillips, who about a
hundred years later has a lady in *The Mysteries of Love* (1658)
fear that her lover will one day say, 'Would my eyes had been
beat out of my head with a cricket ball the day before I saw
thee.' So we know the cricket ball was hard. The Lewes find
may be a junior ball, being only about three inches in diameter
(the irregular shape makes it impossible to specify). The absence
of the stuffing makes it impossible to determine the weight.

A quality ball is made of a number of natural materials with
a leather outer casing stitched with twine. The centre was
formerly a square of cork which was wound round with layers
of cork and worsted. Five layers were used, the last wound
damp so that it contracted in a gentle oven. Today the centre is
usually made of a compressed-granulated round cork *squab*.
The *quilt winder*, or *quilter*, makes the *quilt*, which is the whole
inside of the ball. This is hammered round. Then the quilt is
weighed and gauged. Then, preparatory to adding the false
quarters, they are *skived*, by the *skiver*: OED gives the meaning
of 'pared or shaved (of hides)', but bevelled is more exact in

this case. False quarters are pieces of leather the same shape as, but smaller than, the quarter themselves. They are necessary because the cover will be sewn, when it is turned inside out, with six-stranded hemp, a thick twine, which makes a ridge around the edges where it is sewn: the false quarters compensate for this. 'To *skive*', of course, has a different meaning, to be set a task and instead 'skive off to the pub' defines it and the *skiver*.

But before this can happen, the leather, cow-hide, must be treated. It comes in half *culattas*, this Italian word having an etymology apparently to do with the word *culo* (vulg.), and referring to the part of the cow or horse between the saddle and the tail – the rump. It is then alum tanned. The hide is stretched across, and then *straked*, a term cognate with *stretch*, both coming from OE 'streccan' with palatalised 'cc'. (One is reminded here of the difficulty with the palatalised and hard middle 'c' of 'cricket'.) Straking applies to lengthwise stretching over a knife, using winding rollers. The noise the leather makes then is said to be the ball 'talking', or the leather 'barking', as it is straked over a knife. Then the *knocking-out machine* punches out the four leaf-shaped segments of the cover and shapes and bevels them. The cover-maker sews the four quarters together, into two halves, using six-stranded hemp. The false covers are fitted, and the halves moulded on a press. Now the *trimmer* takes the flashing off, the two hemispheres are fitted and seamed together (the small seam) and wax-dipped. The stitcher, using nine-stranded flax twine, which comes solely from Northern Ireland, sews together the small seam and the big seam of two rows each side of the ball, 80 stitches each, saddle-stitched with awls using a nylon bristle. It was formerly a hog's whisker, imported from Russia, as the only material supple and strong enough to go through the stitch holes. It has now been supplanted by nylon, one reason being the cost, measured in pounds per ounce. It is split at the tapered end (the hogs' whiskers were frequently split already), the twine fitted into it between the legs of the split, and then the bristle twisted on and looped round through the twine for the stitching. The wax on the twine is a mixture of lard and tree resin, and is classified (in descending grades of hardness): *straight, peak* and *wobble*. This process is all carried out by *ball snobs*, the old term for ball makers, from snob, a shoe-mender, cobbler, or his apprentice. Then waxing takes place. This was done with buck fat from Scotland until the supply dried up, but the British Wax Institute supplied an adequate substitute. The ball is then milled and weighed and checked on an MCC-approved gauge. The weight for an adult ball has to be $5\frac{1}{2}$ oz. to a tolerance of 2 drams ($\frac{1}{8}$th of an oz.). The ball is then gold-stamped. Ladies have a 5 oz. ball, which must be manufactured to the same tolerances, and the junior ball is $4\frac{3}{4}$ oz.

ball²   a delivery made by the bowler who bowls six balls an over in England, formerly eight in Australia, now six: many years ago the over was of four, then of five balls. *A good ball* is one of the right length and direction, or of some kind of difficulty, which threatens the dismissal of the batsman.

ball doctoring, tampering   a term applied to three methods of inducing greater movement in the air to the ball. This applies particularly to *reverse swing* bowling, when the ball moves late and at high speed. According to Imran Khan, speaking to David Frost on television in 1994, there are three types: gouging or scratching; smearing with unguents such as sun-oil, lip-salve, or sweat: and seam-lifting. The first is definitely illegal, but the other two are in common use. The smearing is done on the smoother side, its effect being to make it smoother still so that the boundary layer separates earlier. The most common, seam-lifting, 'had almost become accepted in the game' (Imran Khan, *Daily Telegraph*, 20 November 1993). The quarter seam may be lifted with the fingernails, although botttle-tops have also been used. The practice has gone on for many years: according to Khan, nearly every seamer picked the seam, but he could not remember an umpire taking action over his 21 years in the game.

In a lecture to the Cricket Society in May 1994, Alec Stewart of Surrey and England said the process could be observed because the different substances left a different coloured stain on the bowler's flannels as he polished the ball. Simon Hughes pointed out in the *Independent on Sunday*: 'there are several first-class players who have imported oily substances from their clothes onto the ball, and one team used non-scented talcum powder'. This seems a sensible precaution, as Don Oslear (p.33) found that with lip-salve the ball gives off a distinct odour after a time: more difficult to detect is the wax spray applied to trousers beforehand, on which the ball is then rubbed.

The doyen of fast-medium bowlers, Sir Richard Hadlee, writing in the *Sunday Star Times* of New Zealand (February 1995), suggested legalising minor forms of tampering such as using a fingernail to scratch the ball. It has to be remembered there is no law against restoring the ball to its original condition, or lifting the stitching (as opposed to the seam) which has been flattened by use.

balloon, ballooner   a high rather than merely long hit. 'After all, he [Jim Bridges] had made 99 not out against Essex on his native sward, mostly by huge high balloons' (Robertson-Glasgow, speaking of Weston-Super-Mare). It also used to describe a score of zero, or duck.

banana, banana ball   a delivery that bends violently in the air, a ball that swings a lot, cf. 'banana kick' in football.

bandy wicket   a simplified form of cricket, played in East Anglia. 'A game with bats or sticks, and ball, like cricket – but with bricks ... or ... hats, instead of bales and stumps, for wickets' (E. Moor, *Suffolk Words and Phrases*, 1823). The etymology is to bandy balls or words, OED deriving it from the Fr. *bander*, another pointer to French influence.

bang   to *bang it in*, of a quick bowler. Tony Greig speaking of Dennis Lillee and the 1974–5 tour of Australia: 'He got more and more exhausted with the effort of trying to bang it in short ... If he hadn't allowed himself to be psyched out of it he'd probably have got me out' (Francis, 26).

  For the batsman to give the ball *a bang*, is to bang the bowling around.

Barmy Army   a group of young Englishmen who travel to Test Matches and divide opinion. Seen by some as soccer-style hooligans, but welcomed in Australia in 1994, where they first were given their name at the first Test in Brisbane (they had previously been to Barbados in the 1993–4 series). Nowadays they market their own T-shirts, and have their own label for beer. As the origin of *barmy* is 'full of barm', which is 'the froth that forms on the top of fermenting malt liquors' according to the OED, their name seems well chosen. Developing out of soccer, the core, or corps, numbers some twenty, though forty went through the Australian tour. Organised, to some extent, by a 'general', thus named at the Melbourne Test.

barnacle   a batsman who clings to his wicket. Top *barnacle* in Tests at the moment is Michael Atherton, the England captain, who in the Johannesburg Test of 1995 batted for 185* in 645 minutes to save the match. His Lancs team mate Jason Gallian has the longest county innings: 11 hours and 10 minutes. T.E. Bailey was named 'Barnacle Bailey', once staying 255 minutes to make 71 and save the Lords Test of 1953. P. W.-T. has 'barnacles' as a *pair*, 1861.

barndoor   'of a defensive style, so that the bat looks like a barn door' (OED). Can be used adjectively of a bat: 'The Gentlemen's wickets were 27 in. by 8; the Players' 36 in. by 12 in. This was called the Barn-Door Match, and was won by the Players, by an innings' (Box, *Theory*, 91).

barrack   vigorous vocal support for a team. Generally supposed to be from native (New South Wales) *borak*, banter: ('to poke borak' = to make fun) – *ODEtym*.

But Hele gives a more picaresque and likely explanation in *Bodyline Umpire* (120): 'When cricket matches were first staged by Sidney's Military Club outside the Victoria Barracks in Paddington, those confined to barracks were permitted to watch them from the uncomfortable broken-glass-topped barrack walls. They were a particularly vociferous coterie, and they came to be known as barrackers.' Which explains why they were such a feature of Sydney, and may explain: 'They all to a man "barrack" for the British Lion' – *Melbourne Punch*, 14 August 1890. Originally, the meaning was to *barrack for*, 'to support and encourage by jocular comments'. But one may suppose that the glass lent a certain acerbity to the remarks.

Barrackers were notably found on the 'Hill' at Sydney, where the famous Yabba roared at Mailey, 'O for a strong arm and a walking stick!' as he bowled at Trumper for the first time. The above would explain the emergence of the term at Sydney and the quote, for if the soldiers were British, they would – presumably – support their country. It seems likely that the *ODEtym* has the less satisfactory derivation.

barter   either verb, to hit a half-volley, or noun, the ball itself, a half-volley. Belongs to that minuscule number of words that come from a name of a practitioner: Robert Specott Barter, who entered Winchester College in 1803 and held the post of Warden from 1832 to 1861. He was famous for his despatch of half-volleys. The first mention is in the *New Sporting Magazine* as early as 1836, when 'Mr Stent of Winchester lashed out and barter'd forty-five runs . . .', followed by Fred Gale, this time writing not as the 'Old Buffer' but as 'A Wykehamist' in *Public School Matches 48:* 'If I could be a boy again, and lay well hold of one "straight barter" with an old bat I once had, which drove like a racket.' But it also seems to have a variation: 'steady and straight, without the usual Winchester swipe or "leg barter"' is in *Lillywhite's Scores* in 1863, and by 1896 the word was being used at Eton. It seems that this may have figured in a grant of arms to the Warden, for Gale writes of 'a descendant of a former warden' (surely Barter) showing 'an old coat of arms with a pair of shoulders "extended", and a ball "volant", and a motto "Well bartered" underneath.'

basil   medium-paced *off-breaks*, named after Glamorgan's

Steve ('Basil') Barwick (Steve Rhodes to Michael Parkinson, *Daily Telegraph*, 8 October 1994).

bat   originally a club, stave, with sense as from Fr. *battre*, to beat: 'He nemeth is bat and forth a goth/Swithe sori and wel wroth' – *Beves of Hamtoun* ('nemeth': cf. Ger. *Nemen*, to take).

The bat in cricket probably started off as a hockey-stick sort of shape, in the rude fashion of those times, shaped to deal with *trundling*, but longer, so that taking the long handle really meant something. Then, as *length bowling* came in, the bat was straightened and given shoulders, then the handle was spliced in, sometimes with whalebone, and then always with cane. The first batmaker is said to have been Pett of Sevenoaks, who made 'the best sort' of bats and sold them for 4s. 6d in 1773.

Bats now are, or should be, made from willow; of the 100 species of the *salix*, only *Salix Alba Coerulea* is used. The trunk is first cut into rounds, then riven into billets, or clefts. The pod of the bat refers to the thick bit at the bottom, the *sweet spot*, but a pod-shaver shapes the whole of the bat. He uses draw-knives, block plane, finishing plane, and a spoke-shaver for the finishing touches.

The cane used in the handle is Manau cane, and the best comes from Sarawak (also used for garden furniture). It is often split into three pieces, sometimes twelve, and rubber strips are inserted between them, apart from the very top, where a cork and rubber compound (which sticks better) is used. Towards the inserted end of the handle, the rubber finishes and a wooden laminate (hickory, ash, etc.) is inserted to avoid any moving parts within the bat itself.

The bats are kiln-dried, and then pressed to $1\frac{1}{2}$–2 tons per square inch. Three passes are made to start with, then the bat is tested with a mallet, to judge whether more is needed. This hardening process is supposed to do away with the need for *knocking-in*. The hardness of a bat is partly determined by the grain of the willow: the narrower the grain, the harder the bat, and the longer it will last, but a wider grain, with its softer surface, hits better. The soft part of the grain should be on the inside edge of the bat, which is why left- and right-handed bats are cut differently. The weight of the bat is a subject of much discussion: Compton's sole bat in his record-breaking season of 1947 weighs 2lb. 2oz., Hutton's for his 364 at the Oval in 1938 hardly more, and has a grain extraordinarily fine. One of Grace's bats, also in the museum at Lord's, has 2 $4\frac{3}{4}$ written on the back.

Other woods have been tried, but without success: the willow is the only consistency which allows the ball to be hit hard without destroying the bat or jarring the hands. And it has to be the female tree: the male is too hard and heavy. An aluminium bat was produced and taken to the wicket in a Test by Denis Lillee, but was rapidly outlawed. Among the problems it caused were the speedy disintegration of the ball, and, when jammed down on a *yorker*, of the covered concrete pitch.

Bat can also refer to the wielder: 'someone makes some comment about having seen better bats in a cave' (Wilde, 19).

bat basket   'G. Parr was obliged to play with a bat basket on, his finger being very bad' (*Bell's Life*, 10 August 1856).

bat gauge   an implement used to measure the width of a bat, which must be $4\frac{1}{4}$ inches or less. An eighteenth-century cricketer called 'Shock' White once came out to bat with a bat as wide as the wicket, and it is said that his enraged opponents from Hambledon shaved his implement down to the allowed width.

bat mugger   a wooden instrument for working oil into a bat. (1912, P. W.-T.).

bat-pad catch   a catch given to a fielder, usually close-in, but not always, given the resilience of some modern pads, from a ball which has hit the bat, thence to the pad, thence to a fielder. Often from off-spin bowling, and a difficult umpiring decision. 'If he has to play forward, he will have the front foot some distance in front of the bat so that if the ball hits the inside edge of the bat it cannot bounce from the bat to the pad and from there into the hands of the leg-side fielders' – C.L.R. James on Bradman playing Laker (*The Nation*, Trinidad, 30 October 1959).

bat's end   'point of the bat's end' was the original name for the fielding position known now as *point*. 'The old bat used to be heavy at the point – very requisite for picking up a Grounder' Revd James Pycroft, 1862 (OED). Thus the end of the bat was called the 'point', and the old illustrations show the heavy curved bats held so that the end was in the direction of what we now call 'point'. Lewis has this as Hampshire dialect, but it is plainly descriptive: *The Young Cricketer's Tutor* has 'point of the bat' as the place for point to field.

batsman   as Cardus defines *batsmanship*, below, Peter Roebuck says of Brian Lara: 'Unlike Gavaskar, though, technique is never Lara's master. Gavaskar was a creature of science and will. Lara is nature's creation. He is not a man batting, rather a batsman' (*Sunday Times*, 12 June 1994).

batsmanlike   cf. workmanlike: 'Thanks to McCool's undefeated and most batsmanlike century, [the Australians] reached 365 on the second morning' (Whitington, 194): contrast, without being unfair to the magnificent McCool, the next entry:

batsmanship   the batsman's art: the art of batting at cricket; batting performance. 'The Rev. F.H. Gillingham ... has done splendid service for Essex by his vigorous batsmanship' (*Westminster Gazette*, 30 May 1907) – OED.

Cardus describes Frank Woolley of Kent and England: 'His batsmanship, like all fine art, can be enjoyed by everybody, because it is fresh and natural. To add up the runs made by Woolley – why, it is as though you were to add up the crotchets and quavers written by Mozart' (*Essential Cardus*, 110). He sums up (in Moult, 46): 'Coaching is a curse ... Batsmanship is to batting what poetry is to verse.' Nyren (p.73) describing Beldham: 'It was the beau ideal of grace, animation, and concentrated energy.'

But it need not always describe elegance: 'batsmanship such as that of ... in his stubborn days, Charles Hallows, which flowed on ... without ever the hope of an anacoluthon' (Robertson-Glasgow, *Crusoe*, 248).

batspeed   'The crucial figure in your calculation for despatching a cricket ball to the boundary is the speed of the bat.' Simon Hughes, reporting from the congress of The Institute of Physics, goes on: 'Batspeed. The key to Lara's genius ... he picks the bat up extremely high ... Everything is cocked' (*Spectator*, 2 September 1995).

batter   'one who bats, or is batting' says Lewis indisputably, and gives an early use of the phrase, from the magazine *Temple Bar* (1861): 'And there is the quack on a muscular Christianity basis, who ... ranks a good batter ... before a Smith's prizeman.' The first use of the word seems to occur in the verse of J. Duncombe, the *Surry Triumph* of 1773: 'At last, Sir Horace took the field,/A batter of great might'.

batting   as a word, applies to the whole art, as painting to paint. 'Our batting was at a very low ebb by then. Tyson, Statham and the rest, on the other hand, had their confidence boosted ...' – Ian Johnson, Australian cricket captain, on the end of the 1954–5 Ashes series (*WCM*, October 1994).

batting average   see *average*.

batting crease   another name for *popping crease*.

batting order   the order in which the batsmen go in, from 1 to 11. There is an old captain's saw: 'Never change your order when chasing runs.'

batting points   see *bonus points*.

battyman '"Skipper! My skipper done played a battyman shot man!" said a West Indian at the Oval as Richie Richardson played and missed' (Andrew Baker, *Independent on Sunday*, 28 May 1995).

beamer a ball aimed high by the bowler, often to the height of the batsman's head. 'Let us not confuse orthodox fast bowling with bouncers and beamers' (*The Times*, 21 March 1962, OED). The *beamer* reaches the batsman as a high full toss, and as it hasn't bounced is that much faster, apart from being difficult to pick up as the line is so different – more difficult than one thinks: 'When he let go of that ball, I just didn't see it,' said Mark Ramprakash, who received one on his visor from the fast-medium Glenn McGrath, in the bright light of the Perth Test, while making 72 in 1995. Philippe Henri Edmonds of Middlesex and England was thrice heavily bruised through his body armour by beamers in the West Indies. Derived most probably from hitting somebody with a beam.

bean ball is either a *bouncer* or a *beamer*, *bean* meaning the head.

beat has two meanings, the first shown by Grace (*Cricket*, 246): 'Try to have sufficient command of the ball so that if it beat the batsman it will hit the wicket.'

The second as exemplified by Geoffrey Boycott on BBC television, when England wickets were falling to the West Indies in the Third Test at Edgbaston, 1995: 'You've just got to stay in for the first hour . . . not beat the ball . . .'.

beauty 'Spofforth was bowled by a "beauty" from Mycroft' (OED: *Australians in England*, 1882, 46). Mycroft, a Derbyshire bowler, is thought to have given his name to Sherlock Holmes's elder brother, the intelligent one, although whether this was because of the cunning of his deliveries is unknown. Also 'beaut', especially in Australia.

beer match a match which takes place after the main game, usually because one side has won so quickly there is time to spare: '"We don't want the embarrassment of being half-way through the beer match when he [John Major] gets here," observed Mike Watkinson in his usual dry manner' (*Cricketer International*, March 1997); Lancashire were scheduled to play India A on their tour of the subcontinent, and proceeded to win the *one dayer* in the last over.

behind the pace scoring at too low a rate for the situation.

belter a pitch where the ball comes on straight after bouncing so can be belted: '[Sri Lanka's] batsmen opt for vertical take off in the first fifteen overs, not the last fifteen . . . A belter of a

pitch is one essential prerequisite . . . Jayasuriya hit 13 fours . . .
and three sixes, from only 44 balls' (Scyld Berry, *Sunday
Telegraph*, 10 March 1996).

bend   the movement of the ball in the air (see *swerve*), but
implies more of a single movement than a curve, which can
gradually increase as the seam angle changes in relation to the
angle of the line of flight as the swing pushes it round.

beneficiary   the recipient of testimonial appreciation: see below.

benefit   a testimonial in the form of the gate receipts, or other
monies, as a personal gift and not remuneration for his services,
which is awarded to a cricketer of some years' service with his
county. Nowadays it is usually after ten years' service after
being capped; previously it was at irregular, and spontaneous,
intervals. William Bestwick of Derbyshire took all ten wickets
against Glamorgan in 1921, and collections were taken up at
his next two home games; he gave half the proceeds to Arthur
Morton, his team-mate who had had a motor-cycle accident:
'give this to owd Arthur, he needs it more than me.' At this
time the invested sum was always handed over to the professional cricketer when his career was over, or when he found
an investment, such as a share in a business or a farm, of which
the trustees approved. 'Its purpose was not to encourage the
cricketer to further exertions, but to express the gratitude of his
employers and the cricket-loving public for what he had already
done and their appreciation of his personal qualities . . . If the
benefit had taken place after Seymour's retirement, no one
would have sought to tax the proceeds as income . . .' so said
the Lord Chancellor in 1927, deciding by a majority of four to
one in the Court of Appeal that the proceeds from benefits
were not taxable. But in 1954, in the case of Bruce Dooland,
the Australian leg-spin, googly topspin, and flipper bowler,
playing as the club professional in the Lancashire League, the
decision differed. A key clause in the contract may have been
'collections shall be made for any meritorious performance by
the professional with bat or ball'. It was held that the collections
were part of the earnings of Dooland's profession under the
terms of his contract (*The Times Law Reports* 1927 and 1954).

The proceeds of testimonials vary enormously, from the
equivalent of £100,000 for Cyril Washbrook at Lancashire
when he had been an established England player for some time,
to those who barely break even. As county gates fell, new
methods such as the 'benefit season' with special games and
attractions, 'personal' appearances, and so on, were introduced:
sometimes a team-mate would help. Compton, year after year,

would entertain the Whit Monday crowd at Lord's, either for himself or a fellow professional; on his own benefit day in 1949 he made 182 and collected £12,000.

beneficiaire   man receiving a benefit (1843, P.W.-T.).

bias   obsolete: 'turning of a ball in its course from the leg side towards the off after pitching' (OED). 'The bowler was not slow to take advantage of the opening by developing anew the old "bias" or break from leg' – J. Mitford, *Runs*, (1833), v. 135.

Bill's Mother's   used at Old Trafford when the clouds start building up, and it looks as if rain is coming, say from Altrincham, but generally from an unspecified direction: 'it looks a bit dark over *Bill's Mother's*', is how it is described (David Green of the *Daily Telegraph*, interviewed by the author in 1995).

bite   grip of the surface of the ground on pitching. J. Lillywhite's *Cricketers' Companion*: 'If the ground is soft, slow bowlers will tell best, the ball hangs or bites' (1867).

bits-and-pieces player   bats a bit, bowls a bit. 'Roger Twose, the county bits-and-pieces pro, jokingly hung a sign on his own changing-room peg, proclaiming "World's Second-best Left-hand Bat", Brian Lara being the best' (Frank Keating, *Spectator*, 20 August 1994).

blackwash   when West Indies completed their 5–0 defeat of England at the Oval in the 1984 Test series, a banner was displayed by the West Indian section of the crowd with the single word 'blackwash'.

blade   of a bat, the part which is not the handle: 'by the handle of the bat being nearer the bowler than the *blade* . . .. the ball will be prevented from rising' – *Practical Hints on Cricket*, by William Clarke, 'Slow Bowler, and Secretary to the All England Eleven'. Clarke, born 1798, appeared in the Nottingham Eleven when 17, touring with his eleven until late middle age.

blaze   a hard shot: origin possibly from the dual sense of blazing a trail by scoring trees, and of a blazing torch. The sense is that the ball is so hard struck it scorches the grass.

blazer   the jacket, of classic cut, worn by teams to denote membership. At international level the colours are green for Australia and South Africa, with the national coat-of-arms; blue for England, with St George and the dragon; black for New Zealand, with the fernleaf. Originally, HMS *Blazer*'s crew wore them to distinguish them from other crews.

blind   in a limited-over game, i.e. in which the winner is the side that scores most in the given overs; the side that bats first thus has no target to aim at.

blind spot   'that spot of ground in front of batsman where a ball pitched by the bowler leaves the batsman in doubt whether to play forward or back' (OED). More exactly, the spot on the eyeball with no receptors, because the optic nerve runs from there to the brain. Usually reckoned as around middle and leg. 'Now the great difficulty of slows, besides being (as they ought all to be) "in the blind spot", consists in the elevation . . . of a dropping ball' (*Baily's Magazine*, 1864); 'Too often would come a ball on the blind spot' (Grace, *Cricket*, 73).

blinder   OED defines this as 'something "dazzlingly" good or difficult, esp. a piece of play in Rugby Football or Cricket'.

'Striking out an an innocent looking ball, I've sent a blinder – dead into the fieldsman's hands' (Hammond, *Cricketers' School*, 35); 'You played a blinder . . . it was the best game I ever saw' (David Storey, *This Sporting Life*, 1960); 'they dropped one easy catch and caught three blinders' (*The Times*, 16 February 1963). The word implies the ball was travelling fast when referring to a catch.

blob   a batsman's score of no runs, so called from the zero placed against his name in the score-sheet = duck's egg. 'Mr Foster . . . taking the first wicket of the tour by bowling Mr E.R. Mayne for a "blob",' (Hobbs, *Ashes*, 19). Still in use.

block[1]   to stop (a ball) with a bat, so as merely to protect the wicket, without attempting to hit it so as to score runs. H.T. Waghorn, in *Dawn of Cricket*, referring to a game in 1772: 'As the lame man could only block his wicket' (OED).

block[2]   Australian: the *square*, or area of the ground where the pitches are laid.

blockhole   the dent made in the *popping crease* by taking guard; it may have been originally the hole into which the ball had to be 'popped' to run a batsman out, although from a print at Lord's the hole seems to be in the wicket crease.

blow away   to destroy an innings by bowling. 'Ambrose would have blown Bradman and Boycott away' – Simon Hughes (*Daily Telegraph*, 31 March, 1994), in the wake of England's total of 46 in Trinidad. The origin of this is probably lost in pulp fiction, referring to American gangsters and their habit of using large-caliber sub-machine guns to deal with their rivals.

blue   to win his *blue* or to be a *Blue* is to be chosen to represent his University or School in rowing, cricket, etc. 'An old Blue' is one who has rowed or played in an inter-University contest.

board   short for *scoreboard*.

body-break   obsolete form of *action-break*.

bodyline, body-line   after the young Don Bradman had completed his first Test series in England, his aggregate of runs was 974 and his average 139. How to contain him in the next series, in 1931–2, on his own pitches?

Nottinghamshire had two fast bowlers, Harold Larwood and Bill Voce, both England players. Larwood could not swing an old ball, so he would break it back and switch his field for catches on the leg side. And it had been noted that the Don had seemed a bit unconfident playing fast balls on the leg stump at the Surrey Oval, though he made 232. George Duckworth, the England wicket-keeper, admitted to Archie Jackson that he had the original idea after watching him there. News of the new bowling technique got out, and Douglas Jardine, appointed captain for the series, took Carr (the Notts captain), Larwood and Voce out to the Piccadilly Grill to quiz them about it. He also saw F.R. Foster, the left-handed fast bowler of the 1911–12 Ashes tour, who later said publicly, 'I would like all my friends in Australia to know that I am sorry my experience and advice were put to such an unworthy use.'

Although the packed leg-side field had already been tried, the row really erupted at Adelaide in the Third Test on 14 January 1932 when the Australian captain, Bill Woodfull, was hit over the heart by a short ball from Larwood, who did not at that time have a leg-side field. To the Australian umpire, George Hele (see *Bodyline Umpire*, 130), it was a ball that was a bit short and pitched on the leg stump, to Larwood it was a straight ball, and Woodfull had moved towards the off; to Jardine it seemed Woodfull stepped across outside his off stump to a ball which Larwood brought back from the off. Larwood was bowling at that time to a normal field, but soon after this incident the **short legs** were brought in, which by itself nearly caused a pitch invasion.

Then the Australian 'keeper, Oldfield, was hit on the head, although the ball was not aimed at his body. Indeed he appears to have been hooking from slightly outside off stump. Again, it was touch-and-go whether the field would be invaded by spectators.

Curiously enough, the English bowler who finished with the best **analysis** was G.O. Allen with 8 for 121. Although a key man in the leg-trap of up to six short legs, at just forward of square, where he caught Bradman for 8 off Larwood in the Test, he refused to bowl *bodyline*.

After this match the Australian Board cabled the MCC: 'intensely bitter feeling . . . in our opinion it is unsportsmanlike . . . unless stopped at once it is likely to upset friendly relations existing between Australia and England.' The MCC disagreed, but ended their cable saying that if the ABC thought the remainder of the tour should be cancelled they would with great reluctance consent, to which the Australians replied they did not think that necessary. The next MCC cable asked if they could 'accept that as a clear indication that the good sportsmanship of our team is not in question?' To which the Australian Board of Control rather backtracked, saying they did 'not regard the sportsmanship of your team as being in question'. Jardine's determination to have the charge of unsportsmanship withdrawn (or he would not lead the team out in another Test) probably had much to do with the last MCC cable. The Dominions Secretary, J.H. Thomas, said that the bodyline question had given him more trouble than anything else.

It wasn't all Jardine's fault: umpire Hele observed that when Jardine threw the ball to Allen after Larwood's first over, Sutcliffe walked up to Allen, who was supposed to bowl from the other end, took the ball from him, and threw it to Voce. Jardine looked surprised but did not interfere. Led by Sutcliffe and Hammond, the field moved to the leg side.

But was it intentional aiming at the batsman's body, or just fast leg theory from the man regarded by Hele (who saw them all, up to but not including Marshall and Hadlee) as the best, let alone the fastest, he ever saw? Larwood himself said: 'with Bradman it was like trying to trap a wild duck, his movements were so swift. In the final split-second before my arm whipped over I used to watch him, trying to anticipate his intentions. If he moved one way or the other, I would vary my direction at the last instant to keep it in line with his body' (p.99). Hobbs thought the bowling was aimed at the batsman. 'Bradman was not tall enough to prevent the ball cocking up to Allen at forward short-leg,' said Hele.

Larwood's best match analysis was 10–124 in the first Test (when Bradman was absent), but in the second innings he seldom bowled short for his 5–28. But the tactic did succeed in reducing Bradman's series average to 56.57. Was it unsporting, given what McDonald and Gregory had done to England soon after the Great War? Without moral relativism, the answer must be yes. Larwood said that he wouldn't have bothered if he could have swung the ball, but he couldn't in Australia, perhaps because the superior product of those days had much neater stitching, making a lower seam.

While this is probably wrong, because a lower seam does not necessarily hinder swing (as shown in *swing* below), he may point unwittingly to the correct reason in the same paragraph when he observes that 'many bowlers today can swing the ball long after the sheen has gone' – when differential air pressure is, if anything, easier to achieve if one side of the ball is kept in fair condition. A better understanding of aerodynamics might have averted bodyline.

The term itself was apparently coined either by the father of Chester Wilmot, 'Buns', or by Jack Worrall, a former Test batsman, referring to a match before the Series began. Worrall used the phrase 'half-pitched slingers on the body-line', which was copied by Hugh Buggy of the *Melbourne Herald* on the evening of the first day of the first Test at Sydney, and picked up by his sub-editor Ray Robinson, later one of the best-known of all Australian cricket writers. This seems to be the first use of bodyline bowling as a single word.

The legislation in the original Law 46 put the onus on the umpire: 'The persistent bowling of fast short-pitched balls at the batsman is unfair if in the opinion of the umpire at the bowler's end, it constitutes a systematic attempt at intimidation . . .' This owed a certain amount to the talks held by the Australian captain Woodfull, George Hele, and the Melbourne *Age* cricket correspondent, Frank Maugher, on the beach at Sydney on the evening of the last day of the Series. Jardine himself stood up well to the bodyline attack of Martindale and Constantine in the Old Trafford Test in 1933, making 127.

bonus points   OED has '?from L. *bonus*', from *bonum*, originally Stock Exchange slang, a boon or gift over and above what is normally due. *Bonus points* are awarded in the County League table for performance in batting and bowling over the first 120 overs of each team's first innings. The batting side gets one point for scoring between 200 and 249 runs, another for 250–299, another for 300–349, and another for 350 and over, a maximum of four. The fielding side pick up their bowling points (still over the first 120 overs) thus: 3–4 wickets down 1 point, 5–6 another, 7–8 another, and 9 and 10 another. The system was first introduced to make for brighter play, reward good performances, and lessen the number of drawn matches, for which no points are given.

booth ball   before boundaries were properly marked, the ball would run out among the spectators from a hard hit. Tents, and booths would be among them, thus the term. Boundaries came in later than one might think; they were not in place when W.G. Grace started playing at Lord's *c.* 1864.

Boot Hill   very short leg. 'Brian Hardie of Essex . . . stood very close and took some fearful blows from the ball. But he also took some brilliant catches in his days at Boot Hill' (Oslear, 200). In the gunslinging days of the West, the dead were buried there: one can only suppose they died with their boots on, and these gradually worked their way to the surface, rejected by even the coyotes.

boots   *boots* also means shoes, which is what they started as, ordinary shoes with nails driven in and buckles which could bear the team's crest or name: in the eighteenth century one unfortunate tore his nail off on the buckle while fielding. Now separate boots are used for bowling and fielding, and batting. They are made from a variety of materials, leather, rubber and plastic, with a variety of grips and attempts at protection both from the ball and injury to the foot from stamping down on the ground, prevalent with fast bowlers (Larwood 1933, Gough 1995). Further work is needed in both supportive and protective aspects.

bore   obsolete: 'to wick a bore in curling and cricket is to drive a stone or ball dexterously through an opening between two guards' (OED). 'He was the king o' a' the core, To guard, or draw, or wick a bore' – Burns, 'Tam Samson's Elegy and Epitaph', 1786. The derivation of 'wick' may ultinately be the same as that of 'wicket'.

bosie, bosey   Australian term for *googly*.

Botany Bay Lad   'early name for an Australian cricketer, from the original settlement of Botany Bay, 1788' (Tyson, 20).

bottom edge   with a cross bat, the inside edge is nearest to the ground and is the *bottom edge*.

bottom hand   the *bottom hand* on the bat: too much of it leads to errors like playing *across the line*.

bounce¹   to *bounce* the ball means to bowl a bouncer, e.g. 'Lillee bounced Brearley twice.'

bounce²   a reference to the degree and predictability of bounciness in the pitch: 'The main problem today is the variable bounce, which can make the best batsman in the world look second-rate' (Boycott, 27).

bouncer   a short-pitched fast ball which rises to the chest of the batsman, frequently well above. Obviously this can be intimidatory if done too often, and the umpires have it within their discretion to call a 'No-ball', and caution the bowler, inform the captain of the fielding side and the other umpire and the batsman. If it goes on, he should give the bowler a final warning and inform as before. On repetition, under section 8 of Law 42, he can direct the captain to take the bowler off. First usage in Lewis is 1928: 'C.K. Hill-Wood ... has a curious delivery ... But he "makes haste off the pitch" and can send down an occasional "bouncer"' (P.F. Warner, *Morning Post*, 2 July).

'[Lindwall's] bouncers were most effective . . . Because of his low action they used to skid through head high and were never really pitched short; as a result you had little time to play them' (Compton, *Innings*, 163).

boundary   'Always agree at starting . . . what are the boundaries' (J. Lillywhite, 7). The Laws of 1884 mention *boundaries* for the first time. There were no fixed boundaries at Lord's as late as 1864. Boundary also denotes a four or six.

In those days a six was only awarded for hitting the ball out of the ground. Many instances are given of large totals being run while the ball, sometimes seeming unnaturally elusive, was retrieved from among the spectators: a practice, says Nyren, to which his men would never, well, stoop. But in 1733 the playing area at Kennington Common was ringed round for a game, and in 1745 the playing field was benched round at Addington in Surrey 'for better regulation', which had something to do with the betting.

bounds   from *single wicket*. Nyren says in *Young Cricketer's Tutor*, 'When the parties consist of fewer than five on each side, the custom of the game is, to make bounds on each side of the wicket.' These were drawn square with the wicket to a length of 22 yards, though exactly where is not clear.

bowl   from ME *boule*, adopted from Fr., and in turn from L. *bul-* to swell, and *bulla*, a bubble, cf. 'bullfrog' (OED). It is the action of bowling. First mention seems to be in the *Weekly Journal*: 'They would not suffer him to bowl' (7 July 1722).

Originally, the ball was actually bowled or 'trundled' along the ground: 'fast sneaks' as Altham says. In the two earliest descriptions of the game, Godwin (1706) has the ball shave the pitch: 'radit iter rapidum', *radit* meaning to scrape, shave (the root for our 'razor'). The next work, James Love's *Heroick Poem* (1744) has 'Four times from Hodswell's arms it skims the grass.' But by around the middle of the 18th century, or just after, the ball was being thrown through the air, bouncing about three-quarters of the way down the pitch: the new 'length bowling', which in its turn encouraged round-arm deliveries because now flight and deception were possible as well as a change of speed.

This brought about a cautionary Law in 1816, which stated that the ball 'must be bowled (not thrown or jerked) and be delivered underhand with the hand below the elbow' (see also *straight-arm*). In 1835 the Law read: 'The ball must be bowled. If it be thrown or jerked, or if the hand be above the shoulder in the delivery, the Umpire must call "No Ball is out"' ... but bowlers continued to transgress. In 1862 Edgar Willsher (not to be confused with Willes) was in his turn *no-balled* by John Lillywhite, in the Surrey v. England match, and all the professionals on the England side left the field in protest. The next day the play was resumed with another umpire. But progress could not be stopped, and in 1864, after *The Sporting Life* had tried to set up a Cricket Parliament to take over the Laws of the game, MCC amended Law 10 to omit mention of the height of the bowler's arm, retaining the provision against throwing and jerking.

John Nyren wrote his 'Protest Against the Modern Innovation of Throwing, Instead of Bowling the Balls' as part of *The Young Cricketers' Tutor:* 'from the random manner of delivering the ball, it is impossible for the fine batsman to have time for that finesse and delicate management, which so peculiarly distinguished the elegant manoeuvring of the chief players who occupied the field eight, ten, and more years ago' (Lucas, 40).

Thus to bowl fast, slow, or medium pace. To *bowl short* means to bowl to a short length (not to be confused with one short, which refers to a batsman not properly completing his run). To *bowl a full length* is to 'pitch the ball up', on or just over the best length for that kind of bowling. To *bowl over the wicket* means the bowling arm is the one closest to the wicket. Thus Terry Alderman's close-to-the-stumps approach, *bowling wicket to wicket*, always gave Graham Gooch trouble hitting round his front pad. To *bowl around the wicket* is for a right-hander to bowl from the leg-side of his wicket. This creates more *angle* and creates different difficulties.

To bowl into the rough means to pitch the ball in the area roughened up by the footmarks of the bowler operating from the other end.

To bowl an over or overs: to complete 6 balls or 8 balls from the same end, formerly 4 or 5 balls. Alf Valentine of the West Indies bowled 80 overs in The Oval Test Match of 1950, then a record. His figures would have been better but for Len Hutton's superb stroke play through the covers to give him 202*.

To bowl to one's field: to have the fielders positioned so the majority of balls hit by the batsman go to a fieldsman. Thus a slow left-armer will usually bowl with a *cover* and *extra-cover*, or *short-extra*, an off-spinner with *short-legs*. Allan Border set a field for David Gower of three *slips*, and two *gullies*, this last being an effort to stop Gower scoring square of the wicket off his faster bowlers.

To bowl a batsman: to hit the stumps and dislodge one or other of the bails, even if the ball comes off the batsman. The stronger form is to **bowl out**, either of a single batsman or of a side, and in the latter case does not refer to the entire side being out by having their stumps hit, but it does imply a low total. To bowl Gatting 'off his legs' (from an in-slanter from Mervyn Hughes) means that in the Test series of 1993, Mike Gatting of Middlesex and England played across the ball coming into him, missed it, and the ball hit his pads and went onto the wicket. This was the last ball of the day. In the next Test Shane Warne showed how to bowl Gooch 'round his legs': Gooch attempted to pad away a ball pitching well outside the leg stump, but the ball spun viciously behind him and hit the leg stump. To *underbowl* a bowler is not to use him as often as circumstances indicate, and to *overbowl* him is to use him too much.

To bowl dry is an Australian term meaning to bowl line and length around the off stump, waiting for the batsman to make a mistake.

bowl-out   when a result is not possible through playing a game of cricket, in some *limited-over* competitions which have to go forward with a result, a *bowl-out* is conducted. Not dissimilar to the penalty shoot-out in football, a number of players are chosen to bowl at a wicket and the side which misses fewest times is the winner, with a sudden-death proviso for a tie. Introduced as a toss of a coin had to decide an abandoned game between Gloucestershire and Middlesex in the 1983 quarter-final of the Benson and Hedges Cup at Bristol.

bowled   the ball has hit the wicket and dislodged a bail, without any intervening substance except a pad, or other part of the batsman's body. If his bat has touched it, it will be *played on*.

bowled out   a strong form, usually referring to a side rather than an individual, implying that they have been dismissed cheaply. Previously used to signify mere dismissal, Waghorn's (*Cricket Scores*, 47) 'James Bryant (bowled out) 0' dates from 1750, and in 1819 the expresssion was used of all such dismissals in the Andover-Stockbridge match.

bowler   one who bowls.

bowling   referring to either the individual, the side, or the *attack* of some of the bowlers. The *Hampshire Chronicle* reported on a match between tradesmen on the North and on the South sides of Winchester High Street on 11 August 1859, which resulted in an unexpected victory for the 'Southmen':

'The Northmen were now become serious and this feeling must have been vastly increased when on succeeding to the wickets the comparatively small score of 36 was only obtained, Messrs. Naish and Blakes's *bowling* evidently confusing the batsman'.

bowling average   the number of runs scored against a bowler, and extras awarded against him, divided by the number of wickets he takes, whether in a match, a season, series, or lifetime: see *average*.

bowling crease   marked in line with the stumps, 8' 8" long but considered of infinite length, i.e. its jurisdiction does not stop at the end of the line but at the boundary.

bowling machine   the first bowling machine was the *catapulta*, used to give practice to the batsman, especially in the art of the *draw shot* and against 'perfectly straight bowling'. Probably from Greek *kata*, against + *pallain*, to hurl (OED). It first appears as an invention of Nicholas Wanostrocht, whose transparent *nom de jeu* was 'Felix'. His invention was described in the *New Sporting Magazine* of 1837: 'an instrument for bowling, which has been invented, during the last cricketing season, by Mr. Felix, and given by him to that deserving servant of the Marylebone Club, Mr. Caldecourt.' Felix himself used it to practice against the fast bowling of the giant (over six foot and eighteen stone) Alfred Mynn.

That, and its smaller and lighter descendant the *balista*, resembled Roman siege engines of that name except that they did not have their projectiles in a sling at the end of an arm. Rather the arm sprang up, with a rubber pad at the end which hit the ball, which was on an adjustable plate, in the direction of the batsman. As it needed constant reloading, its virtue must have been its constancy of aim. Mr Caldecourt seems to have had quite a flourishing and profitable relationship with Felix (see *glove*).

The modern bowling machine has two spinning wheels, between which the ball is passed, or in between which it is dropped by a coach or from a hopper. The speed of the wheels determines the speed with which the ball is spat out, at up to 90 m.p.h. By altering the speed of one wheel relative to another, the dimple ball, like a giant golf ball, can be made to swing, or spin at lower speeds.

bowling points   see *bonus points*.

bowling restrictions   the amount of overs, or the proportion of the total, that any one bowler can deliver in certain types of competition. A one-day match can consist of 55 overs for each side, of which the maximum permitted total per bowler is 11.

box¹ 'Hobbs was caught in that nondescript position which is variously known as "the box" and "the gully"' (*Daily Mail*, 29 June 1926).

box² the abdominal protector, used in fact to protect the genitals, and which fits into the front pouch of the athletic supporter or *jock-strap*. Bowling which comes *into the box* is bowling slanting in to the area of the crotch.

brace to bag a brace: to get a *duck* in each innings. See also *pair*.

brain box, brain bucket colloquial and jocular for the helmet worn by batsman or close fielder such as short-leg. 'Box' is supposed to refer to the much earlier appearance of the lower protector, thus, again jocular, the priorities for defending the different organs.

bread and butter shot is the most profitable shot of a batsman: 'Wessels has soft hands, and exemplary control ... back, then leaning in as the ball comes to him, he uses the angled bat to fade the ball down to third man ... this has become his staple run-getter, his bread-and-butter shot' (Slater, 2.i. 4).

bread and butter wicket a plain no-nonsense *pitch*, adequate for many runs.

break the ball *breaks* when it changes direction after bouncing. Thus an *off-break* goes from off to leg and a *leg-break* from leg to off (breaking from off or leg): they can be said to *break back* or *break away* respectively, or *break in* (the off-break). Also to *break the ball* means to make it turn.

The term *on-break*, for leg-break, is no longer used. The sole occasion given by Lewis is from Fred Gale's entry in the Badminton Library's *Cricket* of 1888: 'One thing I am certain of, which is that there was an on-break from Farmer Miles' bowling, for I watched the balls pitch and curl.' In the early days of the game the word used was *twist*.

To *break the wicket*; to dislodge a bail or the bails in stumping or running out a batsman: 'He took her [the ball] close to the bails and just broke the wicket' (F. Gale, *Baily's Magazine*, September 1875.

To *break his duck*, to get off the mark, open his account: not used of breaking a brace, or pair.

breakaway a ball which breaks away from the batsman. Not listed in Lewis.

breakback today usually applied to a faster type of ball, which pitches on the off and then turns back into the area of the wicket. But at the turn of the century it was applied to this great slow-medium off-spinner, a candidate for the all-time Australian team: 'Hugh Trumble, who in the match took fifteen wickets, was bowling grand break-backs' (Giffen, 21).

break-necker   an obsolete term, a large off-break: 'It was what is commonly termed a break-necker, pitching about a foot wide and turning onto the wicket' (Alverstone & Alcock, 150).

bring¹   to put (someone) on to bowl. 'Hayward and Parr were then brought on [as bowlers]' (*Baily's Magazine*, September 1860).

bring²   to get the ball back onto a line which might endanger the batsman's wicket. Richard Hutton writes of Matthew Hart of New Zealand, bowling left-arm round the wicket, from 'wide of the crease. At present he has to bring the ball a long way to straighten, and it was only towards the very late stages of the game that the ball showed occasional signs of turning sufficiently' (*The Cricketer*, August 1994).

Broad-Halfpenny Down   was the original site of the Hambledon ground, but 'the Duke of Dorset and other gentlemen ... complained of the bleakness of the old place.' It must indeed have been so, for the next ground was windy enough to support a windmill, yet Windmill Down was 'one of the finest places for playing on I ever saw' (Nyren, in Lucas, 63). The original word was *bord-halfpenny*, 'bord' being an obsolete form of 'board', and was the toll exacted by the lord of the manor for setting up booths and stalls at a fair. The annual fair of St Giles's Down at Winchester had hundreds of booths and lasted sixteen days.

broomstick   to make which, take an old bat and shave the sides until no wider than the handle. Teaches ball-watching; also used to equalise sides, as in father and son games at preparatory schools. The Revd James Pycroft reports that at Cheltenham College the first Eleven plays the second Eleven a 'broomstick match' (p.120).

Brumbrella   the Test and County ground of Edgbaston, seat of the Warwickshire County Cricket Club (WCCC), boasts a very copious covering over the pitch. 'Brum' being slang for Birmingham (and 'Brummie' for a denizen thereof), *Brumbrella* is a portmanteau word.

BLSP   'bad light stopped play': see ***bad light***.

bucolic   'That was an agricultural hoik, rustic, bucolic ...' said David Bairstow BBC Radio 4, Natwest Trophy semi-final, Lancs v. Yorks Old Trafford, 13 August 1996. From Gk *boukólos*, a herdsman or shepherd.

build   to put together, with patience and fortitude, an innings. 'The innings was set back to square one when the two [Titchard and Harvey] departed in consecutive overs bowled by Greg Mike . . . but it was re-built successfully around the resilience of John Crawley' (Jon Culley, *The Independent*, 27 August 1994).

Bulli   Bulli is a town south of Sydney, NSW. The name is used to designate a type of soil used especially for cricket pitches. 'This Bulli soil is wonderful in its resistance to wet . . . The wet does not run through the Bulli' (*Westminster Gazette*, 18 April 1904). The soil had another quality: 'Larwood seemed to skim off the hard Bulli soil surfaces of Australia like a pebble skimming off water . . . one out of every three or four deliveries would skim off the surface to be chest height . . . if Voce, Allen or myself wanted to . . . it bounced like a tennis ball and with all the speed taken out of it' (Bowes, 212).

bullshot   a cross between a pull-shot and a cow-shot, the ball being hit between mid-wicket and mid-on: 'Botting's bullshot steepled into the golden haze . . .' (*Wandsworth Borough News*, 3 September 1993).

bump   the rise of a ball from the pitch to a greater height than is usual. 'A man who plays fairly straight . . . and can meet the ball with the bat when it comes on straight with no hang or bump' (Lyttelton, 31).

bump ball   a ball which hits the ground immediately after the batsman has hit it, then flies up into the air, so it looks a catch (see also *crowd catch*). Almost always comes off the very bottom of the bat, but can also come from the very end, under the bat, making it difficult for an umpire to judge

bumper   a bumping ball, rising off the pitch. *Bell's Life*, on 19 August 1855, writes as follows: 'From the fact of the ground not being a good wearing one, the "bumpers" of Lillywhite could not be mastered.' So it seems the ball was in use at that time, although full over-arm bowling still had to be developed.

bumpy   an archaic use of a ball that rises abruptly from the pitch: of bowling; using or characterised by 'bumpers', also emerging from round-arm and crossing the globe in round-arm days. 'The batsmen seemed afraid to look at him, especially after the first bumpy over' (*Australasian*, 9 March 1867).

bunsen   rhyming slang: bunsen burner – raging *turner*. 'Jimmy [Hindson] is a genuine spinner of the ball . . . while the rollers need a raging "bunsen" to cause major problems. Jimmy is capable of beating the bat when things are not so helpful . . .' (Alan Ormrod, Notts coach, *WCM*, July 1995). Professor Bunsen of Heidelberg invented it, claimed for cricket apparently by G. Gooch.

business stroke   a sound, no-nonsense, safe stroke. Cardus deplored the loss of the cut to Rhodes: 'Well, it never were a business stroke,' said he (Ball & Hopps, 74). Another usage is given by Arlott: 'the average batsman played the leg-spinner defensively and waited for the bad ball before he hit. This was "business", but it was not adventurous' (*Playfair Cricket Annual*, May 1962). This argues a rather gradgrind approach to an occupation which has a great deal to do with risk-taking.

butter-fingers   OED dates it from 1615, but the earliest cricket mention seems to be in Charles Dickens's account of the match in Dingley Dell in 1837, where Mr Jingle 'launched his personal displeasure at the head of the devoted individual, in such denunciations as – "Ah! ah! – stupid" – "Now butter-fingers!" – "Muff" – "Humbug" – and so forth' (*Pickwick*, vii). *Muff* is still used of missing a catch.

butterfly mark   a bright orange stain which appears on bats, often causing their rejection by potential customers. It is in fact a sign of first-quality willow. see *heartwood*.

buy   *to buy a wicket* is to give the batsman opportunity to score runs, and temptation to get out doing so: for a fast bowler the predilection for the *hook*, with two men back or a deep fine leg. More often the art of the spinner: 'Wardle, of course, is always prepared to buy his wickets. Today he bought eight. Upon his success in finding purchasers among the better batsmen in the matches ahead I fancy a good deal may hang' (Swanton, *Report*, 23).

bye   'run scored for a ball which passes the batsman, and which the wicket-keeper and long-stop fail to stop' (OED). *To steal a bye*: to make a run from a ball by starting the instant it passes the wicket-keeper, or even earlier. OED is incomplete here, as *byes* frequently are run from a rebound from the wicket-keeper's person.

Whether byes were scored or not in the dawn of organisation appears to have been a matter of individual contract; Waghorn's *Cricket Scores* refers to a 1749 match where 'five of Addington Club challenge any five in England for 50 guineas, to play bye-balls and overthrows' (p.43). In the 1770s they were recorded.

C abbreviation for 'caught', e.g.: Saeed Anwar c. S. Warne b. McDermott. In the dawn of the game, the name of the fielder was sometimes not given, and in the 1769 scorecard of the Duke of Dorset's XI v. Wrotham, the abbreviation is ct. At the same time C is recorded in Nyren's *Tutor*, and in Waghorn's *Cricket Scores* from 1772 (p. 86): 'Turner 1st ins. 11 c.', without mentioning the fielder. Also an abbreviation for the captain.

c&b abbreviation for 'caught and bowled' a slight misnomer, the bowler himself catching the batsman. This applies even via a fielder: thus when a ball rebounded from the head of silly mid-on to the bowler, who accepted it with some astonishment, he was credited with the c&b (London evening game, Colliers Wood 1988). As in *catch*, the bowler was apparently not given credit until the 18th century.

cafeteria bowling 'True, England offered cafeteria [help yourself] bowling on Friday' (Graeme Fowler, *Sunday Telegraph*, 18 August 1996). See also *gimme*.

call[1] of an umpire: to declare (a bowler) to have bowled a 'no ball'; to declare (a delivery) illegal, either by overstepping the mark (nowadays the popping crease) or by incorrect action such as not having a straight arm at delivery.

call[2] a shouted direction by a batsman to his partner either to run or not. It was said of Compton by Ian Peebles (see *googly*) that his first *call* was akin to an opening bid in bridge. 'Let men run by some call; mere beckoning . . . leads to fatal errors' (Pycroft, 1854; OED). But see also *steal*.

call[3] *call* for a catch, or tossing the coin to decide choice of innings at the start of the game.

Cambridge poke seems to be what it says, mainly to the *on* side. In 1868 *St Paul's* reported: 'the cut, the old leg-hit, the draw, and . . . "the Cambridge poke", supplemented the original drive.' And in 1896 BLC mentions "the Cambridge Poke", so called, I believe , in contemptuous irony.' See also *nudge, nurdle, Pilch's poke*.

camel-footed of a fielder, whose ungainly and slow stride resembles that of the camel.

cane malacca or manau for bat handles. To *cane the bowling* means to hit it all around the ground, to give it a good thrashing.

cannon obsolete: a ball that glances off the striker's legs or pads into the wicket. 'Bowl at the leg stump and the chances are . . . you will score a "cannon" off the batsman's pads onto the wicket' (Jessop, 1925, Lewis, 73).

canteen bowling see *cafeteria* bowling.

cap   *to be capped* means to be a regular member of a county side, or to have played, even if only once, for your country. Brian Lara is the only recorded player to have been awarded his before he played for his county, Warwickshire. The first record of *capping* as a reward seems to be from 1746, when John Fuller of Uckfield wrote to the great promoter of the game, the Duke of Richmond, saying that he proposed a cricket plate 'as a Diversion more calculated to the Genius, and more agreeable to Sussex men, than a horse race . . . the proposition was to pay each man that play'd, and a guinea and eleven black velvet caps for the Conquerors . . .'. He hoped to arrange matters by playing over three days, which is perhaps the germ of the idea, but in this case it was so as not to disturb the Ball, his Grace's '(Newcastle) Clarett, and the Race' (Marshall, 9). See also *colours*.

captain   started off as *general*, but by 1823 Mary Mitford was saying 'Samuel Long, a bowler comme il y en a peu' had come to live in her parish and 'Our captain applied to him instantly to play; and he agreed at a word' (*Lady's Magazine*, July, 387/1). She was also that year referrring to 'our impartial general' (see *cricketal*).

By 1843, 'A Wykehamist' in *Practical Hints on Cricket*, vi, makes it seem as if this was not always so, saying ambiguously that the wicket-keeper or the captain 'should take the greatest pains in laying out the field.' The reason for the demotion seems unclear, especially considering the responsibilities of the position, but these days the only general on the ground is either retired or commanding the *Barmy Army*.

A captain's lot is not a happy one, in the international theatre demanding active chess in four dimensions over a period which can last five days, success on the field, and diplomacy off it. Peter Roebuck criticises the practice of limited-period appointments: 'Atherton . . . should not be permanently on trial. It is an insult. Back him or sack him' (*Sunday Times*, 14 May 1995). On the same page Robin Marlar reported the fatiguing effect on Richie Richardson, whose lassitude seemed partly due to the effort of captaining the West Indies.

A *captain's innings* is one which makes the entire innings, or staves off defeat. The epitome is the 185* at Johannesburg against the South Africans in 1995 to save the match, in over 10 hours at the crease, by Michael Atherton, captain of England (see *barnacle*).

capture   for a bowler to take a wicket: 'McDermott captured 4 for 74' (*Independent*, 8 October 1994).

card   or *match card*, or *score-card*. Contains the score of the match, to date. 'The printing tent was introduced at Lord's, on June 26th, 1848, by Frederick Lillywhite, and the public, for the first time, could secure a "correct card" of the game' (Taylor, 111). Pratt (see **scorecard**) was selling his cards at Sevenoaks in 1776, so they may antedate the race card.

carpet   the surface of the field, the ground, also carpet drive. 'His hits . . . are never high; on the contrary they are mostly, to use the slang of the cricket field, "on the carpet"' (*Cricket*, 22 June 1882, 93).

career best   batsman's or bowler's best performance.

carry one's bat   to bat throughout an innings without being dismissed: all 10 wickets must fall. The only man to have done this twice for England is Sir Leonard Hutton, 202★ v. West Indies out of 350, Oval 1950, and 156★ out of 272 at Adelaide 1951: 58 and 57 per cent of all the runs, including extras, of the two innings.

cart   to hit the bowling all over the field. 'Half-way through the over I carted a half-volley into the pav.' (Wodehouse, *Tales of St. Austin's*, 35).

cartwheel   viewed from side-on, the bowler's lead leg is forward, the lead arm comes over, followed by the bowling arm, and the effect is that of the start of a cartwheel. Fred Trueman of Yorkshire, Derbyshire, and England, was noted for this. As was Derek Randall's cartwheel in the field to celebrate catching Marsh off Hendrick, 15 August 1977, in the Ashes.

castle   the wicket a batsman defends: 'In support came . . . Alfie Hall . . . with a low action which ensured his hitting the castle' (i.e. not bouncing over the top of the wicket) (*Sunday Times*, 31 May 1959; OED). If a batsman is *castled*, he has been bowled.

Castle Cup   the domestic first-class competition of South Africa, formerly the Currie Cup after Sir Donald Currie.

catapulta   see *bowling machine*.

catch   from the late L. *captiare*, from *captus*, as capture, captive. The start of Law 32, not here quoted in its entirety, says 'The striker shall be out *Caught* if the ball touches his bat or if it touches below the wrist his hand or glove, holding the bat, and is subsequently held by a fieldsman before it touches the ground.' It continues to say that the fieldsman must be within the field of play throughout, with no part even touching the boundary. But in the 1947 Code the fieldsman only had to have his feet 'entirely within the playing area at the moment

when the catch is completed'. So jumping to catch a possible
six, one could tumble back over the line with the ball and have
made the catch, a minor encouragement to spectacular play.
Before that the Law seems to have been laxer, the Revd Pycroft
exclaiming of William Yalden, a licensed victualler from Chertsey, that 'he once when fielding, jumped over a fence, and when
on his back still caught the ball!!!' (*Hambledon Men*, 218).

And before that, the situation seems to have been positively
dangerous: the first printed Laws, those of 1744 and 1755, both
state that 'If [the striker] runs out of his ground to hinder a
Catch, it's out', and also 'When the ball is hit up, either of the
Strikers may hinder the Catch in his running Ground; or if it is
hit directly across the Wickets, the other Player may place his
Body any where within the Swing of the Bat, so as to hinder the
Bowler from catching it; but he must neither strike at it, nor
touch it with his hands.' This may have something to do with
Jasper Vinall, killed at Horsted Keynes in Sussex, in 1624, by
Edward Tye's bat, while Vinall was going for the catch.
'Ground' and 'running ground' presumably means the pitch, so
see *running* for a possible upshot, and explanation of why
obstruction was first limited to the area of the crease and then
in 1884 outlawed.

In 1836, the bowler had finally been given credit for the
wickets caught or stumped off his bowling. Before that 'Edm.
Elton caught out by Trodd 2' was the best he could expect
(Simons). The first mention of *caught* to appear is in the
Goodwood MS of the Duke of Richmond, 1727.

A *good catch* refers to either the act of catching or is the
quality of the named player. A *dolly*, or *sitter*, is an easy catch:
to *butter a catch* is to miss it or *put an easy one down*. The
poet Wodehouse describes how heinous this is in 'Missed!':

> The batsman with grief from the wicket
> Himself had begun to detach –
> And I uttered a groan and turned sick – It
> Was over. I'd buttered the catch.

Moreover:

> Ah, the bowler's querulous mutter,
> Point's loud, unforgettable scoff!

Another form, *catched* or *catched out*, was also used in the 18th
century.

catching positions   are those nearer the bat, such as slips,
short legs, gullies, and the *silly* positions.

Catherine-wheel, Catherine wheeling action see *cartwheel*. Now referring to the bowling position seen from side-

on, with the leading leg extended, the lead arm ditto, and the other arm and leg coming straight over. The 19th century use appears to have meant all overarm bowling, as Fred Gale uses it in *The Game of Cricket* (1877): 'We may all admit public bowling . . . to be more varied than formerly, before catherine-wheeling was allowed' (177).

The derivation is from Catherine, saint and martyr, broken on the wheel, then beheaded, thence to a rotating firework, from which the resemblance to a lateral somersault can be seen.

caught and bowled   *see* c&b.

caught behind   by the wicket-keeper.

centurion   scorer of 100 runs. Originally the Roman commander of half a maniple, or 100 men. Appears to have transferred itself to cricket in the 1880s, with the first reference given by OED as 1883, and in 1886 *The Graphic* has 'Some other "centurions" have been Chatterton (108) for MCC . . .' (Lewis, 45).

century   appears about 15 years before *centurion*: 'By his careful and manly style it looked as if another century was coming off but Willsher stopped him' (*Bell's Life*, 12 July 1863). Original probably 100 Roman horsemen.

champion   the Champion was W.G. Grace. The word comes from L. *campus*, a field, which was where combat was joined between two men. The king's champion was his deputy. It came to have a general use for an athlete, as in Chaucer's friar: 'Therto he strong was as a champioun,' so it could have applied to Ian Botham.

chance   a *chance* to dismiss the batsman, almost always by catch, sometimes by running out: 'Hassett was not at first comfortable and gave an easier unaccepted chance to Hutton' (Swanton, *Victory*, 230 on the Fifth Test, 1951). First use found in *Bell's Life* 'without giving a chance' (6 September 1829). Then in *The Young Cricketer's Tutor* of 1833: 'The real beauty of hitting, is to see a batsman go in, and get many runs, without giving a chance.'

chanceless   an innings without opportunity being offered to the attack or fielders to dismiss the batsman. 'Constantine once more took the game by the throat with a savagely struck but chanceless 103 – out of 133 – to win it by three wickets' (Arlott, *Essential*, 222). Also found in *Bell's Life*, 28 August 1875.

chancy   of a shot, risky; of an innings, replete with opportunities for fielders, and near misses for bowlers. 'White was decidedly chancy. He mishooked Malcolm . . . Another mistimed hook barely evaded square leg...' (David Hopps, *Guardian*, 13 May 1995).

change   of the bowling or bowler. A *change bowler* is one who is not in the front line of attack, and the usage seems to date from before Nyren in 1833: 'we reckoned [Aburrow] a tolerably good change for bowling' (Lucas, 49).

channel   'He's got it in the right channel,' said Robin Jackman as Darren Gough bowled from round the wicket to the left-handed Jayasuriya, on a line around the off stump (Sky TV, World Cup quarter-final, 8 March 1996). See also *corridor*.

charge   to go rapidly down the pitch to get to the pitch of the ball with aggressive intent; a more vigorous movement than the next entry.

chassé   'a gliding step, executed by bringing one foot behind the other while this is at the same time advanced' (OED). Thus Geoff Boycott's commentary on the Third Test, Adelaide 1991: 'Gooch chasséd down the wicket to Border' (ABC TV). The purpose of the *chassé* also being to get to the pitch of the ball.

cheap   said of a bowler to mean he is thrifty, does not give many runs away in his *spell* of bowling. The early Teutonic meaning included 'cattle' (OE only) or 'market-place' (thus Cheapside). *Cheap* itself is shortened from 'good cheap'.

check, check-drive   to check a front-foot shot, not giving the full follow-through, thus reducing its power. 'Hick, looking a natural No. 3, check-drove Gary Kirsten for six...' (David Frith, *WCM*, September 1994).

cherry   slang for ball: Bob Willis in Second Test, in Melbourne 24 December 1994, referrred to 'the shiny cherry' – the new ball (Sky TV).

chest on, chest-on   a bowler's action, when he delivers with chest square to the batsman. Used mainly by faster bowlers, sometimes to help the inswinger. Mike Procter of South Africa was the prime example of the recent *chest-on* action, but some West Indies bowlers of today, notably Courtney Walsh, approximate his action.

chinaman   in England, the *chinaman* is the left-hander's wrist-spun *off-break*. In Australia, it is the left-hander's *googly*, spinning away from the batsman, which is incorrect. We can do no better than take it from the man whose delivery gave rise to the term, Ellis Achong, a left-arm off-spinner from Trinidad, who spun his island to victory over the MCC tourists of 1930, and was selected for the 1933 England tour. He was the first, and it seems so far the only, Chinese to play cricket at international level. At Old Trafford he had Walter Robins stumped: 'It pitched perfectly and turned back nicely and when Robins saw it coming back at him, he opened his legs and the ball went through. On his way from the wicket, Robins turned to Learie [Constantine, who was fielding at point] and said: "Fancy being out to a bloody Chinaman!" because it had been reported in the Press that I was the first person of Chinese origin to play Test cricket' (Lawrence,13). Obviously, then, an off-break, and the googly is never mentioned in connection with Achong. Thus it would appear not to refer to Oriental guile, except as a later, secondary, and thus less satisfactory meaning.

Having been immortalised in Lancashire, Achong remained there for many years, taking over 1,000 wickets in League cricket, and returned to Trinidad after the war, where he stood as umpire to Compton's chinamen and googlies in a test there: Compton thought he had the opener caught (off his googly!) by Graveney in the slips, and so did Graveney. Achong did not, and the difference precluded any further discussion of the origin of the term. No really effective bowler of this type at Test level has arisen for some time, in fact since Fleetwood-Smith bowled Hammond neck and crop to tip a series Australia's way, although the Australians George Tribe and Walsh played in England for many years after the War. They gave way to Johnny Wardle of Yorkshire and England, who bowled either *orthodox spin* or *chinamen and googlies*.

Chinese cut   a shot which hits the inside edge of the bat and runs down towards long leg. More advertently, some cricketers, although on a fairly low level, practise it against a *yorker*, by moving their feet aside and jamming the bat down at an angle, making the ball shoot in the same direction. In Yorkshire this is called a *Lancashire cut*, and the compliment is returned. 'Oakman edged an intended off-drive past the leg-stump for four, a stroke variously described as a *Chinese cut*, a *Surrey cut* or a *Staffordshire cut*' (Alston, 62). See also *dog shot*.

chin music   see *throat theory*.

chip   as in golf, but hitting it over the fielders or the inner ring without full power. Graeme Hick of Worcestershire and England did it twice in succession at the Oval in 1995, and Ian Botham commented that 'Glenn Turner of Worcester was a fine exponent of that many years ago' (Sky TV).

chirping   euphemism for *sledging*. 'Although the Australian team developed a reputation for "chirping" during the latter part of Allan Border's career as captain . . .' (Brian Murgatroyd, *Sunday Telegraph*, 23 November 1994).

chop   a shot between a cut and a back-stroke, coming down on the ball and putting it into the general gully area.

chuck   a thrown ball, an illegal delivery: 'Slow underhand "chucks"', 1862 (*Lillywhite's Scores*, II, 30); 'Did you think that ball that bowled you was a chuck?' (Wodehouse, *Tales*, 1903, 22); 'One of Griffiths's most effective deliveries was a (doubtless unconscious) "chuck" which has now been umpired out of his repertoire' (*New Statesman*, 1 July 1966) – OED. Griffith was warned by umpire Elliott in the Fourth Test at Leeds in 1966, but *called* only in Barbados. See *throwing*.

chucker   used to describe a bowler who throws: see *throwing*.

circle   something of a misnomer, because it is in fact two semicircles, radius 30 yards, with the respective stumps at centre point. Only employed in some *limited-over* games.

claim   another slight misnomer: for a bowler to *claim* a wicket does not mean he considers it rightly his own but that he has taken it.

clay   type of soil from which pitches are made. Although heavy enough to stand up to rolling, its sticky quality makes for a slow pitch, with the ball turning slowly off it. It is mainly aluminium silicate, and formed largely from the decomposition of felspathic rock (OED). The verbal root is *kli-*, meaning *to stick, cleave*.

clean bowl   'a ball that hits the wicket without having touched the bat or the body of the striker. (Implying that the batsman was completely beaten by the ball)' (Lewis, 48.) P.W.-T. has first use 1854.

clinker   a very good ball. 'Tom Emmett was bet half-a-crown he could not bowl a Light Blue, sent down a clinker which nearly did, and claimed fifteen-pence, half a half-crown then . . .' (Standing, 2).

clip   invariably used of a shot to leg: 'when finally he clipped Andy Pick off his legs to deep square-leg, he had plundered 17 fours and four sixes,' Christopher Martin-Jenkins wrote of Tony Wright (*Daily Telegraph*, 13 May 1995).

close of play, closure   sometimes shortened to *close*: the end of a day's play, the end of a match, life's terminus: 'and at the close of play I'll meet the scorer in the sky' (Australian).

club   a large bat, or a forceful, not particularly elegant shot, as when Kevin Curran 'clubbed and stroked 92 at four per over' for Northants v. Somerset (*Daily Telegraph*, 13 May 1995), or an association of cricketers. Both from a seemingly Proto-Germanic form of a root 'form a lump, lump together'. This went through the meaning of a weapon, a heavy tapered stick, then was used in the 15th century for a sporting instrument. It was in the 16th and 17th centuries that the word became closer to its original meaning, with 'club' meaning to pool resources, gather together (*The Private Lives of English Words*). *Club cricket, a club cricketer, club player*, implies a fairly high standard, an established club, although amateur: not like *league cricket*.

coach   an instructor in the arts and skills of cricket, often a retired cricketer installed in one of the fee-paying schools, and remembered, like George Geary at Charterhouse, by generations; sometimes forgotten, as Tom Emmett was, 'allowed to die without a single tribute worth the name being written,' as E.V. Lucas wrote in *The Hambleden Men* (120); sometimes feted as Patsy Hendren was at Harrow when the school beat Eton at Lord's for the first time in decades, and the school insisted he was on the balcony to receive the plaudits of the crowd for one last time (Heald).

It is the only word in cricket known to come from the Magyar. Kocs is a place between Buda and Raab, *kocsi* is the adverb, and the original meaning was a conveyance with passengers inside and outside (OED).

coat of varnish   to miss the stumps by a *coat of varnish*, a near miss. See also *thin stumps, thick stumps*.

cob   obsolete: a gently bowled ball. 'The captain ... bowled slow cobs to old Mr Aislabie' (Hughes, *Tom Brown's Schooldays*, 1857).

coffin   the large rectangular container, often of leatherette or papier-mâché, in which a cricketer's or club's gear is carried. It is larger than a normal bag.

coil   the position of the fast bowler preparatory to strike. But not always: Malcolm Marshall of the West Indies had to get a coaching certificate before he could register as an overseas player, and was told of the importance of bounding and coiling: 'I've obviously never coiled,' said he (Bill May, *Mail on Sunday*, 12 June 1994).

coir   the prepared husk of the coconut fibre; from Malayalam *kayar*, cord. It is like *jute* but thicker and knitted, and turns more. This gives a hard artificial surface: 'His bowling that day was the fastest I've ever faced, and that was on coir matting, not jute ... but Constantine was a gentleman bowler: he wouldn't bowl more than two bouncers an over' – Lala Amarnath, India's first Test *centurion*, on making 104* in 1934 (Subroto Sirkar, *WCM*, September 1994).

collapse   Stories abound of the stranger to our shores seeing huge black headlines 'ENGLAND COLLAPSE' on newspaper vendor's boards, a surprisingly cheerful hoarse voice reiterating the fact, and crowds of men (formerly top-hatted, and in the City) rushing to buy the paper. Their agitated conversations with their neighbours, their distraught faces as they scan the stop press news, terrify him. Jardine and Leyland removed – two of the bastions of trade and industry: other apparently vast enterprises at astonishing lows: Hammond gone for twelve, Sutcliffe fighting desperately, Paynter on nine: a nation-wide market bust. He sells all his shares, moves out of sterling into gold and Uruguayan bonds, his broker so distracted he hardly seems surprised . . . good schoolboy stuff.

'Australia had collapsed to 5/184 . . . In three balls, a game and three careers . . . had changed. These events served to remind students of the game that cricket can never be taken for granted. A collapse is never more than five minutes away' (Roebuck, 192).

collar   to *collar* the bowling is to take it by the scruff of the neck and hit it all round the ground.

colours   club, county *colours*, as in blazers, ties, caps, meaning simply membership. The natural conservatism of the Englishman asserts itself in the red and yellow of MCC, pink school blazers, and so on: the Chelsea Arts Cricket Club assemblage of Cerulean, Cerise, and Sand might have come straight from the palette of J.M.W. Turner, via Chelsea Reach. Presentation of colours marks the recipient as an established member of the XI.

come in   of a batsman, to *come in* to start his innings. 'The Duke's hands came in first, and got 79 before they were out' (Waghorn, 4). Also of a delivery, to come in, *come back, nip back*, describes a ball pitching on the off and moving towards leg.

come off, come off quickly   'Amarnath came off the pitch like the crack of doom', Hammond used to say of the great Indian all-rounder's medium-pacers. Scientists tell us that no ball can *come off* the pitch quicker than it hit, unless *top-spun*, so the illusion must be due to coming off quicker than expected, or skidding, some of which can be produced by *back-spin*.

come up   see *pick-up*.

conker   the ball: 'So much depends upon the battles over the new conker' (Peter Roebuck, *Sunday Times*, 13 November 1994).

cordon   a ring of (usually) close fielders, or slips, around the batsman. See also *Death Valley*.

corner   to *tuck* a delivery around the *corner* is to deflect it onto the leg side behind square.

Cornstalks   was the way in which the visiting Australian teams in the 19th century were described in the Old Country.

corridor of uncertainty   first mention in public print seems to be that of John Woodcock in *The Times* when reporting from Brisbane on 18 November 1986: 'Dilley talks of Terry Alderman, the Australian who has had a couple of seasons with Kent, advising him always to bowl in the *corrridor*. By this, the Australian means "the corridor of uncertainty" . . . the one just outside the off stump which most batsmen like the least.' And on 23 June 1990: 'a lot is made these days of the "corridor of uncertainty", a term . . . first coined I believe by Terry Alderman, who seldom strays from it. When the West Indians try to bowl there, they are not themselves. When Hadlee does, the batsmen wish he would not' (*The Times*). See also *channel*, *alley, patio*.

country   a deep position anywhere on the field. Also, a place of banishment. Lewis quotes A.G. Steel: 'Grace, and Reid, and Barnes, must all be in places somewhere near the wicket, as none of these are quick enough . . . for fielding in the country' (BLC, 1888, 215). This can have distinctly rustic connotations, such as fielding in the country to the minatory bellow of rutting stags at the end of September in Hampton Park.

county   from AF, *counte*, present Fr. *comte*: the domain of a (foreign) count OED. The first county cricket club formed was Northamptonshire in 1843: though some claim Sussex was first in 1836, more generally they are dated as 1857.

county championship   contested by 18 first-class counties, although there has been talk of splitting into two leagues. The county championship as a league was born at a meeting of the moribund Cricket Council, held at the Oval on 11 August. Eight counties were pronounced to be first-class, and as the competitors for the championship in 1891. Before that counties were proclaimed champion on various unofficial bases, such as the least number of matches lost. Surrey was the first proclaimed champion by Wisden in 1864. *County cricket, cricketer*, applies only to play and players involving first-class counties (see also *Minor Counties*).

cover   short for *cover-point*. A fielding position to the off-side of the batsman at roughly 45 degrees to the pitch, or the fielder who fields there. *Short cover* is close to the batsman, *silly cover* closer, and *deep cover* on or towards the boundary. Revd James Pycroft: 'cover is the place for brilliant fielding' (x, 193).

cover-drive   generally considered the most elegant shot off the front foot that a batsman can play. Walter Hammond was the acknowledged master of the *off-drive*, hitting the ball very hard to where the fielders were not. The left-hander's off-drive is considered particularly attractive, the master of this sinistral art being David Gower, also master of the more difficult *cover-drive* off the back foot, as shown in 12 off one over from Terry Alderman in the Third Test, Adelaide 1991. 'Donnan made some excellent "cover" drives and cuts' – Ranjitsinhji (1898, 71).

cover-nips   see *nips*.

covers[1]   describing the general area of *cover point, square cover, extra cover*, deep extra, etc.

covers[2]   pitches nowadays are often covered to protect them against the elements, and against the loss of revenue a curtailed match would mean. As well as making for an easier batting strip, it means fewer spectators are disappointed. It was not always so: when Australia were put out at Brisbane for 58 in 1936, the bowlers' footholds were covered but the pitch was not: Allen 5–36 and Voce 4–16.

cover slip   obsolete for a position of third man.

cover up   to place one's pads in front of the wicket as a first or second line of defence against the ball. See *pad-play*.

Cowden   'In Limpsfield and the district the rustics . . . will always call out *Cowden* if the ball comes to a fieldsman first bound . . . an umpire from Cowden must have given a wrong decision . . .' (G. Leveson-Gower, *Surrey Words* 1893). Cowden is a small village on the Kent-Surrey border.

cowshot, cow-shot   F.B. Wilson dated it back to 1904: 'Very generally put down to me but . . . I have been told . . . the real author was Gerald Winter' (pp. 169–71). Winter was a well-known eccentric of the cricket field. Similar in effect to the *Stogumber mow*, the ball is dispatched off the front foot, turning it into more or less a half volley, towards *cow corner*, that part of the field which lies between square-leg's left and and mid-on's right, or into pastures beyond.

cow corner   where the *cow-shots* go. Or worse, in the case of the visitor player at Lewannick CC (Cornwall) who, chasing a cow shot, leapt the boundary wall into a deceptively crusted slurry-pit. Fortunately it was only knee-deep, so he was back on the field before he suffocated from the fumes.

crack, a cracking shot   hard and cleanly struck: 'Royle began to show his hitting powers, cracking him to sq. leg . . .' report of 'Mr. Hornby's English Eleven vs. Eleven of New York and

Philadelphia' (*American Cricketer*, 1879). 'Originally echoic' says the OED.

cradle   a device for improving short-range fielding. It resembles half a very large barrel with the ends and alternative staves removed. Into the concave side of this, a ball is thrown to careen out of the other end at an unpredictable height and angle. It is said to have been invented by the Reverend Gilbert Harrison, a Victorian clergyman.

cramping   the batsman: bowling a line that gives him no room to play his strokes, and can *tuck him up*. Often from a ball that comes into the batsman.

crease   originally a (s)cratch in the ground. The OE form was *cratch* or *cracche*: H. P.-T. has 'crack and cratch' as doublets, with interesting implications for the derivation of 'cricket' itself: the AS. is *cracian*, and *cracchen*, to scratch, is related to the Dutch *krassen*, and the old form shown in *Piers Plowman*, where a cat 'Wol cracchen us or clawen us'.

The first recorded description of a match is in Latin, in 1706, and was written by William Godwin, a proficient Latin scholar, and in it there is no mention of a *crease*. Rather it appears that the umpire had to be touched, probably with a bat, as the Latin suggests:

>   Stant Moderatores bini stationibus aptis
>   Fustibus innixi, quos certo attingere pulsu
>   Lex jubet . . .

The two sides were in dispute about the rules of the game until a watching Nestor was brought in to settle all. The agreement details the wickets being set (twin uprights with a clean bail atop). But there is no mention of any crease being cut, so it seems that creases were not yet in use, at least in that part of the world (the poem was written by an old Etonian and alumnus of King's College Cambridge). By 1744, the crease(s) were being cut in the ground: 'When ye first Wicket is pitched and ye popping Crease cut, which must be exactly 3 Foot 10 Inches from ye Wicket . . . Ye bowling creases must be cut . . .' say the first Laws, of that date. The white line was brought in in 1862 by Alfred Shaw of Notts and Sussex, originally by marking with chalk.

See also *popping crease, return crease*.

crease frame   a large wooden stencil used as a guide for marking the creases. An iron three-pronged guide can be used for setting the stumps.

creeper   see *shooter, mulligrubber*.

cricket   a contest between two teams of eleven players each on

a pitch twenty-two yards long. Not a sport, nor a pastime, nor
quite a game, nor ritual . . .

cricket ground   'London play against Deptford and Green-
wich in Mr Siddle's new cricket ground at Deptford.' Dated to
1748 in Waghorn, *Dawn of Cricket.*

cricketal   Lewis finds nothing but nonce-uses, from Mary
Russell Mitford's three rich young farmers who 'presented
themselves, and were all rejected by our independent and
impartial general for want of merit – cricketal merit' (*Lady's
Magazine*, July 1823). Also *Cricket in the West; or, the Twelve in
America* (1873) by R.A. Fitzgerald: 'The juncture was critical,
not cricketal.'

cricketalia   a nonce-word, described things to do with a
festival of cricket. Occurs in the 1747 letter of Horace Walpole:
'Lord John Sackville . . . instituted certain games called *cricketalia*, which have been celebrated this very evening in honour
of him in a neighbouring meadow.'

cricketana   dating from 1862, when according to the OED it
circumscribes literature, sayings, and items of gossip about
cricket. Then in 1929 it came to describe collectables, and one
of the reasons for the founding of the Cricketana Society in
1929 was to make a register of collectors.

cricketer   one who plays at cricket. There is no other qualification, except disparity in the definition. One of the joys of the
game is that *cricketers* come in all sizes and inclinations: the first
mention so far found being 'Wm Pullen, the cricketer, hang'd
at Maidstone' in 1742. They vary from the small and rather
fox-like giants (Lillywhite weighed only six stone) such as
Grimmett, Bradman, 'Tich' Freeman at 5' 4", Larwood the
same at eighteen, to the 6' 7" of Curtly Ambrose, the 6' 9" of
Joel Garner, the mass of the later David Harris, who would be
provided with an armchair between overs, or of Ian Botham.

   Tom Walker's hard, ungain, leg-of-mutton frame; wilted,
   apple-john face (he always looked twenty years older than he
   was), his long spider legs, as thick at the ankles as at the hips,
   and perfectly straight all the way down . . . the driest and
   most rigid-limbed chap that ever I knew; his skin was like the
   rind of an old oak, and as sapless. I have seen his knuckles
   handsomely knocked about from Harris's bowling; but never
   saw any blood upon his hands – you might just as well
   attempt to phlebotomize a mummy. This rigidity of muscle
   (or rather I should say of tendon, for muscle was another
   ingredient economised in the process of Tom's configuration)
   – this rigidity, I say, was carried into every motion. He moved

like the rude machinery of a steam engine in the infancy of construction . . .

Nyren thus described a cricketer over two hundred years ago, a man so imperturbable that Reverend the Lord Frederick Beauclerc dashed his hat on the ground in a fit of temper when Tom blocked an over of his.

Supposed to imply moral character, (cf. *not cricket)*, as in the song from the *Canterbury Festival*: 'Your cricketer no cogging practice knows / No trick to favour friends or cripple foes . . .'

Nyren, archetypical cricketer, to whom the game was not all, shows us what it was like to live at the end of the eighteenth century and start of the nineteeenth, with Noah Mann galloping up to the ground, leaning to pick up handkerchiefs, the wagering, and Nyren himself, splendid pointsman, whose fingers carried the marks to his grave, but also a violinist to whom Vincent Novello inscribed several pieces. He himself composed three pieces Novello published, and the accompaniment to Byron's 'Fill the Goblet Again'.

However tenuous the claims for cricketers may be, the term does at least imply a certain cheerful vigour: the game is so difficult that it is stupid to play it, but you have to be quite bright to do so. An art critic 'once cuttingly declared that he had time to be interested in art because (like Mr. Shaw and the Sitwells) he took no interest in anything that anyone did with a ball. In which sweeping statement he did not, I take it, include the amazing manipulation by the Omnipotent of this terrestrial globe' (Farjeon, 96). One might prefer an afternoon on the field with Byron, 'together joined', as he puts it in *Hours of Idleness*, 'in cricket's manly toil', or with the great Duke of Marlborough who preferred it to Moral Philosophy, and produced some 'Master stroaks' before he was caught out (according to a 1712 broadsheet), or on the sands with Virginia Woolf's trusty forward stroke, to the pallid secchities of Shaw, the Sitwells, or Alexander Pope ('the senators at cricket urge the ball' runs the line in *The Dunciad*).

cricketress Lewis: a woman cricketer. The first recorded match seems to be on 26 July 1745, when eleven maids of Bramley met eleven of Hambledon (which by bizarre coincidence was not *the* Hambledon but a hamlet close to Godalming in Surrey). 'The girls bowled, batted, ran, and catched as well as any men could do', said the report in the *Daily Mercury*. The married women won. 'So famous are the Bury women at a cricket match that they offer to play against any XI for a sum', said a report of the same year.

But there must have been many contests before for the women's games to be so well organised. In 1747 the manager of the Artillery ground charged a whole sixpence for admission; nevertheless there were 'the greatest number of spectators ever seen at any public diversion' as Charlton and Singleton beat West Dean and Chelgrove. All these villages are on the South Downs (the Downs again!), so it was apparently worth their while to travel a long way to play.

In 1775 Six Single beat Six Married at Moulsey Hurst, and in 1777 the youngest daughter of Sir Peter Burrell top-scored in her match 'and so bewitched' the Duke of Hamilton that they were married in spring 1778. On 5 August 1827 XI Old Ladies of Southborough played XI Young Ladies of Tunbridge for 3 bottles of gin and nine pounds of gunpowder tea 'completely outgeneralled them and won by 52 runs' (H.P.-T., f 10).

The standard of women's cricket is higher than some might think: a good judge once considered a woman, Mollie Hide, to be the best slow bowler in the land for some years.

cricket house   'a very commodious cricket house has been built at considerable expense at Newark' (1848, P.W.-T.).

Cricket Max   a new version of the game, in which double runs are given for some scoring strokes: a six through the *V* counts as twelve. Played mainly in New Zealand at the time of going to press, the main protagonist being Martin Crowe, the former Test batsman, it seeks a livelier tempo to cricket. Each side has two innings of 10 overs with a break in the middle, so the game is over in an afternoon.

Cricket week   A festival Week of cricket, arranged by some of the county clubs annually, such as the 'Scarborough Week' of Yorkshire, the 'Hastings' Week' of Sussex, the 'Bristol Week' of Gloucestershire, etc., the progenitor of these being the famous 'Canterbury Week' of Kent. See *festival*.

cricket wicket   a misnomer, because it refers to a pitch which will, during the course of a game, help both batsmen and assorted types of bowlers.

cricketting   'A cricketting between the Weald and North Downs' (1640, P.W.-T.).

crocketts   Winchester College phraseology, in latter half of 19th century, for a version of cricket; also when a boy made no runs at a cricket match, he was said to have *got crocketts* (Lewis, 63).

crooked bat   (to play) *with a crooked bat,* meaning it is not perpendicular, or (a meaning which seems obsolete) with the face of the bat turned at an angle and not fully opposed to the ball. 'Observe the rule of not playing with a crooked bat, which means that the full face of the blade is not offered to the ball' (BLC, 1920, 22).

cross   three obsolete meanings: the first, losing a contest through trickery: *The Times* of 28 July 1827 said of the men of Sussex playing All-England, 'the cricket match which has just ended was a cross, and that it was lost purposely by the men of Sussex.' The second is to impede a batsman trying for a run. The third, still vital but now found as *across the line* is stigmatised – 'to cross a ball is the worst of bad play' – by Nyren in *The Young Cricketer's Tutor.* The modern use refers to batsmen *crossing* on the pitch while attempting a run: the one nearest the broken wicket is *run out.*

cross bat, cross-bat   *cross-bat* strokes are those made with the bat horizontal to the ground, e.g. hook, cut.

crowd catch   occurs when the spectators think the batsman is out, habitually when a close-in fielder has caught the ball but it has come off the batsman's pad.

crumble, crumbler   a dry crumbly pitch: it takes spin as the ball can bite, and is usually hard, so 'the dry crumbling pitch, barring rain, will be fiery until the hose is put on it' (Marriott, 113).

crust, crusted   to be hit on the head or helmet: 'The tail took the total beyond 200, Greg Blewett and Ian Healy both joining Taylor in being "crusted" or "sconed" as the Australians call being hit on the head . . .' (Paul Newman reporting from Antigua, *Sunday Telegraph,* 9 April 1995).

curator   Australian term for head *groundsman.*

curl   generally used of slower bowling to denote the lateral movement in the air of a ball, because of its spin, as in Arthur Mailey's encounter with Victor Trumper: so different from swing, which is caused by the seam. *Curly* is obsolete, Lewis's last definition being from 1898.

curve   the way a spun ball moves in the air before bouncing. Described by Arthur Mailey in 'Opposing My Hero' (he bowls Trumper a leg-break): 'The tremendous leg-spin caused the ball to swing and curve from the off and move in line with the middle and leg stump.' Trumper hits it for four and a few balls later Mailey bowls him with a 'wrong 'un' or 'bosie': 'As with the leg-break, it had sufficient spin to curve in the air . . .' (Ross, 359, 360).

cut[1]   a stroke made by the batsman on the off-side which can be in any area between very fine, e.g. first slip, and square. Bill Edrich excelled at the shot, which is less often seen now. The cut off the back foot is made by taking the right foot back and across, slashing with the bat horizontal or nearly so, and rolling the wrists over to keep the ball down. J. Lillywhite's *Cricketers' Annual*, 1879: 'to cut well requires a flexibility of wrist that cannot possibly be transferred to paper' (W.G. Grace). 'His wrist seemed to turn on springs of finest steel,' was how the Revd Mitford described that of Beldham (Lucas, 125).

cut[2]   of a bowling action which cuts the hand rapidly down one side of the ball at the moment of release, imparting spin; see *off-cutter, leg-cutter*. Originally *cut* was synonymous with spin, but recently it has denoted the spin imparted as above by faster bowlers.

cut drive   Sometimes, and more frequently in the past, the cut was played off the front foot with the left leg well across. But it is, as F.C. Holland says in *Cricket* (1904), 'a stroke difficult to class'. Now obsolete.

cut over   of unknown origin, meaning especially to be hit in the groin and temporarily disabled, dating back to at least 1859, as well as to destroy the effectiveness of the bowling. P.F. Warner used it in 1904 in *Recovering the Ashes* (249): 'Duff was very badly *cut over* by Hirst.'

cut up   to *cut up* the pitch by the action of the ball hitting it, often rotating so the seam digs in: '[S.F. Barnes] was literally cutting up the pitch with his fingers spin and the ball was flashing right across the wicket' (Duckworth, 60).

cutsman   A batsman who 'cuts' the ball or makes the stroke called a 'cut' (see *cut*[1]); an adept at making this stroke. This may be a nonce-word, employed in *Felix on the Bat* (1.iii.15): 'One of the finest cutsmen that ever graced a cricket field.'

cutter   either of a batsman who employs the shot, or a delivery, as in *cut*[2].

cut through   an obsolete term meaning to skid off a wet wicket.

D **ab** a shot played with little force, on either side of the wicket, as in Gower hitting four off Fraser through the *covers*, Hampshire v. Middlesex, July 1993: 'That went with no more effort than a cat dabbing at a goldfish.' Conversation in Lord's pavilion.

daisy-cutter a *shooter*, or a low under-arm ball. But also and previously, it refers to the action of a horse (G. Hammond, *Horse Racing, A Book of Words*, Manchester: Carcanet, 1992).

danger area has a specific meaning of that part of the pitch whch is roughened up (see also *rough*) by a bowler running on it after his delivery.

dart to have a *dart* at a bowler means to take him on, try to hit him around. Speaking of Darren Gough's predilection, Geoffrey Boycott said on BBC TV: 'He's got to decide whether to duck or have a dart and hook it . . .' as Gough started batting in the Second Test at Lord's, 1995. And in the same Test, Richie Benaud spoke of Brian Lara as immediately below:

dash 'he had a dash at that one', as he tried to *hook* early in his innings.

day-night match, daynighter Australian: a match which starts in daytime and ends under floodlights at night. 'We won the first final, a day-nighter in Sydney . . . I thoroughly enjoyed making 127 not out, easily my best one-day innings' (Border, 142).

dead ball when the ball is out of play, and no runs can be scored and no wickets taken. First mentioned in Lewis as from 1798, Law 27: 'If any person stops the ball with his hat, the ball is to be considered as dead.' Whether this applies to bystanders as well as *watchers-out* is unclear. The present concept is in the 1744 laws, when the batsman 'may do as he pleases' in the interval between the bowler gathering the ball and delivering it.

dead bat to play with a *dead bat*, relaxing the hands at the moment of impact so the ball drops dead.

dead wicket one which contains no *devil*.

dead stand obsolete: a stand in which no runs are made: 'Noah hit it out in his grand style. Six of the ten were gained. Then there was a dead stand . . . ultimately, however, he gained them all . . .' (Nyren, of Noah Mann; Lucas, 64).

death ball the special ball a bowler pulls out of the hat to take a wicket. See below.

death bowler '(Angus) Fraser does not have the slower ball to be a "death" bowler in one-day cricket' (Scyld Berry, *Sunday Telegraph*, 11 December 1994). This presumably refers to the batsman misjudging the speed of the ball when going for runs.

death rattle   the sound of the stumps the batsman hears when he misses and the ball hits.

Death Row   the row of slips and gullies waiting for their prey: 'Lillee's bowling was only eight miles an hour slower than Thomson's, which meant Marsh, the Chappell brothers, Mallett and Co. in Death Row still standing over thirty metres from the bat . . .' (Wilde, 35).

declare, declared, declaration (abbreviated as **dec**)   when a captain *declares* his side's innings closed, the other side goes in to bat. Before the Laws of 1798 a captain had to tell his batsmen to hit their wickets down. Under certain conditions, he may also *forfeit* his seond innings. Norman Gifford, the left-arm spinner capped fifteen times for England, when captain of Worcestershire, once declared when exactly 150 runs behind, to find himself asked to *follow on* (*Slow Men*, 154). A famous *sporting declaration* was that when Gary Sobers left England 215 in 165 in the Port-of-Spain Test in 1968, and England won with a few minutes to spare.

deep   either in the outfield, or a deeper position, e.g. *deep cover*, than normal (see also *sweeper*).

deep field   far behind the bowler, usually fairly *straight*, or *long-off, long-on*. Almost obsolete, but 'I was caught in the deep-field by the Australian captain' as used by A.A. Lilley (p. 152) retains its sense.

defence   'A good defence is the secret of batsmanship,' says Denis Compton. Thus the art of the batsman in not letting the bowler dismiss him. *Defend, defensive*, to describe this type of play seems to be first mentioned in 1830, in Mary R. Mitford's *Our Village*: 'His hits were weak, his defence insecure, and his mates began to tremble' (ch.iv, p.29), and the Revd James Pycroft in *The Cricket Field* of 1851: 'The old players did not play the steady game . . . The *defensive* was comparatively unknown: both the bat and the wicket, and the style of bowling too, were all adapted to a short life and a merry one' (ch.iv, p.58). Nyren mentions *blocking*, as above, but not defence. A *defensive field* is one set to stop runs being scored rather than wickets taken.

deficit   from the L. *deficit*, something wanting: the amount by which one team is behind another in runs.

deliver, delivery   a bowler *delivers* the ball. This can be fiendish, lifting, etc., but a *high delivery* means the bowler has kept his arm up: this combined with a straight front leg means greater speed, and, since the arc of the high arm swings on a wicket-to-wicket axis, greater accuracy. The word seems to have been in general use in the time of Hambledon: 'delivering his ball straight to the wicket, it curled in, and missed the Duke's leg-stump by a hair's breadth', and '[Richard] Francis was a fast jerker; but though his delivery was allowed to be fair bowling, still it was a jerk' (Nyren, in Lucas, 65).

depth   in both bowling and batting means a number of players who can do one or the other or both.

devil, devilry   a pitch with fire in it: pace, bounce, and perhaps a tendency to do the unexpected. From the Gk *diabollein* which had an original meaning of 'to throw across'. 'Twice David Nash . . . was struck in the face, indicating the devilry in the pitch' (*The Times* on the England-New Zealand Under-19 match, 3 August 1996).

devil's number   87, or thirteen away from a hundred. Said to have been started by Keith Miller and a friend just before the Second World War, when they noticed an unusual number of batsmen getting themselves out on this score. The legend persists, even though checking back on the original scorebook, Miller is said to have found the score he first looked at was 89 (Tyson, 45).

dex   'There is a sport known at some schools as "stump-cricket", "snob-cricket", or (mysteriously and locally) as "Dex", which is a degenerate shape of the game': Lewis quotes Andrew Lang (BLC, 1888, 1).

didapper   'A name formerly applied by the old Kent and Hampshire players to an under-hand ball that kept near the ground, and bounded more than once before it reached the batsman. (So called after the small water-fowl, the diving dabchick or Little Grebe, locally known in Kent as the "Didapper" or "Divedapper", and in Dorset, Hampshire, and Norfolk as the Diedapper.)' – Lewis, 75.

diddle   for a bowler to remove a batsman with cunning. It may come from the OE *didrian*, to delude. 'J.W. Hearne and Aubrey Faulkner, two of the great all-rounders of cricket, diddled us out twice' (Robertson-Glasgow, *Crusoe*, 25).

dig   an innings (Australian): 'Colin McDonald made 80-odd in the second dig' (Mosey, 18). Also, a successful attempt to deal with a *yorker* is to *dig it out*. *Digging for runs*, less often heard, is to be getting them with difficulty.

dip   particularly *late dip*, is a very useful thing for a bowler to have in his armoury. It means the ball pitches shorter than the batsman thinks it will, thus giving it more space to turn before it gets to the bat. See also *loop*.

dirt   or dust: a substance which was formerly quite freely rubbed onto the ball. C.J. Kortright of Essex, supposedly the fastest bowler of his day – around the turn of the century – averred that he rubbed the ball in the dirt to get a grip on it. This is now illegal, but desirable with the advent of reverse swing, as this depends on having one side of the ball as rough as possible. Thus when the captain of England, Michael Atherton, was seen to take something from his pocket and apply it to one side of the ball at Lord's, in the 1994 Test against South Africa there, enormous controversy ensued. Atherton said it was to dry the ball for the bowler, who was Gough of Yorkshire, the fast bowler, who can reverse swing the ball. His action was not illegal, Law 42.5 stating 'No one shall rub the ball on the ground or use any artificial substance or take any other action to alter the condition of the ball.' Dirt is not an artificial substance, and Atherton only had it in his pocket. But why he should have been drying sweat from the ball is an unresolved question.

dismiss, dismissal   the removal of the batsman or the team: 'only the resolute White, with 62, extended the innings beyond tea because Hampshire's second innings dismissal had been swift' (Michael Austin, The *Sunday Times*, 2 July 1995).

divot   as in golf, a lump with grass on it knocked out of the pitch. Originally used for roofing cottages (OED).

do   for a bowler to *do* a batsman means to undo him, with cunning or skill. 'Fred Titmus does 'em in the air,' said Alfred Gover *c*. 1975, referring to his ability to flight the ball. 'He did him with one that came back off the seam,' refers to movement from off to leg, dismissing the batsman. A pitch that *does* something helps spin and movement off the seam.

dog shot   played by Victor Trumper of New South Wales and Australia in the 1890s and 1900s. The ball was dispatched between his bat and his legs to the fine-leg area. To facilitate the passage of the ball, his right leg was cocked, hence the name.

dolly, dolly-drop   an easy catch, a high lobbed full-toss in bowling. OED has 'designating an easy catch, etc.', from 1895, but also gives *dolly* as an Anglo-Indian word, from 1860, roughly transliterated from Hindi *dali*, meaning 'an offering of fruit, flowers, sweetmeats, etc.' Curiously, both *dolly* and *lolly* (Australian) are derived from the last. Thus a bat may be lured to his downfall by an exotic tracklement. The jacket illustration shows a *dolly catch*.

Don, the   Sir Donald Bradman, A.C.A.

donkey drop   a high lobbed ball, whether over- or under-arm. The derivation would seem obvious, the first use in Lewis being

1888, A.G. Steel writing: 'As the slow bowler walked up to the wicket to bowl, the big hitter turned to him and said, "What, are you going to bowl your donkey-drops? I'll hit them all out of the ground"' (BLC, 1888, 128).

dot ball   a ball which is not scored off, thus making a *dot* in the score-book.

double   the feat of scoring 1000 runs and taking 100 wickets in a season, rarely done now. Wilfred Rhodes was the *double* champion of his time, passing the figures sixteen times, and heading the bowling averages for four consecutive years 1919–22.

The double double of two thousand runs and two hundred wickets has only been done once, by G.H. Hirst of Yorkshire, who in 1906 took 208 wickets at 16.05 and made 2385 runs at 45.86.

The wicket-keeper's double is 1000 runs and 100 dismissals in the season, and Leslie Ames of Kent and England performed it thrice, with 2,842 runs in 1932.

double century   200 runs. The only man to have made a double double century, or two hundred runs in each innings, was Arthur Fagg of Kent, in 1938, when he made 244 and 202 v. Essex at Colchester. But it also appears to have meant a century in each innings: A.E. Knight writing 'that double century is the scoring of two separate centuries in the same match' (p.342). Sunil Gavaskar of India became the first man in Test cricket to score that double thrice, when in the 1974–5 series against the West Indies he scored 107 and 182* in Calcutta. Alan Border made 150* and 153 against Pakistan, another unique feat.

double egg   a pair (*Bell's Life*, 31 August 1862).

double figures   of a batsman, to make ten or more runs.

double wicket   the present game, as opposed to *single wicket*. It is not clear when this form developed, but Joseph Strutt, who can claim to be the first historian of sport, says in his *Sports and Pastimes of England*, 1801, that cricket 'consists of both double and single wicket' (II.iii.83).

down   a fallen wicket, by whatever means. Seven wickets *down* is self-explanatory.

Also batting position: No. 3 bats at first wicket *down*, 4 at second-wicket *down* and so on.

drag   the dragging of the trailing foot, especially a fast bowler, with particular reference to dragging it over the *popping-crease*, and sometimes over the batting-crease, thus shortening the distance over which they bowl. See also *front-foot law*. 'I sat opposite his delivery for some time and found that he was still dragging over . . . the English umpires were immediately satisfied that if he brought his back foot down behind the line, that was all that concerned them' (Fingleton on Lindwall's action, Don, 47). The *drag line* was drawn in the ground some way behind the wicket crease, some feet in fact, and the bowler was *called*[1] if he overstepped this line with his back foot, which would mean that at the moment of delivery his dragging back foot would be over the the bowling, or return, crease. The *drag plate* is a metal toecap on the bowler's boot, from 1963.

It is also obsolete for **backspin**, and here opinions diverge, for Lewis quotes E.R. Wilson: 'Drag is rare and of little practical value' (BLC, 1920, 84), while Armstrong (1922) says of a ball with drag that it 'never seems to arrive as soon as it is expected' (p.45). Perhaps he was referring to early *flippers*, but those seem to arrive early.

There is an obsolete use for what appears to be the *pull* stroke, rather deprecated by W.L. Murdoch: 'Often have I seen Lockwood and A. Bannerman, two of the best exponents of the short straight ball drag stroke, sacrifice their wickets in attempting it' (*Longman's Magazine*, January 1883, 289).

draw[1]   a game which for reasons of time does not achieve a result, i.e. not a *tie*. To *draw stumps* is the end of play for the day. To *play for a draw* usually happens when one of the sides realises it cannot win but does not wish to lose.

draw[2]   obsolete: a shot played to a straightish or legside ball which deflects it down to long leg. The bat is held behind the legs, nearer to the wicket, at a fairly acute angle.

dressing-room   each side usually has one. This can lead to some confusion, as in the case of Alan Border, a trifle dissatisfied with his dismissal lbw by Botham at the WACA, 1986–7, where the dressing rooms were side by side. He displayed his mastery of vernacular while divesting himself of his protective equipment, throwing his bat and gloves on the floor. He was astonished to see himself being gazed at by a doubly astonished Alec Bedser, manager of the England team, whose dressing-room he was in.

drift, drifter   a finger-spinner's ball, not spinning, which drifts in the air in the opposite direction to the usual spin. Also used to denote the way in which a spun ball curls in the air in an opposite direction to the way the ball will go after bouncing.

drinks interval   one, or when very hot sometimes two, short pauses for drinks to be brought out to the fielders and batsmen. Formerly the job of the twelfth man, now a caparisoned trolley.

drive   the ball is played with the bat fully swung (except for the *check-drive*) and perpendicular to the ground (except for the *pull-drive*). 'The top hand is the important one in the drive, and the drive is still, and always will be, the best paying stroke in cricket. The bat meets the ball full face, minimising risk, and no bowler likes to be met with a full and flashing blade' (Fingleton, *Cricket*, 222). Driving is usually off the front foot, but to drive well off the back foot is a mark of the complete batsman. 'Thorpe produced 84 towards England's win in Barbados, when he drove off the back foot with great elan' (David Hopps, *Guardian*, 15 October 1994).

drop   has three meanings: to say a fielder *dropped* a batsman means he dropped a catch put up by that batsman. To be dropped from a side means not to be chosen for it. And W. Lillywhite's *Young Cricketer's Guide* of 1849, shows a bowler's trick: 'The bowler on seeing you leave your ground will *drop* one short' (p.16) i.e. make it pitch on a shorter length.

duck   dating from at least 7 July 1856, when 'Wright gave another duck, forming a pair' (*Bell's Life*). A score of zero, but only when the batsman is out, the shape of a *duck's egg* when written. Possibly the pale blue of an empty sky helped the symbolism. *Golden duck*, a, or to get, is to get out first ball (not to be confused with *king pair* which is to do it twice in one game). You may then join the Primary Club, started by Beckenham CC in Kent, a charity to help visually disadvantaged cricketers. Members wear the distinctive tie on the Saturday of the Lord's Test, one of the few sights as reassuring as it is awe-inspiring. The Australian club provides facilities for the disabled and holds functions at the Lemon Tree Oval at Dooralong in New South Wales. There is no known organisation for the holders of the king pair.

In June 1989 David Gower became the only man to play 100 consecutive Test innings without a duck, a run he extended to 119, according to Kersi Meher-Homji (p.53), who also lists 'zoinks', 'blongers', 'glozzers', 'globes', 'potatoes'. For *duck-shooting* he has the supremo as Ray Lindwall with 0.80 per Test, followed by Sir Richard Hadlee with 0.77 (and the top duckster in tests with 66 to his name) and Fred Trueman with 0.74. And *duck pie* was tasted by John Ikin after 99 consecutive innings when bowled by Eric Hollies.

The other meaning 'Are you a *ducker* or a *swayer*?' is attributed to Ian Redpath of Australia, referring to ducking under a ball rising at the body, or swaying out of its line.

duckmasters, ducksters   (see also *quackers*) are adepts.

dustbowl   (Australian) word taken apparently from the dust-bowls of the American Depression, and here meaning a dusty pitch, suitable for spin bowling. Also *dustheap*. See also *crumbler*.

dusty   see above.

Easy single   one run taken without much hurrying.

easy-paced   a pitch which does not offer much to the bowler in that deliveries do not come off fast, achieve much bounce, or generate much *anti-batsman behaviour*.

edge   edge is from the Indo-European root *ak-* to be sharp or pointed. An *edge* can be voluntary and involuntary. The edge of the bat, usually the outside, is applied to the ball, which flies off into the slip or leg-slip area. An *educated edge* is when the batsman uses a spot near the edge to deflect the ball to score. Also used as a verb.

eighty-seven   supposed to be unlucky as thirteen short of a hundred, as are 187, 287, etc., but there is no evidence to support this. See *devil's number*.

eleven   'A match is played betwen two sides each of eleven players' are the first words of the Laws of Cricket. Thus eleven signifies a team here: the word comes from roots meaning 'one leftover' (from ten): the OE is *endleofen* corresponding to Gothic *ainlif* and Common Germanic *ainaz* + *lif*, 'plausibly related to Indo-European *liq-* to leave' (*ODEtym*). The number itself is often thought to refer to the eleven good apostles, in the same way that thirteen is unlucky as the number at the Last Supper. Or it may be simply the fingers of the hand plus one, a captain. The roots of the numbering system based on eleven may have the same origin (see Introduction). The first eleven-a-side match known for certain is in Sussex in 1697 for 50 guineas. Whether this was then firmly established or not we don't know: *The Postboy* advertised a ten-a-side on Clapham Common for 28 March 1700.

emergency   obsolete for *substitute*: recording the term, Lewis quotes Grace's encomium of his brother E.M., who 'played as an emergency', taking all ten and scoring 192*.

emperor pair   term suggested by Kersi Meher-Homji for the performance of Kim Hughes at Johannesburg in 1983–4, dismissed first ball in both innings, and also first ball when he went in as Rodney Hogg's runner.

end   each pitch has two *ends*. Bowling from them has different advantages, as in the Nursery end at Lord's, the slope of the ground helping the ball to cut or spin to the off. William Caffyn, writing of Old Clarke, the early Notts professional and slow-medium trundler says: 'He was always eager to get the best end of a wicket to bowl on. "I'll have this end, and you can have which you like!" he would say to his fellow bowler' (Lucas, xx). Applies to either bowler's or batsman's end.

even time   to score in *even time* is a run a minute.

expensive   an *expensive* spell is one which has many runs scored off it: the implication being for few or no wickets. Seems to emerge in the 1890s: in 1900 P.F. Warner said, 'Vyfhuis, the fast bowler [of British Guiana] was expensive' (p.64).

express   either a very fast ball or bowler: maybe another influence of the railways on cricket, coming from a train running expressly to one station, then a fast train stopping only at a number of stations. Lewis's first mention is in 1895, Pentelow's *England v. Australia*: 'the Australians could do little with Ulyett's expresses.'

extra cover   to the right of cover, and the left of mid-off.

extras   byes, leg-byes, wides, and no-balls. They are not scored by the bat, so not added to the score of the batsman: no-balls and wides are debited to the bowler and show up in his analysis (since 1994). *Lillywhite's Cricket Scores* records a match at Lord's on 14 July 1842 when the Royal Artillery Club gave away 48 wides, supplemented by 58 no-balls. In Australia the term is *sundries*.

F **ace** facing the bowling, or the face of the bat. *To open the face* is to twist the bat around its vertical axis so that the ball is hit more towards the off side, e.g. through *point* rather than *mid-off*. *Closing the face* directs it more to the leg side. 'Brian Lara opening the face of the bat and hitting it over the top' (Michael Holding for Sky TV: Lara sliced it deliberately over backward point, World Cup semi-finals, 14 March 1996).

fag a fieldsman. Not heard with this meaning outside Winchester. *Long fag* is *long field*. Cf. Carthusian and general public school slang *fag*, meaning a younger boy employed on menial tasks for the prefects. Lewis dates it back to at least 1840, where Olympian cricketers are assigned fielding positions: 'Great Jupiter [shall be] long fag, because he can shy the ball like a thunderbolt straight through the air' (*Sporting Magazine*, August 1840, 332).

fair play the unwritten code, not infrequently emerging more in the breach than in the observance. It has a long history, the 'Old Buffer' (Frederick Gale) in *Echos from Old Cricket Fields* 1871 has Dr Grace trying an early *spedegue*, 'leaving the batsman powerless. It was within the laws of cricket, but that was all.' If it was E.M., however, he did frequently bowl underarm. Sir Jack Hobbs gave himself out at the Oval against the Australians when the umpire didn't, and even more surprisingly seems to have got himself out against them after another wrong decision, letting himself be bowled. John Nyren says in 1833, speaking 'in behalf of Hambledon men, I cannot recall to recollection an instance of their wilfully stopping a ball that had been hit out among them by one of our opponents. Like *true* Englishmen, they would give an enemy fair play.' The phrase 'it's not cricket' is pretty well synonymous with 'it's not fair play'. See also *cricket, not; walk; gamesmanship; umpire.*

fall wickets are said *to fall* when taken, possibly referring in the early instances to the displacement of the bail. See also *wicket.*

fall away used of a bowling action when the bowler, instead of remaining side on, with his left shoulder pointing towards the batsman (if a right-handed bowler), drops it, letting it swing outwards to the offside. This makes his bowling less accurate, and can cause the bowling arm to be dropped lower, so at an angle. 'West Indies won despite Ambrose being out of rhythm. Most of the time he was falling away, and rarely did he hit the seam' (Imran Khan on the First Test at Edgbaston, England v. West Indies, *Daily Telegraph*, 17 June 1995).

farm to keep a weaker batsman away from the bowling. 'When . . . Denis was "farming" the bowling, he resolutely – and rightly – refused to take a single except near the end of an over' (W.R. Hammond, 65, on the Adelaide Test 1947). Compton, the last surviving recognised England batsman, was making his second century in the match, had Godfrey Evans as a partner much of the time, and Bradman had strung out a *wheel field*, to keep him away from the strike.

fast¹ a *fast* pitch, or track: the ball comes off quickly, or 'comes on to the bat', and has a bit of bounce.

fast² a *fast* bowler, one who delivers the ball with great velocity. 'First you had Snow and Garner. Then, one step higher, you had Roberts, with Michael Holding one step above him. Then, three steps above Holding, there was Thommo [Jeff Thomson of New South Wales, Queensland, and Australia]. He was the only bloke I saw hit a sightscreen after bouncing only once . . .' – Greg Chappell talking to John Thicknesse (*Evening Standard*, 24 October 1994). He is borne out by Thomson's clocking 99.68 m.p.h. when tested and Holding 87, although to put Thomson's feat in perspective, it was at the WACA, and the Perth pitch is rock-hard. Other time trials show Larwood at 96, but in the 1930s the equipment might not be so accurate as today's. Wes Hall of Barbados and the West Indies clocked 93, Trueman 92, Statham and Loader were in the 80s, and Alan Davidson in the 70s. Godfrey Evans reckoned Tyson faster than Trueman, who points out that he was not tested in his prime and reckons he might have topped the ton.

Alec Stewart sees his former team-mate Sylvester Clarke as the quickest; and David Gower says 'I think he might receive my vote on the strength of several deliveries at the Oval one day. He ripped the top of my glove off, and he would also bowl you the occasional delivery you simply never saw' (Gower, 30).

fast bowlers' union not only interchange of information, but also unspoken agreement not to bowl *bouncers* at each other. *Quickies* are often *rabbits* and *ferrets*, few more so than Devon Malcolm, who took a pounding from Courtney Walsh in the final Test in the West Indies in 1994. Then, brought in for the Oval Test against South Africa in August, he was hit on the helmet by a first-ball bouncer from de Villiers. 'You guys are history, you're going to pay for this,' he said, and nine did as he took 9–57 in the second innings (the only one he didn't get was de Villiers).

fast-footed two contradictory meanings, the old one being as Felix in *How to Play Clarke* (1852) puts it: 'If you are a fast-footed man, i.e. if you fix your foot down near the crease, and resolve not to move it under any circumstancces, you are his easiest victim.' But *fast-footed* today means to use your feet quickly to go down the pitch, or right back – e.g. to hook.

fast hands   'The vagaries of the pitch and its relatively slow pace gave compact back-foot players with fast hands the best chance' (Simon Hughes, *Daily Telegraph*, 31 August 1996), i.e. hitting at the last possible moment with great force. See also *wrist, wristy*.

fast-medium   a bowler, or bowling, that is slower than fast but quicker than medium-fast, at around 75 m.p.h./115 k.p.h.

feather   a shot in which the blade of the bat is drawn across the ball, or the ball slides off the angled face, down into and through the slips area. See also *late cut*.

featherbed   some pitches are very soft because of a thick layer of grass, too much *scarifying*, too much manure, or loose soil. They are thus difficult for the bowler to get much turn and bounce.

feed   to *feed* a shot: to bowl to a batsman's weakness. Thus at Edgbaston 1995 Darren Gough let himself be tempted into a *hook* shot, and was caught, it being obviously the plan of the West Indies to feed him with short balls.

feel for   Lewis's first reference is to Ranjitsinhji, 'to feel at', but by 1904 Pelham Warner was writing 'feeling for that off ball with the happiest results for us.' The meaning is to stick the bat outside the off stump. See also *fishing*.

feigned names   in the early and mid-19th century, numbers of players used false names. In one of the earliest of Haygarth's *Scores and Biographies* we find 'The following is the list of cricketers who have occasionally played under other names, in *Bell's Life* and other papers, owing to their profession, &c.' And we then see that W. Pickering Esq., chose to be W. Pluckabrooch Esq. (surely rather incriminating), H. Aite Esq., to be Love Esq., and A. Law to be A. Infelix Esq., obviously a reference to Felix, itself a feigned name. The disapprobation of cricket, because of its association with drink and gambling in those early days, was probably the reason for this. 'Felix' was a schoolmaster and indeed school proprietor at 19 on the death of his parents (his curious and enviable career is described by Green in *A History of Cricket*).

fend   the word is a short form of 'defend' and applies to a batsman doing just that, usually from a hostile bowler who is making the ball rise. The batsman *fends* it off.

ferret   very late order batsman; goes in after the *rabbits*. Can be also referred to as 'the one before the extras', 'above the extras'. It may come from the L. *fur*, thief; thus 'furtive'.

festival   from the Latin *festus* a feast, through to an occasion for merriment. The first cricket *festival* was held at Canterbury. On 1 August 1841, Kent v. England was played on a ground on the outskirts of Canterbury belonging to the family of John and W. de Chair Baker. John suggested to the Hon. Frederick Ponsonby that he should bring down some of his Cambridge friends, then becoming famous for their amateur acting, to entertain the large number of visitors the cricket attracted. Scarborough, from 1876, was the first to be actually called a festival, and traditionally touring teams played their last match there – having 'bid adieu in the south' at Hastings, where Compton scored his seventeenth century of the summer. Cheltenham staged its first festival in 1878, Folkestone between the wars, and Kingston-upon-Thames between 1948 and 1953 – including a North v. South game (see Altham, Sawnton (ed.)).

According to Lord Harris, I Zingari were the founders of the Canterbury Week. 'The best of the Zingari would play on the field all day, play on the boards at night, and keep up the fun at the Old Stagers supper to latish hours.'

fetch   in batting: 'The right foot must be moved when a ball is fetched, i.e. when we jump out to drive a ball, hoping to convert the good length into a half-volley' (Knight, 69). Applies also to a bowler bringing the ball back into the batsman, *fetching* it back a long way. From OE *fecc(e)n*, showing again the palatisation of the *cc*.

field   derived from AS *feld*, originally meaning just an open space as opposed to woodland, or hurst – as borne out by the frequent place names ending in either. The original, and correct, term for the place where the match is played, as used by Revd James Pycroft in *The Cricket Field*, 1851. Can also be used to mean *fielder*.

fielder, fieldsman   one of the team fielding. The word started out as *fieldsman* though **watchers-out** was in use in 1768. *Outscout* as out-fielder was also in use early, as in 1798 in Horne Tooke's *Diversions of Purley*: 'Is an Out-scout at cricket sent to a distance, that he may the better listen to what is passing?' (p. 405). **Look out** was also in use (see entry referring to Dickens in 1837), as were **seek out, seeker out**, dating from 'James Love's' *Heroick Poem* (his real name was Dance): after the ball had left Hodswell's arm (see **bowl**) four times: 'Then Mills succeeds. The Seekers-out change place.' OED has mention of 'fieldsman' in 1824, implying that it is the first, but the

Nyren quote below seems to show it was in use in Hambledon days, and moreover we have from 1767 the *Cricket Song of Hambledon Club*, ix: 'Ye fieldsmen look sharp ... Move close like an army, in rank and in file.' It seems that the most descriptive term took over from about 1840.

fielding   one of the three great departments of the game: the act of stopping, retrieving or catching the ball after it has been hit by the batsman, and returning it to the appropriate place.

> If a ball be hit very hard in the direction of the long field, the safe way to play it is by dropping on one knee with both hands before him: should these miss it, the body will act as a rampart to prevent its further progress. To the young cricketer I cannot too frequently repeat that activity, observation, and steadiness are the most valuable qualities in a fieldsman, and allow me to add, as an old 'Tutor' – in any other man. (Nyren, in Lucas, 88).

Less demanding is that great gully fielder, captain of Surrey, P.G.H. Fender: 'Of the three great departments of the game, there is one thing that can be said without any fear of contradiction, and that is that in fielding alone, of the three, proficiency can be achieved by anyone' (p. 61).

The homage to Vic Richardson for his fielding in 1928 at the Second Test in Sydney, where at the end of every session the Hill stood and cheered him, and he was carried off shoulder-high at the end of the day, is probably unique, and Hele took care to record it for posterity. Hele thought the young Bradman the finest outfielder of all time (and he saw Colin Bland). Bradman, who once ran out Hobbs, himself no mean cover-point, when he thought there were two runs and didn't even make one, considered Learie Constantine, later Lord Constantine, the greatest all-round fielder: 'Speed of foot, agility, balance, good throw, confident catching – he had the lot' (Bradman, 138).

fielding machine   advertised in *Ayres' Cricket Companion* of 1910, the 'Kachaball' Cricket Machine (pat. 1905) has passed into obscurity.

fielding positions   where the fieldsmen are placed.

fiery   used now of a pace attack (Cardus spoke of a 'vehement' Notts attack in the 1930s), but formerly more of the pitch: Lewis in 1934 only quotes the former: 'The wicket was very fiery ... and ball after ball went over Mr Webbe's head.' 'Fiery Fred' is F.S. Trueman.

figures   generally used of bowlers. Thus, the best *figures* for

any debutant England bowler are 7–43, Dominic Cork for
England v. West Indies, Lord's Test 1995.

filth   refers to slow bowling, especially 'Two early wickets by
Ron Stern and a lively spell by Nick Kirwan put the XL Club
behind the rate and they were unable to cash in sufficiently on
the subsequent flighted filth' (Cricket Society *News Bulletin*
October 1994). See also *muck, tosh.*

fine   defines fielding positions that are more behind the wicket.
Thus *long leg* is at an angle of about 45° to the line of the
pitch, but *fine leg* is further round behind the batsman. This
may not be true in Australia, Frank Tyson in *The Terms of the
Game* defining long leg as another term for deep fine leg.

finger   for the umpire to give the batsman the *finger* is devoid
of rudery other than giving him out.

finger-spin   used of a spin-bowler who spins with his fingers.
Current examples are Eddie Hemmings of Sussex, Nottinghamshire, and England, and Phil Tufnell of Middlesex and England.
Both spin in the orthodox way, using mainly the first finger to
make the ball spin, turning their wrist outwards, away from
their bodies. For Hemmings this produces an *off-break* to the
right-handed batsman, for Tufnell a *leg-break*. This is not the
only way that *finger-spin* is used: Eric Hollies of Warwickshire
and England rolled his fingers over the ball at the moment of
delivery to produce a leg-break. But as Sir Donald points out,
referring to this method, 'the harder, truer wickets of Australia
demand more than finger-spin if the ball is going to turn
sufficiently to be dangerous' (Bradman, 107). S.F. Barnes,
regarded by some as the greatest bowler of all, used very much
the same grip for leg-break, off-break, and *top-spinner*, wrap-
ping his unusually long fingers and his thumb around the ball
roughly equidistantly. More of the difference was in the angle
of the wrist, in both cases angled to prduce some top-spin as
well. The similarity of grip enabled him to change his mind and
bowl either break without readjustment. Both, therefore, came
out of the front of the hand. The top-spinner had something of
the same grip, little finger rather further down the ball, and that
too came out of the front, making it difficult to spot. 'All my
fingers did something. I don't know how I did it myself, so how
can I tell other people?' said he (Duckworth, 159).

first change   the bowler who comes on to bowl after the
opening bowlers: thus a *fourth-change* bowler is one who seldom
is given a bowl.

first-class   describes the standard of cricket played. *Tests*,
County Championship, *Shell Trophy*, *Red Stripe Cup,*

Castle Cup, *Sheffield Shield*, University matches (at present), some Festivals and games such as North v. South and Gentlemen v. Players from the past. In 1864 the 19th edition of *Lillywhite's Guide to Cricketers* gives 'Names of Batsmen in first-class matches only'.

first slip   the *finest* of the slips, next to the keeper, and sometimes a little further back than him and the other slips; should have the best reactions.

fishing   dangling the bat outside the off stump, which often results in a catch to slip. A major sin, much castigated by Geoffrey Boycott on television, exemplified from Johannesburg: 'In goes Cork . . . Hudson's fishing . . . there's a big appeal . . . he's caught by Russell' (BBC Test Match Special, 26 December 1995).

fiver   five runs off a ball, given if a fielder stops the ball with his hat – originally a topper, one presumes. Viv Richards stopped a certain boundary by throwing his famous maroon cap at it, and the batsman was duly awarded five runs. This comes from the first sentence of Law 41.1, which states: 'The fieldsman may stop the ball with any part of his person but if he wilfully stops it otherwise five runs shall be added to the run or runs already scored; if one run has been scored, five penalty runs shall be awarded.' (Law 41 makes many other points regarding The Fieldsman.) Five runs are also awarded if the ball hits a helmet on the ground behind the keeper.

fizz   a wicket with *fizz* in it is liable to produce a

fizzer   a ball with pace and devil, especially off the pitch. First OED mention is the verb 'to fizz' from 1864, but in cricket the use comes later, Lewis finding in 1920 E.R. Wilson in the Badminton *Cricket* p89: 'A fast bowler takes a wicket "with a fizzer"; a slow bowler, owing to a bad stroke: but both achieve the same end.' The first use is echoic, from 1656 (OED).

flannels   the material from which cricketing trousers were formerly made. Curiously, if the OED's putative derivation from Welsh *gwlanen* from *gwlân*, wool, is right, it might show why Flemish weavers came over in the first place, as flannel is defined as 'an open woollen stuff, of loose texture, usually without a nap'. English cloth was inferior at this time. Flannels are now made largely from synthetics, or a mixture. Trowsers are regarded as inconvenient as well as unbecoming by the Revd John Mitford in 1833, as they might 'be in the way of the ball'. The advantages of knee-breeches and stockings are clear. However, the fashion for flannels continued, the first apparent mention being from 1888, when James J. Payn ch. ix, has 'He had worn cricketing flannels' (OED). *Flannelled fool* comes from Rudyard Kipling's 'The Islanders', 1902: 'Then ye returned to your trinkets; then ye contented your souls / With the flannelled fools at the wicket or the muddied oafs at the goals.'

flash   an active form of *fishing*, not in Lewis, so probably of origin after 1945. A typical *flash* would be a cut at a ball too close to the off stump and too well pitched up to be safe, while a flashing drive or cut is one with panache.

flat   in bowling, a *flat* trajectory, without air or loop: 'Flat Jack' Simmons, the Lancashire off-spinner, **pushed the ball through** in this way. In fielding, a long hard return by a fielder from the boundary.

flat bat   *to hit with a flat bat*, or *to flat-bat* usually implies a shot made with a *cross-bat* and the bat's face perpendicular to the ground, and that the ball has gone on the off side or straight back over the bowler's head: 'Rollins ... flat-batting Angus Fraser over cover-point for another six' (Charles Randall, *Daily Telegraph*, 6 June 1995).

flick   a wristy shot, played late without full power of the forearms and shoulders. The face of the bat is turned with the wrists at the last instant as the blade descends, and the ball forced away, usually at an angle, usually on the leg side, although also to the off: 'Tendulkar continued in attacking vein, until he flicked Walsh to mid-wicket, where Brian Lara held a difficult catch' (*The Times*, 3 December 1994).

flight   a slower bowler's way of inducing a deceptive trajectory so that the batsman is uncertain of the length of the ball, e.g. by keeping the arm action as quick or quicker, but making the ball come out more slowly (Ray Illingworth, commentating, BBC Television, Old Trafford, 1993), or giving it more of a loop, or flatter to deceive.

Cardus seems to include sideways movement, as in reporting the first Test of 1938 he has Sinfield 'flighting the ball with the craft and pretty curve of long tradition'. And in his panegyric on Wilfred Rhodes: 'Flight was his secret, flight and the curving line, now higher, now lower, tempting, inimical ... every ball a decoy, a spy ...' In case one underestimates Rhodes, as one so often does the giants of the past in today's climate of extremely fast bowling, A.E. Knight, the Leicestershire batsman, said in 1906 that he 'turns or breaks the ball on a favourable wicket far more than any left-hander I have met.' He toured Australia with Rhodes, making the catch off him which broke the Trumper/ Duff stand which was threatening to win Australia the game. (*Essential Cardus*, 12, 67).

The purpose of flight is shown in 'but Jimmy Hindson was unlucky not to claim Crawley's wicket with one ball that foxed him in the flight and then turned' (Jon Culley, *Independent*, 27 August 1994).

flipper¹   wrist-spinner's ball that skids through from the pitch, being given a backwards flip by the hand and wrist. Jonty Rhodes of South Africa picks it 'from Warne's grip on the ball, which shows the batsman only the index and middle fingers . . . rather than the four fingers he sees when it is a leg break' (John Woodcock, *The Times*, 17 March 1994).

Richie Benaud describes it as an unnatural action flipped from under the hand, as opposed to the over-the-wrist spinners, a 'backspinning topspinner with the seam of the ball at right angles to the pitch . . . The scientists tell us nothing can come off the pitch, because of friction. It just seems to come off faster.' He would not allow anyone under the age of twelve to undertake it because of the strain it imposes on the ligaments, muscles, and tendons (letter to the author, 29 June 1993).

The first practitioner was Clarrie Grimmett, thought to have produced it *c.*1939–40. He passed it on to Bruce Dooland, also of South Australia, later of Nottinghamshire and League Cricket, who taught it to Benaud. But the old fox showed the grip for it in a photograph in his book *Tricking the Batsman* (1934), so it is possible he was an unknown flippant for some years. It would have been in character.

flipper²   the wicket-keeper's glove: 'It wasn't going to carry to Athers at first slip. I just dived, shot out my left flipper and the ball stayed in. I was really pleased,' said Alec Stewart (*Independent on Sunday*, 2 July 1995), referring to the diving catch which took the wicket of Brian Lara.

floater   a type of delivery used mainly by an orthodox finger-spinner: in fact a slow swinger. The seam is upright, slanting towards slip, index finger resting on top of it. Thus it seems to float away to the slips, movement increased if there is a cross-wind blowing from leg to off.

fluke   a chancy shot, which by luck is either successful in scoring runs or avoiding dismissal. Felix said in his *How to Play Clarke* (1852): 'Hundreds of runs have been obtained by what are very properly called flukes.' 'He *fluked* a shot through the slips' has the same meaning. OED has first mention from 1857, referring to billiards.

flukey   is said in the same way of a shot. OED's first example is 'flukey hitting' from 1879, but Lewis has 'Cosstick . . . playing a very flukey innings' from the *Australian*, 2 March 1867.

fly-slip   a deep slip, to catch the balls that fly over the heads of the slips. First mention of the position is uncertain.

follow-on   Law 13 reads:

'The Follow-On'

1. Lead on First Innings

In a two-innings match, the side which bats first and leads by 200 runs in a match of five days or more, or by 150 runs in a three-day or four-day match, by 100 runs in a two-day match or by 75 runs in a one-day match, shall have the option of requiring the other side to follow their innings.

2. Day's Play Lost

If no play takes place on the first day of a match of two or more days' duration, (1) above shall apply in accordance with the number of days' play remaining from the actual start of the match.

The *follow-on* used to be compulsory, and the number of runs behind has varied with time. Thus after the university match of 1893, MCC amended the Law so that a follow-on was compulsory if the side batting second was 120 behind. First mention in Lewis is from 1865, *F. Lillywhite's Guide to Cricketers*, (86): 'Surrey "followed on" but left only 23 run for Oxford to get to win.' See also *declaration*.

follow through, follow-through   the end of the action of both bowling and making a stroke. Lewis defines it as 'The whole weight and impetus of the body used to effect the delivery of the ball in bowling.' Harold Larwood's fingers were reputed to touch the ground during his. Brian Lara's flourishing *follow through* shows the *bat speed* with which he hits the ball.

foothold   of a bowler, to gain a foothold on slippery grass. Sawdust is used.

footmark   marks made on the pitch by the bowler (very occasionally the batsman). The umpires may *warn* the bowlers about this; it gives the bowlers from the other end a chance to pitch in the marks, just outside the right-handers' leg stump or the left-handers' off stump, and turn sharply, or erratically. 'Just on the right length, but too far outside the leg stump to confer a match-winnng advantage . . . A spot a foot long, and only three inches wide . . .', wrote Hedley Verity, 'the remaining Australian batsmen fell to balls which I pitched in the roughened soil of those footmarks' (p.90).

footwork   the batsman's placing of his feet to counter the bowling. If he can move into position to play his shot quickly, and has seen the ball early, he obviously has an advantage. 'As soon as the ball left my hand he was moving into position with those tiny feet,' said Alec Bedser of Bradman.

'In the past, English batsman have proved tragicallly *foot-tied* against Australia's spinners . . .' – John Arlott, *Playfair Cricket Monthly*, May 1961.

force   see entry above: a shot played with power, implying more power than the ball might expect.

forcing batsman, shot   aggressive. *Forcing game* as an expression is now rare: the first mention of *forcing* being from 1888.

fore right off   an unknown fielding position, from the late eighteenth century, probably silly mid-off: 'James Bray kept wicket for his own club, but when he went to play elsewhere he was generally "fore right off"' (Haygarth, 1, 394).

forfeit   a captain may *forfeit* his side's second innings under certain conditions (Law 14), to achieve a *result*.

forward   any shot which involves going *forward* to meet the ball. It came in when the new length bowling was introduced, and the bat became straight and shouldered: 'The method then [c.1804] introduced was running in at the ball, hard hitting, and a bold forward play' (Denison, 41). The Revd James Pycroft's *Cricket Field* has absorbed this well enough to produce imprudent advice: 'But since the best forward players may err . . . practise the art of *half-play*' (p. 126)

forward cut   a cut shot, with the left leg forward.

forward stroke

. . . move the left foot forward, about three feet, keeping the right foot behind the popping crease. Now move the bat as far forward as you can reach, so as to present its full face to the ball; keeping the bat upright, or rather slanting *the handle* towards the bowler to an angle of about 22 degrees. In order to maintain an upright position of the bat, the left elbow must be turned up. Let me urge the young batsman not to neglect this direction of turning up the left elbow . . . It is likewise the best and safest way for hitting . . . for, if a stroke be made with the left elbow in the position stated, and the bat at the same time upright, the ball cannot rise. I need not point out the advantage of this. (Nyren, in Lucas, 22)

four   runs, either all run or a boundary; *fourer* obsolete for *four*.

fox the ball   the fieldsman tries to mislead the batsman that either he's closer to the ball than he is, or has picked it up already, or conversely that he is further from it. See also *slobber*.

Frank judgment   when playing for the Bengal Governor's XI against a Commonwealth team in the 1940s, Benjamin Frank shouldered his bat to what he thought was George Tribe's googly. It was his chinaman, and flattened his stumps. Thus it is known in the Bangalore leagues.

free hit   either the bowler has bowled a loose ball, or the batsman has manoeuvred himself into position, so the result is a danger-free scoring stroke; thus, facing Warne, the 41-year-old Emburey 'always went back to every ball pitched wide of the leg stump, ensuring both pads made a second line, then taking a free hit' (Dave Crowe, *The Cricketer*, January 1994). If the bowler bowls and the ball stops halfway down the wicket, the batsman has a *free hit*.

free hitter, free-hitting   a stroke player, which goes back to 1851: 'In olden times the freest hitter was the best batsman' (Pycroft, 580). And ibid., 'Many a man, whose talent lies in defence, tries free hitting, and between the two proves good for nothing' (213).

French cut   Australian or NZ: see *Surrey cut, Chinese cut*.

front foot   either of bowler or batsman, the leading foot. Thus a *front-foot batsman* is one favouring forward play.

front-foot law   the law by which a bowler must not bowl with his front foot over the batting crease. If he does, it is a *no-ball*.

full   *on the full* means a full toss. A *full length*, though, is a ball of goodish length, up to the batsman.

full moon   obsolete since the mid-19th century: a duck.

full pitch, full toss   a ball which reaches the batsman without bouncing, either because he's gone to meet it or because it is too full a length.

Game   the noun has been identified as having a Gothic root *gaman*, meaning 'together', identical to the L. *com-* prefix. The likeness is illustrated in the *ODEtym* with L. *communis*, Gothic *gamains*, OE *gemaene*. *ODEtym* has the Teutonic preface *ga-* (Ger. and Dutch *ge-*) plus *man:* fellowship. This gives a meaning of togetherness, suitability, and also collectivity: i.e. **team spirit**. The dropping of the final 'n' is as in 'eve', 'maid'. 'Game' as in hunting is from the same root. Thus the sense is of co-operation rather than competition.

gamesman   a player who engages in *gamesmanship*, the art of gaining an advantage, or of putting an opponent off his stride, without cheating. Skimped in cricket by Stephen Potter, who perhaps knew the subject was too big for him. The only really practical advice given by Potter is for the bowler to shout 'No ball!' in the accents of the umpire, as the ball leaves his hand, a merely average 'ploy' (p.97–8).

His researcher, Lord Tile (brother of E. Tile), claimed to have found 8,400 instances in a game between Sussex and Derbyshire at Hove, but this is doubtful, the low observed score probably owing more to the naïveté of the observer than the absence of a Pope. Tile's difficulty, naturally, was in finding a game in which gamesmanship was not rife.

'Parlettes' and 'ploys' have an obvious place, however, and some observations from research indicate further possible lines of development. There is the international skipper said to have developed a word which sounds like 'Hells!', which he follows very quickly with 'We'll bat' or 'We'll bowl.' W.G. Grace is said by Tyson (p.168) to have called 'the Lady', and since the pennies of the time had Victoria on one side and Britannia on the other, he seldom lost a toss.

gamester   in the earliest known form of laws of the game, those drawn up in 1727 between the second Duke of Richmond and Mr Brodrick, the players are referred to as *gamesters*: 'If any of the gamesters shall speak or give their opinion on any Point of the Game, they are to be turned out . . .'. 'Gamester' meant a player of any game from the 16th century.

gardening   refers to the batsman's attempts to improve and repair the pitch, tamp down irregularities, or replace divots, and so on (sometimes to gain time). See also *pitch-smacking*.

gate   the gap between the bat and batsman's forward leg; frequent mode of dismissal for an off-spinner. 'Amir Sohail became [Damien] Fleming's second victim, bowled through the gate' (*Independent*, 8 October 1994). Also, according to Lewis, an Irishism for the wicket: 'his Gates fell as flat as my hand'

(W. Bolland, *Cricket Notes*, 1851). The meaning has circled back to the original.

gauge   an instrument for determining the bat is of the correct width, $4\frac{1}{4}$ inches. Sometimes the bat spreads slightly with usage, and the bats of both W.H. Ponsford and W.G. Grace failed 'spot-checks': in the former, the trouble was remedied by scraping with a bottle-top. In Grace's case, he had asked for the bats of Percy McDonnell and Alec Bannerman to be tested, so was hoist with his own petard.

gauntlets   term for the gloves of the wicket-keeper, and, it seems, long-stop too. 'Wrist gauntlets are of great use, and no hindrance to catches, which often come spinning to the long-stop' (Pycroft, 226). This may refer to the time when the bowler *kept* at his end, and was the *general* in charge of the field placings, and so onerous may those duties have been that he rather neglected his keeping. But Pycroft may have been rather out of date, as he certainly seeems to be in the next entry.

general   old term for *captain*, the first mention being Nyren talking about his father in *c.* 1770: 'Richard Nyren was the chosen General' (Lucas, 44). Pycroft was using it in 1851 ('The general must place his men . . .', 16), and Mary Russell Mitford had used both terms in 1823.

gentleman   formerly, an amateur, or one of gentle birth: 'The *gentlemen* always played in breeches and silk stockings; the *players*, as at Lord Winchelsea's, wore hats with gold binding, and ribbons of particular colour' (Revd John Mitford, *Gentleman's Magazine*, 1833). Both wore white.

Gentlemen   1. the side raised from amateurs which until 1962 played the Players. 2. a club side, equivalent perhaps to a Fourth XI, often comprising older, more casual players, who play a leisurely game, supposedly in that spirit, e.g. Gentlemen of Hampstead.

get big   when the ball arrives quicker (and sometimes further up) than expected: 'That got big on him very quickly . . . and Lara realised the delivery was too far up to hook' (Richie Benaud commentating from the World Cup as McGrath bowled to Lara, 4 March 1996).

get in   has two meanings, first of a batsman *getting set*, getting his eye in; second a very early expression describing how to play David Harris's fast bowling, which actually means to come out, play forward: 'you were obliged to get in or the ball would be about your hands, or the handle of your bat' (Nyren, in Lucas, 77).

G.H.O. *got himself out*: the batsman who has required little help from the bowlers to remove himself from an innings.

gimme   syncope of *give me*, used by Charles Colville on Sky TV in the Brisbane Test, 26 November 1994, as Philip De Freitas of Derbyshire and England put one in just outside Mark Waugh's leg stump, which he hit for four to square leg: 'a gimme to most decent Test players'. See also *cafeteria bowling*.

give   his wicket away. A common Teutonic form.

given man   to match sides more evenly, some teams from a particular village to a county side, would have one or two *given men*, players of great ability. Particularly important 'when stakes were high and genuine; later on they came to be regarded as showmen's bluff . . . John Hammond, at a later date the greatest player in Sussex, hardly ever figures in his own team in important matches.' Thus H. P.-T., who also notes that the stake of five hundred pounds a side of the Hambledon club may have been occasional rather than regular. It was, after all, a colossal sum, say a hundred times more in today's money. But promoters will be promoters.

glance, glide   usually to leg, but sometimes to the off: the ball is diverted *fine*. Came in at the end of the 19th century, P.F. Warner saying, 'The back glance and the forward glance have practically taken the place of the leg hit' (*Cricket*, 64). In 1888 Grace wrote that it had taken over from the *draw*[2] (BLC, 1888, 67). 'Constantine takes a long stride with his left foot across the wicket and leaning well forward glances McDonald from outside the off-stump to long-leg for four' (C.L.R. James, 132).

glove   '. . . The fingers of an old cricketer, so scarred, so bent, so shattered, so indented, so contorted, so venerable! are enough to bring tears of envy and emulation from any eye, – *we* are acquainted with such a pair of hands, if hands they may be called, that shape have none.' So said the Revd John Mitford, echoing previous words in his review of *Nyren's Book* (Lucas, 121, fn. 2). Obviously, protection had to be given, particularly from round-arm bowling. The first attempts were padded finger-stalls. The first mention of gloves being made commercially is in *W. Lillywhite's Hand-book of Cricket* (1844), in an advertisement for W.H. Caldecourt's India Rubber Padded Gloves, which he sold from his shop in Pond's End Lane. Felix, designer of the *catapulta* which he passed on to Caldecourt, is also said to have invented the gloves, which were of kid with strips of india-rubber glued to the back of each finger, in about 1835, as well as the first tubular gloves for batting. He may have passed the idea for gloves on to Caldecourt, who seems to have been the first of his genus, the *pro* who keeps a shop; he was frequently a *given man* for clubs such as Percy when they played Marylebone. The Earl of Bessborough wrote that Caldecourt was selling leather gloves stuffed with wool in *c.* 1834–8. One supposes they emerged in a number of different ways, with round-arm or over-arm bowling.

Bill Ponsford, currently the only man to score over 400 twice, is shown in the 1920s with only a right glove on. Things have changed since then: an additional layer is sometimes added to the first two fingers of the lower hand, and a slow-reacting plastic foam used to take some of the sting out of the blow. Sometimes plastic strips are put on top of the foam, sometimes in the middle to make a sandwich. A silicate gel will soon be added to some gloves to spread the impact.

The frequency of finger injuries to English batsmen caused considerable concern: shortly after the Edgbaston Test, Robin Marlar wrote: 'Batsmen's gloves are woefully inadequate against the fastest bowling. The padding used to be horsehair, a semi-rigid material that spread the impact. Horse hair is expensive and hard to work and today's substitute is little better than cotton wool . . .' (*Sunday Times*, 9 July 1995), which, in many cases is just about what it is, kapok, a fine short-stapled cotton wool otherwise known as silk cotton; cashmillon, a similar stuff, or cotton waste being often used in the cheaper gloves.

As the time between a full-length ball bouncing and hitting the hand is too short for the batsman to react, it is possible that all efforts really to protect fingers from the fastest bowlers (and particularly the very tall) with gloves are in vain: we managed with the help of Mr Alan Harding of the British Standards Institute to establish that a direct impact from the fastest bowlers (rather than the more common glancing blows), has much the same amount of energy (100BTU) as that needed to heat a thimbleful of water from freezing to boiling – and this is concentrated over a small area and in a fraction of a second. It seems unlikely that fast bowlers will diminish in height and speed, and undesirable that a man with the talent and bravery to face a great deal of this type of bowling should have his career shortened, so possible developments with shock-absorbers such as those used in running shoes can only be welcomed. Several types of guards, in front of the gloves, which could then be less obtrusive, have been suggested.

gloved   '[Ian] Chappell gloved a nasty lifter down to third for a single and was very annoyed when the umpire signalled a leg-bye' (Boycott, 107). Thus a batsman can get caught out off his glove.

gloveman   slang for the wicket-keeper. Rare, mannered, facetious.

gluepot   see *sticky*.

golden duck   to be out first ball. Steve Herzberg of Kent 'had begun his debut with a golden duck...' (*Sunday Telegraph*, 14 May 1995).

golden pair   of a batsman, out first ball in each innings, an unusual instance being Barnes in the Sheffield Test of 1902: 'I took only one wicket for fifty, but strange to relate it was that of Joe Darling, out first ball in each innings and in the same way, caught by Braund in the slips' (Duckworth, 54). Barnes also had the Durham captain out first ball in both innings in 1906. Synonymous with *king pair*.

go through (a side)   to get a side out quickly and cheaply. Also *run through*.

googly   see also *bosie, wrong'un, chinaman*: a ball, bowled by a wrist-spinner, which bounces in the opposite direction to normal. Thus a right-hand leg-break bowler's *googly* will be an *off-break*, and a left-hander's a *leg-break*, in England: in Australia the 'chinaman' refers to the googly of the left-hander. The action mimics the normal wrist-spinner until the last moment, when it is exaggerated, and the wrist turned further over, and the ball spins from the back of the hand. Some bowlers combine both deliveries with *top spin*, and obviously a ball which goes the 'wrong' way – and quickly – is very dangerous. A very few, such as 'Tich' Freeman of Kent, who once took 304 wickets in a season, have two googlies, and Alf Gover reports spotting one, the shown googly, but being lbw to his hidden one. And some claim to have two, to confuse.

The googly was developed by B. J. T. ('Bertie') Bosanquet from about 1892. It was thought to be with a billiard ball, as the family billiard table was being recovered, but his adoring cousin Louise who, when he developed the delivery outside had the task of fetching and returning the ball, is quoted by her son, the author Nigel Dennis: '"Not a billiard ball, a tennis ball" were among my mother's last words to me', he wrote to *The Times* in 1963. This was confirmed by Bosanquet's brother, N.E.T. Dennis also pointed out that another relative, Bosanquet, B., had introduced German idealism to England in 1886, and that A. C. Bradley's *Appearance and Reality* of 1893 dealt with something of the same problem exercising Bertie at the time. He goes on to say Bosanquet's Ashes-winning 6 for 51 at

Sydney was 'German idealism's first and last sporting victory.'
This claim for a philosophical base may be going too far, but
Dennis (who wrote *Cards of Identity* on a like theme), is further
evidence of the strong imaginative streak in the family, perhaps
necessary for the birth of the googly.

Bosanquet unleashed the new delivery at Lord's in 1900,
having his first victim stumped off a four-bouncer, and was in
due course selected for the MCC team to tour Australia in
1903–4: his pale dreamer's face, gazing into a further and
other distance under a Panama, stands out from the capped,
bronzed, and mustachio'd other members of the team looking directly into the lens. Apart from winning the Ashes, he
bowled Victor Trumper with the first ball he sent him. In 1905
he took 8 for 107 for the very strong English team in the first
Test, and the same year retired, although he did come back
to play for the Gentlemen in 1911, making 105 off an attack
which included S. F. Barnes. His early death was a great loss
to the game, but he had had one pupil, the South African
R.O. Schwarz, and from this sprang the famous quartet of
Schwarz, Vogler, Faulkner and White, instrumental in their
4–1 victory over England in 1905–6, and again, 3–2, in
1909–10. Then the Australians took it up with Hordern, Mailey,
Grimmett, O'Reilly and Fleetwood-Smith. Bradman considered
'Tiger' Bill O'Reilly to be the best bowler he ever batted against:
he delivered leggies, googlies, and top-spinners at a brisk
medium pace which didn't allow the batsman time to get out at
him.

In fact, if we consider who gave Bradman most trouble, the
googler would be top, for Ian Peebles had him completely
baffled at Manchester in 1930, when the Don could not detect
his googly: the first ball nearly bowled him and went for four
byes. Then he gave a chance to Hammond, was beaten the next
ball, and was then caught at second slip from an attempted late
cut – for 14, a tenth of his average for the series. With
characteristic modesty, Denis Compton, put on to bowl in the
Fourth Test at Leeds in 1948, also found 'for some reason
Bradman couldn't tell my chinaman and googly apart' – and
had him twice dropped at slip in two overs (Compton, 54).
Fingleton thought it ranked as the Don's 'most uncomfortable
over in his whole Test career' (*Don*, 163). And in the next Test,
Bradman's last, Eric Hollies, who had deliberately not used the
googly when his county earlier played the Australians, bowled
the Don second ball with it: a murmurous groan of amazement,
disappointment, and of shame ran round the whole ground,

then shocked silence when he had gone the first few yards towards the pavilion, and then applause.

The googly certainly produces drama, and is perhaps the most interesting type of bowling to watch, particularly on television. The more pity, then, that it is seldom seen, the last great practitioner before the advent of Australia's Shane Warne being Abdul Qadir of Pakistan. *Googly merchant* is mentioned by Archie Maclaren in *Cricket Old & New*, 1904 (105).

The word may be largely onomatopoeic, a dialect form of 'goggle'. It was thought to be a Maori word, but the aide-de-camp to the Governor-General of NZ pointed out that the Maori tongue has neither 'g' nor 'l', and thought it might be an Aboriginal word *Yooguli*, meaning 'I rejoice'. But already before 1890 several had produced the ball, though probably without realising quite what they were doing, and the word *googler* was used in Australia in the 1890s to describe any high, slow, teasing ball (Frith, *Slow Men*, 60), preceding Bosanquet, who thus produced a delivery that fitted into a prepared niche. A combination of all derivations at least allows the ball to emerge from, as it engenders, mystery.

goose game   an ultra-cautious style of play: 'the Victorian third wicket partnership existed until tea, Hassett playing the goose game and Harvey batting with all the ease and polish that comes to him so naturally when he is in his stride' (Swanton, *Victory*, 230). Lewis's first mention is from 1899: 'Whatever you do, don't play the goose game. Hard slogging's the sort of thing for Grace' (Snaith, *Willow the King*, 224).

gozunder   as used by Geoff Boycott on BBC Radio 3 from Pretoria on 17 November 1995 during the first England–South Africa Test: a ball that *goes under* the bat, often a *yorker*, but also one that keeps low: a creeper, grub, shooter, or mulligrubber.

Graces   the three Graces were the brothers W.G., E.M. and G.F. All three were notable cricketers, from Thornbury in Gloucestershire, and all played together for England v. Australia at the Oval in 1880. W.G. was the first colossus to bestride the game, playing in 1857 at nine for West Gloucestershire, and continuing to play for the next forty summers and more. Scarce a record remained unbroken by him, or ground unvisited. On one bank of the Humber he scored 400, on the other hit the ball into a passing train.

graft   for a batsman or bowler to proceed by application and accuracy or caution rather than stroke making or *death balls*. 'Saxelby . . . showed he could graft if necessary, but he looked happiest *picking up* leg-side boundaries with the power of a howitzer' (Charles Randall, *Daily Telegraph*, 8 May 1994). See also *pick-up shot*. Probably from the meaning 'to dig', a spade's *graft* being the depth of earth that may be turned up with one stroke of the spade, thus to the meaning of *grafter*, a hard worker, and so to: 'He is a grafter rather than a fluent striker, with little back-lift, plenty of concentration, and a willingness to use his feet' (*The Times*, 24 June 1959; OED).

grass   the surface which should be on the pitch: but also *to grass a catch* means to drop it onto the field: 'England dropped ten catches . . . on paper they have cost 362 runs . . . Graham Thorpe at first slip grassed Steve Waugh on 99 then kicked the ball . . .' (Robert Craddock, *The Advertiser*, Adelaide, 7 February 1995, on the Fifth Test, Perth).

grasser   a daisy-cutter (from 1843, P. W.-T.).

gravedigger   the last batsman. Lewis has this as a nonce-word from 'The Old Buffer' in the *Game of Cricket* (1887): 'grave-diggers. I am not the only man in England who thinks they grow despondent for lack of encouragement . . .'. (See also *Hercules, jack*).

grassy   see *green*.

greasy   a ground or pitch slippery after rain, which may affect the soil as well as the grass. The ball skids and bounces unpredictably.

green   pitches looks *green* because of the covering of grass, preferably moist grass, so the ball *comes off* quickly. Tiny pieces of grass lodge in the seam, swelling it, making it more liable to move off the seam, but whether the enlarged but more rounded seam would cause the ball to swing more is not, on the present state of research, known. This does not always happen, as Gower saw at Old Trafford: 'The pitch had a tinge of green but I have seen them like that at Old Trafford before, and all that happened was they got lower and slower' (p.142). Other-wise, the ball grips and whips.

greentop   frequently used with 'lush' to denote a pitch off which the ball will come quickly because of the damp in the grass.

grip[1]   the rubber *grip* on the bat handle which absorbs some of the shock of the ball, or makes a thicker handle (Botham is said to have used three, Clive Lloyd five).

grip[2]   the *grip* of the hands on the bat. This varies with the batsman, and the same batsman will change his grip for different shots. Bradman would have the left hand turned more clock-wise, to behind the bat, and the right anti-clockwise, which would keep the ball down, and photographs of Hobbs show his left hand turned the other way, knuckles toward the bowler. The other sense is the bowler's grip of the ball, which is how he produces either swing, spin, or gets the ball to go straight on.

gripper   rare: refers to the nature of the surface of the pitch which allows the seam to grip. See also *slipper*.

groove   of either bowler or batsman, but mainly of a bowler settling into consistent line and length: 'The metronomic West Indian, Lance Gibbs ... always settled into his groove before deploying his variations' (Robin Marlar, *Sunday Times*, 13 August 1995).

ground[1]   the entire area on which the game is played, including room for spectators etc.

ground[2]   to *ground one's bat* is to run it in at the end of a run, to avoid being run out. To *ground a catch* means to drop it.

grounder   in cricket and other games, a ball sent along the ground. OED cites 'Grounders and home tosses' from 1849 (*Boy's Own Book*, 69), and Revd Pycroft, 'The old bat used to be heavy at the point – very requisite for picking up a Grounder' (1862, p. 8).

ground bowler, ground boy   the first was a professional attached to the club; as for the second: 'There were no nets [at Lord's in 1845], but ground boys did the scouting' (Gale, *Hon. R. Grimston*, 77).

ground fielding   fielding balls that are hit along the ground, picking them up and throwing them in.

groundsman   started life as *ground man*, and seems to have meant either a *pro* attached to the staff, and/or a man engaged to keep the ground in good repair: 'About 1841 he was offered the situation of one of the "ground men" at Lord's' (*Lillywhite's Scores*, 1863, III, 8).

groundstaff   are employed to keep the ground and surrounds. Lord's ground staffers number some 24 teenagers, who get some cricket and coaching in between running the scoreboard, selling scorecards, and washing the pavilion windows (Denis Compton's least favourite task). They are on the bottom rung of a professional ladder, which has seen among others Dermot Reeve, Philip De Freitas and Phil Tufnell. Ian Botham's initiation rite was a 'whitewashing': stripped, pinned down at the Nursery End, and covered with whitener (Ian Hawkey, *Sunday Times*, 18 June 1995).

grub   an underhand ball which runs along the ground. See below and *mulligrubber*. First seen in *Bell's Life*, 7 September 1862.

grubber   common in the days of under-arm bowling. The last recorded instance in first-class cricket was in 1981, in a one-day match between Australia and New Zealand, who needed six to win off the last ball. Greg Chappell told his brother Trevor to make it a *grubber*. A young girl in the pavilion is said to have observed 'Daddy, that man cheated.' Armitage of Yorkshire also bowled one in the first Test of 1877, after an attempted *spedegue* had been called a wide (Frith, *Slow Men*, 27).

guard   the position of the bat in the *blockhole* relative to a line between the middle stump from the bowler's end to his. 'Centre' denotes middle stump, 'middle-and-leg' covers both these stumps, and 'leg' only the leg. The last two are also known as *two-leg* and *one-leg*, or just 'two' and 'one, please'. To *take guard* is to receive the whereabouts of the bat from umpire and make the relevant mark. In the 1980s, Monte Lynch of Surrey and Gloucestershire adopted a batting position a short distance in front of the stumps, and without taking guard.

gully   a position in the field between point and the slips, formerly known as 'short third man'. A difficult position, the ball coming very quickly, often curving left. From Fr. *goulet*, a channel, or neck (of a bottle).

gun bowler   'he will be our gun bowler . . . he has been thrust prematurely into the role of spearhead bowler' (Allan Border on Craig McDermott in 1986, p.161).

H acker   hard-hitting, unorthodox batsman, generally lower order.

alf-ball   only one side of the ball is gripped, by thumb and first finger, which gives the fast bowler an ability to bowl his slower ball with the same action. Now rare.

half-cock shot   In a video review, Trevor Bailey of Essex and England commented: 'Nevertheless, as the *MCC Masterclass* is aimed at mature cricketers I was somewhat surprised at the absence of any mention of the half-cock shot, which is among the most frequently employed strokes, in particular when it should not be used' (*Daily Telegraph*, 10 June 1994). 'Hutton played forward with his typical half-cock defensive stroke and the ball, skidding but not turning, got past him to the off-stump' (Fingleton, *Don*, 97). As the quotes show, the batsman has played half-forward, leading foot not to the pitch of the ball.

half-pitcher   more common in Australia than England, a term for a ball which bounces half-way down the pitch.

half-volley   a ball pitched near to the bat, or hit just after landing, which stops it turning, and, rising to the *sweet spot*, can be hit hard. It comes from the L. *volare*, to fly. The first mention by Lewis is from *Pract. Hints Cr.* 12: 'All balls pitching between the first line [drawn five feet from the popping crease, for practice] and the crease ... are technically termed half vollies.' This fits in quite well with the introduction of *length bowling*, but the term *full toss* is used in cricket instead of 'volley'.

hands[1]   *safe pair of hands*: a sure catcher in the field, thus by extension a politician who has them is one who, given an awkward situation, can be expected to deal with it without making a gaffe. 'Keep your hands high!' verb. sap., A.E. Gover at his school, meaning to keep the hands above the level of the ball for as long as possible, thus coming down on the ball, keeping it down, and hitting with more swing. See also *soft hands*.

hands[2]   archaic term for *innings*, c. 1740. In 1737, Kent played Surrey and London and won 'at one hands'. Altham points out that the term was the erroneous basis for the supposition that the game of 'handyn and handout' was one of the ancestors of cricket (in the game, boys and girls form a circle, then a boy hits a girl, a girl hits a boy, and then runs off, pursued by the others, until caught, when the process is repeated, so it obviously has nothing to do with cricket).

hands[3]   archaic for player: 'Barber and Hogsflesh were both

115

good hands; they had a high delivery and a generally good length' says Nyren (Lucas, 45).

handled the ball   Law 33 reads:

1. Out Handled the Ball

Either batsman, on appeal, shall be out *Handled the Ball* if he wilfully touches the ball while in play with the hand not holding the bat, unless he does so with the consent of the opposite side.

In the Second Test at Lord's, 1993, Graham Gooch played a ball from Mervyn Hughes down on to the ground just behind him: 'it bounces up . . . looks as if it's going to hit the top of the stumps . . . he gives it a rather cheeky little punch' said Tony Lewis commentating for the BBC on Gooch's reflex action. There have been less fortunate circumstances: in 1978 in a Test against Pakistan, Andrew Hilditch of Australia picked up a ball which had been defensively played back to the bowler and handed it to the bowler. One of the fielders, feeling aggrieved over a decision in a previous game, appealed, and the umpire had no option but to give him out.

hang   Lewis has this as loss of pace from the pitch, but this is not seen now, when the ball being said to *hang in the air* means that it does not arrive as soon as expected – one of the arts of flight: 'if you find the ball hangs, the only thing to do is to plump the bat down as nearly as possible to the pitch of it' (Giffen, 220).

hanging guard   before pads, the back defensive was sensibly played by hanging the bat straight down in front of the wicket, arms outstretched. 'The home-block, hanging guard, or back play as it has been previously called' (*Felix on the Bat*, i.iii.14).

hanging out the bat (to dry)   like *fishing*, or *waft*. 'Saeed then fell to a casual off-side waft . . . Almost as bad was the stroke that Malik played . . . [his] hanging-out-to-dry stroke looked inept as he toughed it to the keeper' (Norman Harris, *The Observer*, 18 August 1996).

harness   two bowlers proffering similar ware, one from each end: 'Spinners' kingdom . . . Giles and Smith were in harness chipping away at tentative Durham batting' (Jack Bailey, *The Times*, 13 August 1996).

Harrow bat, Harrow drive   the *bat* is between the school-boy's size six and the full-size. The *drive*, very rare usage, is variously described as to mid-off, extra-cover, and 'between point and middle-wicket' (i.e. cover). A snick through the slips as well, according to Etonians, and used by Jonathan Agnew as

Alan Donald played an 'old fashioned Harrow drive' (BBC Test Match Special, from Port Elizabeth, 29 December 1995).

hat-trick   the feat of taking three wickets in three consecutive balls. F. R. Spofforth was the first man to do so in a Test Match, at Melbourne in 1878–9. Four wickets in four balls are infrequent: and in 1859, on the first overseas tour, to North America, John Wisden himself took six in six, a double *hat-trick*. The hat-trick can span two innings, or even two matches. 'A white hat used to be given to the bowler who got three batsmen out in successive balls . . .' (*Encyclopedia of Sport*, 1897, I. 246/1). The origin of the custom is obscure, but according to G.B Buckley in a letter to *The Cricketer* of 15 July 1939, a 'really good hat' had long been awarded in wrestling and single-stick. The first recorded award seems to be 1858 to H.H. Stephenson, playing for the All England eleven against 22 of Hallam and Staveley (Meyer-Homji, 21). John Murray records in *Notes and Queries*: 'When I first went to Eton in 1863, the getting of three wickets with successive balls was called "bowling a gallon", and the bowler was supposed to be awarded a gallon of beer' (18 November 1916, 416/2). *The Times* (11 July 1996) reported that 14-year-old Nicholas Causton had taken a very rare double hat-trick, six wickets in six balls, as had his great-grandfather in 1922.

haul   'Devon Malcolm had other ideas, collecting his second ten-wicket match haul in three championship encounters' (Rupert Cox, *The Times*, 13 August 1996).

have a go   at the bowling, to attack it, either generally or a single ball.

head ball, bowler   not a *bouncer*, or *quick*, but an obsolete form, a ball or bowler designed to think the batsman out. 'I must also see another little square man . . . with his tempting pitched-up ball . . . before I believe that a better head bowler ever lived than Lillywhite' (Gale, *New Sporting Magazine*, lx (1870) 35).

headquarters   Lord's, the MCC and in particular the rule-makers and Law-givers at Marylebone. Probably pre-dates Newmarket as the *headquarters*, as Lord's was well established before the first apparent use of the term in horse-racing.

heartwood   some bats have a section of brown wood running down them: this comes from the heart of the willow, is brittle, and the sign of a poorer quality bat.

heave   an inelegant attacking shot, with much body action: 'Fairbrother lost his middle stump after 5½ hours when, wearily he heaved leg side at Brown' (Paul Fitzpatrick, *Guardian*, 13 May 1995).

helmet   originated, as a hard shell, in the 1974–5 season. Lillee and Thomson were the Australian bowlers who prompted an invitation to Mike Denness and Tony Greig to try out a crash helmet. See also **brainbox**.

Hercules   the last batsman, who has to support the other ten (Tyson, 75).

hide the bat   the front leg is advanced to the pitch of the ball with the bat tucked behind it, to give the impression of playing at the ball. This is because part of the *lbw Law* specifies that a batsman may be given out lbw to a ball pitching outside the off stump, and breaking back onto the wicket, if no shot is played by the batsman at the ball.

high action   principal desideratum for a bowler, since the ball will bounce more and the vertical arm directs the ball more easily. 'Peter Taylor, the unheralded off-spinner . . . took six wickets for seventy-eight runs . . . with his high arm [he] was able to flight and bounce the ball' (Roebuck, 195).

high home and easy, home-and-easy   Revd Lord Frederick Beauclerk introduced this type of bowling in the last part of the eighteenth century, but the 'new players' destroyed it by 'rushing in at it, and driving it way' (Revd J. Mitford, *Gentleman's Magazine*, September 1833, 237/2). It is underhand *lobbing*.

hip, hip shot   played by the batsman off his leading hip, the ball being sent to the general area of long leg. *Hiplift*, or *hiplift shot*, as played by Brian Lara, is when hip and front leg are lifted as the ball is hit.

hit, hitter, big hitter   the batsman striking the ball. See also *long hit*. 'Aylward was a left-handed batter, and one of the safest hitters I ever knew in the club' (Nyren, in Lucas 67).

hit-out or get-out   'was the reaction of some England batsmen when their itinerary was overloaded in the 80s' (Scyld Berry, *Sunday Telegraph*, 14 May 1995).

hit the ball twice   a rare method of dismissal. Law 34 states; 'The striker, on appeal, shall be out, *Hit the Ball Twice*, if after the ball is struck or is stopped by any part of his person, he wilfully strikes it again with his bat or person except for the sole purpose of guarding his wicket.'

hit the pitch hard   a *high action* from a *quick* makes this happen, so the ball can lift. 'South Africa have got three bowlers who can hit the deck, bang it in hard . . .' (Geoff Boycott, BBC Radio 4, 2 December 1995, from Johannesburg, second Test).

hit under leg   there seem to have been a variety of cunning devices to deal with the ball on the middle or leg stumps: see *draw shot* for one variation, and *under-leg shot*.

hit wicket   before the *declaration* was allowed, a batsman would 'hit down his own wicket' to get out. Abbreviated now, the batsman is out under Law 35:

> The striker shall be out, *Hit Wicket*, if, while the ball is in play: (a) His wicket is broken with any part of his person, dress or equipment as a result of any action taken by him in preparing to receive or in receiving a delivery, or in setting off for his first run immediately after playing, or playing at the ball. (b) He hits down his wicket while lawfully making a second strike for the purpose of guarding his wicket within the provisions of Law 34.1 (Out Hit the Ball Twice).

hold up   of a ball, *hold up* means to come more slowly off the pitch than is expected; also, not to take a direction from the slope after bouncing, but to go straight on: 'Walsh, from the football stand end [at Headingly], made a ball hold up against the slope to have Atherton caught behind' (Scyld Berry, *Sunday Telegraph*, 11 June 1995).

Of a batsman, to hold up an end – for example, when a tailender has come in to try and keep his wicket up while the better not-out batsman goes on accumulating runs. See also *nightwatchman*.

hole out   from golf, meaning 'to be caught'. 'Close ... decided that the only way to play the ball, with the bowler's dangerous rough patch outside his off stump, was to sweep everything and he soon holed out to Norman O'Neill at backward square leg' (*Boycott on Cricket*, 187).

hollow   a term for the front side of the bat:

> We'd never a penny to toss for choice,
> So we'd chuck up t' bat would we,
>> 'Ump!' says Jim,
>> 'Oller!' says I,
> An' 'Ump it is,' says 'e.
>> – Alfred Cochrane, *Later Verses* (1918).

home   can be the *home side*, or the batsman getting *home to his wicket*. The two archaic uses are *home toss* for full toss, which lasted until 1867 in Australia, and a *Home Boarder*, for **pull**, which 'took the name of the "On Drive", without the fortune which would attend the hit of that name if properly made ... a pull on the on side. It is said to have derived its name from a boy named Webster, a home boarder (that is to say a boy who lived in the town), who was addicted to the stroke' (Lewis).

hook, hook-stroke   stroke played with a cross bat against a
ball of some speed which rises above, say, the hip, usually
because it has pitched short. The batsman swings on the ball,
using (ideally) body, shoulders and arms, often turning the
wrists over to keep it down as it is smashed away to leg between
mid-on and fine leg. A shot demanding bravery and technique,
as the best chance of success comes from getting in line with
the ball, which will hit you if you miss. Vic Richardson could
hook Larwood; Colin Cowdrey was the first to hook the 90
m.p.h.-plus deliveries of Jeff Thomson. Obviously, usually
played from the crease or back foot, but '(Blewett) was so in
form yesterday that he played several hooks and cuts off the
front foot' (Robert Craddock from Perth, *The Advertiser*, 7
February 1995).

hopper   'The term "hopper" usually means the bowler, on
arriving at the bowling crease, is taking off with the right foot
and landing at the bowling crease on the same foot' (Alf Gover,
The Cricketer, September. 1978). This brings on a chest-on
action, like that of Mike Procter of South Africa and
Gloucestershire.

hostile   usually of fast bowling, *hostile* to the batsman's limbs
as well as wicket, although the fiery and aggressive attack of
men such as W.J. O'Reilly can be included. 'Pakistan ... were
undone by accurate and hostile bowling, to which only Amir
Sohail (80) and Wasim Akran (45 n.o.) provided resistance'
(*Independent*, 8 October 1994).

how's that, howzat, huzzat, how wuz her? an appeal to the
umpire to give his decision whether a batsman is 'out' or not.
First mention in Lewis is 1833 from the *New Sporting Magazine*:
'Well thrown by Huddleston!' – 'How's that?' 'Run out!' It is
not clear when the system of appealing first started, but then in
the 1980 Code Law 36 (L.B.W.) does not state 'on appeal'.
The system was evidently in use by 1755: the Laws of that date
say the umpires 'are not to order any man out, unless appealed
to by one of the Players'.

huff   this mode of dismissal made the front pages of both *The
Times* and *The Guardian* in August 1995. Mr Wightman of
Whiteleas CC was marked 'absent huffed' for 0. Apparently the
MCC's Assistant Secretary of Cricket, John Jameson, had
recorded a number of bizarre manners of forfeit, including 'left
to catch train to Continent'.

hump   the back of the bat: see *hollow*.

hundred   100 runs scored by a batsman.

hutch[1]   'to have them back in the *hutch*' is to dismiss batsmen of poor quality – *rabbits*. The famous *lobster*, Digby Jephson, once thought he'd have a little practice at Fenner's nets, but found himself facing the young Tom Richardson, who hit off stump, leg, middle, chest, arm, and ribs (twice). 'Thank you very much,' said the lobster, feeling very like a rabbit, 'I don't think I'll practise any more today,' and he 'walked slowly and painfully back to the "hutch"' (Meredith, 30).

hutch²   scorers sit in hutches, under the scoreboard: 'a match is played double-like, out in the middle for one, and, moreover, in scorers' 'utch as well . . .' (Robertson-Glasgow, *Crusoe*, 73).

I **ffy shot, if-stroke**   Ranjitsinhji has an ingenious explanation for the original shot being into the slips: 'it was called the "but-stroke", after its great exponent the Sussex wicket-keeper [Butt]; but some wag suggested that it should be called in preference the "if-stroke", because if you hit the ball you are nearly sure to be out' (*Jubilee Book*, 165).

independent umpire   in Tests, an umpire who does not come from either of the competing countries. The first, in 1994, was 'Dickie' Bird of England in the Pakistan series in New Zealand.

inducker   an *inswinger* that seems to drop as it comes in late to the batsman.

infield, infielder   now rare, meaning close to the pitch.

in-form stroke   today used of the sort of shot played by a batsman *in form*. But before used of the *square drive:* 'Perfect timing is necessary for the bringing off of the stroke, which is frequently termed the in-form stroke' (Maclaren, 100).

innings   only in the plural in cricket, when the batsman or team is *in*. The highest first-class *innings* is 501 not out, by Brian Lara, the West Indian test player, for Warwickshire against Durham in 1994; he also holds the record for the highest test score, 375★ against England. One of the most remarkable innings ever was by Mr W. Hyman, an amateur of Somerset, who hit 359★ in a total of 466 for 5 in an hour and fifty minutes, for the Bath Association Cricket Club v. Thornbury in Gloucestershire, the home of the Graces, in 1902. His innings included 32 sixes. Dr E.M. Grace, the captain of Thornbury, was hit for 64 runs in two consecutive overs, eight sixes and four fours, possibly a record for six-ball overs, although D.M.S. Wardlaw made 69 off two eight ball overs in Tasmania in 1926, being bowled off the last ball. The most remarkable first-class innings is still that of E.B. Alletson of Nottinghamshire, who in 1911 hit 189. He moved from fifty to his century in thirteen minutes, and his last 142 took forty minutes. The fielders 'by skilful agility,' wrote one spectator, 'managed to avoid contact with the ball.' He wasn't really out, either, the fielder having one foot over the boundary when he caught the ball. Benny Green, in *A History of Cricket*, records these facts, and also that Alletson had a freakish reach of 78 inches, a bat of only 2lb. 3oz., and a sprained right wrist: whether these increased his **batspeed** and explain the power of his hitting we shall never know.

   The Laws of Cricket state that a match shall be of one or two innings of each side, but this is not always the case, as recorded by Simon Raven in *Shadows on the Grass*: 'a two innings match against the King's Own Yorkshire Light Infantry had to be converted into a three and then into a four innings match (so incompetent or "tired" were the batsmen on either side) in order to provide some sort of spectacle for the visitors invited to meals or drinks on the ground on the two days allotted' (p.17).

First mention of innings goes back to 1735, when London 'got 67 *notches* in the first innings' (Waghorn, 10). *Choice of innings* means who bats first, the Laws of 1774 saying 'The Party which goes from Home shall have the choice of the innings.' To *win by an innings* means that the winning side's single innings totals more than the two innings of the losers.

insert   to put the other side in to bat, implying a poor batting pitch.

inside, inside edge   and other related terms all apply to the leg-side, or the side of the bat closest to the batsman.

inside out   turning a batsman *inside out* is not as alarming as it sounds. The batsman, thinking a ball is going down the leg side, turns in that direction the better to place the ball there for runs. But the ball either holds its line or deviates to the off and the batsman has to play with his right side forward (if he's right-handed). 'Boon, in his 100th Test, had already been turned inside out by a beauty from Ambrose, which Richardson clutched high to his left at third slip' (Stephen Thorpe at the Port of Spain Test, *Sunday Times*, 23 April 1994).

insinuator   old term for a high spinning lob, lasting until at least 1867, when 'Hogg played one of Tommy Wills's insinuators very neatly back to him' (*Australasian*, 19 January).

inswing, inswinger   the ball that swings from off to leg, seam pointing to fine or long leg. Mark Nicholas, his former county captain at Hampshire, describes the great West Indian Malcolm Marshall: 'In the early days, his bowling was based on a whippy, sideways action that caused the ball to skid at its target with deadly outswing ... As his action became more chest-on, he developed the inswinger ...' (*Daily Telegraph*, 17 September 1995). The angle of the chest helps to dispatch the ball with the seam in the right direction.

interval   for drinks, lunch, tea. Not only can they refresh, but also undermine concentration. 'The interval's always a good wicket-taker' – Tony Cosier on BBC Radio (Test Match Special, 23 August 1995).

intimidation   the part of Law 42 'Unfair Play' which refers to intimidation goes:

The bowling of fast, short-pitched balls is unfair if, in the opinion of the umpire at the bowler's end, it constitutes an attempt to intimidate the striker ... Umpires shall consider intimidation to be the deliberate bowling of fast, short-pitched balls which by their length, height and direction are intended to or likely to inflict physical injury on the striker. The relative skill of the striker shall also be taken into consideration.

Umpires have various remedies at their disposal, including the removal of the bowler from the attack. Currently a bowler is allowed one short fast ball per over which passes the batsman at over his height while standing upright. Further such balls are counted as *no-balls*, with the consequent penalties and opportunities.

In the end, the umpire may remove the bowler from the attack. Barry Dudleston ordered Somerset and Holland's fast bowler André Van Troost out of the attack in the game against Kent on 10 August 1995.

Irish swing Australian term for *reverse swing*, more common when the phenomenon was not understood (Tyson, 82).

ivory-wristed when Nausicaa and her maidens were dis-covered by Odysseus, they were playing at stoolball 'with wrists of ivory', as Chapman's *Odyssey* puts it. Homer's greatness shows in this unequalled description of fielding.

Jack   the last man in, number 11 in the order. From cards: 1–10, jack, queen, king, ace. Probably from the sense of a man of the common people. See also *Hercules, gravedigger*.

jaffa   a good or unplayable ball, a peach of a ball, possibly from Jaffa orange, but derivation uncertain. Tony Greig, for Sky TV at the World Cup Final in Lahore, 17 March 1996: 'He's likely to bowl a few little jaffas but he's also likely to bowl a few loose ones', as Mike Bevan of Australia came on to purvey some notably short *chinamen*.

jag   used of faster bowlers: 'He [McDermott] got that to jag back a long way,' commented Terry Alderman, the only man to take forty wickets twice in a series, and referring to a ball coming back like an off-break from outside the off stump (Australian Broadcasting Corporation, Third Test at Adelaide, the Ashes 1995).

jerk, jerker   the Notes to Law 24 (No Ball), say, in part, that 'A ball shall be deemed to have been thrown if, in the opinion of either umpire, the process of straightening the bowling arm, whether it be partial or complete, takes place during that part of the delivery swing which directly precedes the ball leaving the hand . . .' It looks as if the ball has been jerked out.

Jessopian   from Gilbert Jessop, mighty hitter and fast scorer (and fast-medium bowler). The term was in use in 1900, before his great innings of 104 in 56 minutes in 1902 at the Oval, where he twice in one over drove no less a bowler than Hugh Trumble into the pavilion. England had been 10 for 3, then 48 for 5 when Jessop came in, with 263 needed for victory. The parallel with Ian Botham's famed 149 at Headingley in 1981 is striking – but it was an uncovered pitch, so difficult, said *The Times*, that no one would have been surprised if any batsman had got out – and Jessop's hundred was the fastest in Tests until Viv Richards's from 56 balls in Antigua, 1985–6. By the time he got out, George Hirst was well set, and he and Wilfred Rhodes hit off the winning runs. Benny Green, in *A History of Cricket*, gives various career hourly scoring rates, with Bradman and Compton at 47, Percies Chapman and Fender at over 60, with Maurice Tate, and Jessop at 79.

jock-rot   discomfort in groin area, sometimes accompanied by an ambergris-coloured deposit, caused by chafing of athletic support. 'Got terrible jock-rot' (Angus Fraser, *Independent on Sunday*, 17 April 1994).

jock-strap   the elasticised belt and pouch which support and protect the genitals, and which contains a pocket for the *box* or abdominal supporter. 'Jock' is a form of fellow, chap, with a hinder meaning of dishonesty in such trades as horse-dealing, thus to the diminutive 'jockey'. 'Jock', especially in American universities, means a student who practises sports for much of his time, an athlete, thus *jock-strap*. The first OED mention is American, from the US Patent Office in 1897, when Charles F. Bennett produced a 'combined jock-strap and suspensory', which latter the Dictionary does not elucidate.

juice 'conditions were ideal for him (overcast and humid) on the first day and there was still a little juice in the wicket when play resumed. But Hadlee used the conditions perfectly' (Border, 176). Hadlee took 9–52 in this Brisbane Test, 1985. The meaning is that there is still moisture in the grass, so the ball is liable to move around more after bouncing.

jump see also *pop, lifter*.

jute a matting laid down, on the pitch especially in Trinidad to render it suitable for play. More placid than coconut. 'From the bark of Indian trees (genus Corchorus)' (*ODEtym.*).

Kanga cricket   see *Kwik cricket*.

eep, keeper, kept   as a single word, simply to *keep* wicket.

keep low   not to rise after bouncing to the expected height. See also *mulligrubber, shooter*.

kick   see *pop, lifter*.

king pair   out first ball in both innings. The quickest is recorded by Kersi Meyer-Homji in *Out for a Duck* when Glamorgan played India in 1947. Peter Judge was out last, bowled first ball by Chandu Sarwate, and Glamorgan had to follow on, but because of rain delays, he and J.C. Clay stayed at the wicket to save time – only to be bowled first ball, again by Sarwate.

knee-roll   the transverse rolls of the pads at knee height: the word occurs on television because the ball hitting on or especially above the *knee-roll* is reckoned to be too high to be lbw.

knock¹   an innings: 'a good knock'.

knock²   *to take a knock* means to be hit fairly painfully by the ball. 'The people who sit in armchairs and criticise cricketers do not realise that a hard knock, for instance on the point of the lowest rib, leaves a sore spot that may hurt, if quite lightly struck, two or three years later. This stiffens batting and means less runs later' (Hammond, *Secret History*, 50).

knocking-in   the way of preparing a cricket bat for use, usually by tapping with an old ball, preferably wrapped in an old sock, and rubbing in linseed oil (though not pouring it into the little hole at the bottom of the bat). See also *shin-bone*.

knock-up   has four meanings: 1. to practise before going into bat. Also knocking-up, to have a knock-up, as above, but also 2. 'knock-up game', an informal game without a specific number of players. 3. In June 1737 Kent led by the Duke of Dorset met Surrey and London led by the Prince of Wales. Kent won easily, *knocking up* their wickets in the second innings, i.e. getting themselves out. This was before sides were allowed to declare. 4. *To knock up runs*, where the meaning is to 'get by labour or exertion', as in Whittock *Book Trades* 1837: '[He] . . . knocks up £3 or 4 weekly', which becomes in *Baily's Mag.* (October 1860): 'Tinley in a trice knocked up 8.'

Kwik cricket   children of both sexes, from 5 to 11, rush onto the ground at intervals in Tests and play it. Started in 1989, following the success of kanga cricket in Australia, it follows the National Curriculum aim of developing throwing, catching, and striking skills. There are now 32,000 sets of gear out. The game is run from Lord's as a non-profit-making subsidiary of the Test and County Cricket Board.

127

Lake, laker Yorkshire dialect meaning 'to play', 'player'. It comes from the ON form *leik-r* meaning 'to play', and shows the Scandinavian influence. Lewis's valuable finding of a reference to 1830 implies also other forms of the stick and ball game: 'The Ripon fielding was excellent ... They then tried their fortune at the wickets with their laking-sticks' (Holmes, 36). And also, 'Now we shall see chaps as can lake a bit ...' (Bleackley, 96). Still in use in 1949, when Fred Trueman dropped a catch and remarked 'That bugger is laikin' wi a steel bat' (Mosey, *Fred*, 17).

lam Wright's *English Dialect Dictionary* defines it as 'a hard hit or swipe. Much used at cricket.' The first meaning given in OED is from the earlier form 'lame', Fr. *lame* a blade, meaning solely 'pieces of wood in a loom connected with the treadles and healds'. It is tempting to see a connection with the Flemish weavers of medieval times removing their lams and repairing to their fields, proof absolute the game is from Franco-Flanders, but a trifle speculative.

lamplight match, gaslight match the 1899 Surrey-Yorkshire match at the Oval was finished when the streetlights were already lit.

lap, lap shot the ball is removed with the bat from the lap area, and dispatched to the leg-side, square-ish. Ian Botham got out to a *reverse lap shot* at the end of his innings of 208 against India in 1982.

last man no. 11, *last man* in, so when a wicket falls the innings is over:

> There's a breathless hush in the Close tonight –
> Ten to make and the match to win –
> A bumping pitch and a blinding light,
> An hour to play and the last man in.
>
> – Sir Henry Newbolt, 'Vitaï Lampada'

late[1] of batting: to play one's shots *late*; a mark of a good batsman is to see it early and play it late.

late[2] of swing: 'but because of movement in the last yard the ball found the inside edge of the bat and went to backward short-leg' (Compton on Bedser, *Cricketers*, 17).

late cut played late and fine, a delicate shot: 'If Dhanraj could have been late cut once on the first two days – not just feathered down to third man – he could have been late cut umpteen times ... but he never was. That is the trouble with today's hulking great bats' (John Woodcock, *The Times*, 14 August 1995).

late order batsman is one who bats beween 8 and 11.

Laws cricket has Laws, not rules, which range from Law 1

The Players, through to Law 42 Unfair Play. The Laws are produced by the MCC and changed, after a great deal of international consultation, to try to cope with the changing conditions of the game. The first Laws that we know of, apart from the agreement made in 1727 (and there are no doubt others) are mentioned in *The New Universal Magazine* of November 1752: 'The Game at cricket, as settled by the CRICKET-CLUB in 1744, and played at the ARTILLERY-GROUND, LONDON.' There is also a silk handkerchief from *c.* 1744 at Lord's, which has around its borders the earliest printed version of the Laws. The first Laws to survive in booklet form are 'The Game at Cricket, As settled by the Several CRICKET-CLUBS, particularly that of the Star and Garter In Pall Mall MDCCLV.' These editions give some idea of how the game evolved: for example, a batsman 'in his ground' was apparently allowed to hinder the fieldsman attempting a catch or other activity. Successive codes have legalised overarm bowling (1864), tried to deal with unfair play, the no-ball, the bowling of fast, short-pitched balls and intimidation, and some of the changes to the lbw Law are set out in that entry. The Laws are supported and amplified by Playing Conditions or Regulations, which specify such things as the hours of play in first-class and Test Matches, and, recently, the banning of underarm bowling in such matches.

lay 'he laid about him with the bat', is common enough, but the word was also used meaning 'to bowl'. Also, in the 18th century, when Fennex was the first to go down the wicket or jump out of his crease, he said 'he went in and laid down a ball before it had time to rise to the bail.' Much to the indignation of his father, who was incredulous of the performance of his offspring: 'Hey hey! boy! what is this? Do you call that play? ... But ... this saves alike the fingers and the wickets from a first-rate top-bailer' (See *bail ball*).

lay off (come off) a stroke Australian term, described by Tyson (p. 85) as leaning back, not getting the full weight behind the shot.

lbw 'one of the best hitters was so shabby as to put his leg in the way and take advantage of the bowlers', said Beldham, referring to Tom Taylor (Lucas, 137). John Ring was also guilty. No doubt this custom grew, as a natural occurrence, purposeful or not, with the new length bowling pitching about three-quarters of the way down the pitch, and the straight bat. Before that, with the long curved bat, it would hardly have been possible to get a leg in the way. The sketchbook of George

Shepheard, *c.* 1790, shows Tom Walker with a straight bat, and what might be rudimentary pads, or paddings. Thus the first lbw rule had already appeared in the revision of the Laws of 1774: 'If the striker puts his leg before the wicket with a design to stop the ball, and actually prevent the ball from hitting his wicket by it', he will be given out. The ball had to pitch wicket-to-wicket and look as though it was going on to hit it. Haygarth, in his *Scores and Biographies*, has the first recorded lbw in the Surrey v. Kent match at Moulsey Hurst in 1795, but remarks that previous outings may have been just recorded as bowled.

In 1902, after the bat had become dominant on the manured and manicured and pitches of that time, a proposal was put forward to give the batsman out if with any part of his body he stopped a ball in a straight line between wicket and wicket which the umpire thought would have hit.

The 'snick-rule' was brought in for a few years at the start of the 1930s, so that a batsman could be out if he hit the ball and it was going through to his wicket. In 1934 it was proposed that a batsman could be out to a ball pitching outside off-stump, but turning in to hit the wicket, and this was adopted in 1937. Under the 1948 Law it was possible to *pad away* a ball if the pad was outside the wicket-to-wicket line. The reason for the change to the present Law 36 is supposed to have been partly prompted by *pad-play*. The Law now reads:

1. OUT LBW

The striker shall be out lbw in the cirmumstances set out below

(a) The Striker Attempting to Play the Ball

The striker shall be out lbw if he first intercepts with any part of his person, dress or equipment, a fair ball which would have hit the wicket and which has not previously touched his bat or hand holding the bat, provided that:

(i) the ball pitched in a straight line between wicket and wicket or on the off side of the striker's wicket, or was intercepted full pitch; and

(ii) the point of impact is in a straight line between wicket and wicket even if above the level of the bails.

(b) Striker making no Attempt to Play the Ball

The striker shall be out lbw even if the ball is intercepted outside the line of the off stump if, in the opinion of the umpire, he has made no genuine attempt to play the ball with his bat but has intercepted the ball with some part of his person and if the circumstances set out in (a) above apply.

leading arm   the bowler's other arm, swinging straight over as counter-poise and – ideally – helping the side-on position for greater accuracy.

leading edge   the edge of the bat, when turned around its horizontal axis, becomes its *leading edge*, usually the outside edge, through playing too soon and lobbing the ball into the air: 'working a full length ball to his less favoured leg side [Hick] used the leading edge to give backward cover a straightforward catch' (Richard Hutton, *The Cricketer*, August 1994).

leather   can be laid into, chased or hunted, depending on whether the batsman or fielder is involved; the ball can also be *leathered*.

leave   the ball can *leave* the batsman or vice versa, in which case a commentator may say 'well left' if the ball is one at which it is dangerous to play.

leg   the side of the field of the batsman's *leg*, the on-side. Applies to field placings such as *square leg*, *leg-slip*.

leg-break, leg-spin, leg-spinner is the break from leg to off, and its bowler. The delivery is named from the way it seems to the batsman, but the bowler is always a *leg-spinner*, even when bowling what are off-breaks to a left-hander.

leg-bye   a run obtained for a ball diverted by hitting the batsman's person. If accidental, a run is given as *extras*, if deliberate, no runs are scored. In the Durban Test in 1948 Cliff Gladwin of Derbyshire and England had one run to score off the last ball of the game to win it: he 'jumped up the pitch and swung his bat wildly as the ball went off his leg ... England had won' (*The Times*, 21 December 1948). (Gladwin had 'scored' two more leg-byes in that over, and he displayed his trousers with the tell-tale marks on them in his sports shop in Chesterfield.)

The *leg-bye* emerged as a separate entity in 1850, when an MCC Committee recommended that 'during the ensuing season, the umpire and the scorer shall be instructed to distinguish on the score, byes made off the leg of the batsman from other byes, by ... calling out and scoring the same as "leg byes"' (Lewis).

leg-cutter   a ball of fastish speed which moves from leg to off by the bowler's hand cutting down the left-hand side of the ball as he sees it, thus spinning it around a horizontal axis. 'On a wet wicket, Alec Bedser had bowled beautifully, using his leg-cutter, which whipped and left the batsman off the wicket'

(Compton, *Innings*, 96), in Lord's Test of 1953 Bedser finished with 14 for 99.

leggie   a purveyor of *leg-spin* bowling or the bowling itself.

leg gully   short and just backward of square on the leg side – mirroring the position of gully on the off.

leg glance, glide   shot brought to perfection by Ranjitsinhji, when the ball is steered with an angled bat down to fine leg, off either front or back foot.

leg guards, leg-pads   'When leg-pads were first introduced they were worn under the trousers' (Harris and Ashley-Cooper, xv). Denison mentions (*Companion*, 1846, p.98) that they are made out of cork and india rubber, which seems to mean they were now worn over the trousers, and Lewis's research turned up a patent of 1856 for 'leg guards of open cross-bar work or net work'. These seem exactly the type worn by Ranji or Grace.

leg-shooter   seemingly a ball pitched on the legs which shot. Alfred Mynn had a certain Butler stumped, because attempting a *draw*, he 'just lifted, for an instant, his right foot' and was stumped (Pycroft, 230).

leg slip   see *fine* short *leg*.

leg spin, spinner   bowling turning from leg to off, a ball which does so, or the bowler who propels it.

leg-sweep   original term for *sweep*.

leg-theory   bowling inswingers, off-cutters, off-spin, indeed any kind of bowling, even *lobs*, to a packed leg-side field. Became notorious when transmuted to *bodyline*, with fast bowlers pitching short to a group of short legs. The first exponent is supposed to have been F.R. Foster with the left-hander's natural inslant, causing batsmen to give catches to his close fielders (Australia, the Ashes 1911–12). But curiously, given the later history of the expression, the first mention seems to be Australian in 1898: 'Cooper bowled the leg-theory almost as remarkably as the off-theory is practised nowadays' (Giffen, 153).

leg trap   a collection of fielders stationed mainly close to the bat on the leg side. See *bodyline*.

leger, ledger   obsolete, from winning the St Leger, referring to the highest score in an innings or highest average: 'I think his [Cameron's] ticket in a Calcutta Sweep for "the Leger" … would fetch a good price' (*Australasian*, 25 May 1867).

length   'if his pace be moderately fast, he should endeavour to pitch the ball about four yards and a half before the wicket: if he be slow, somewhat nearer, and in swift bowling not further off than five yards' (Nyren, in Lucas, 18). *Length bowling* was first introduced around 1770, maybe some time before, because when Hambledon went to play Kent in 1772, verses in the *Kentish Gazette* enjoined the bowler 'be sure pitch a length', and the batsman 'let your bat be upright'. Beldham remembered all the bowling at Hambledon being fast along the ground, around 1780. The new bowling had led to a change in the way bats were made, perhaps sparked off by the indignity suffered by John Small at the hands of one of the first length bowlers, 'Lumpy' Stevens, who bowled him out, 'which had not been done for some years'. This was also in 1772, and 'he changed when about 38 [which would be in 1775] from the crooked bat and scraping style of play to the straight and defensive system' (Lucas, 207). Small 'made bat and ball and would play any man in England' – he was said to make the best balls, at his shop in Petersfield.

Arlott adds, describing the 'very good length' Peter Jackson of Worcestershire would bowl: 'Such a length must be varied for every wicket and for every batsman and it is the measure of the *real* meaning of the expression . . .' (Arlott, 202).

length-ball   a ball bowled which pitches on a length. If a little wide of the off stump, though, Nyren recommends 'the young batsman to have nothing to do with it'.

let off, let-off   a batsman has a *let-off* when he should have been out. He is given another *life*.

life   either as immediately above; also when the pitch has life (see *lively*).

lift, lifter   a ball that gains height from a reasonable length, but not a *bouncer*. 'The Glamorgan captain [Hugh Morris] . . . had no answer to a vicious lifter from Giddins . . . "If there is anybody here able to tell me how to play a ball like that I would be very grateful," Morris said' (Michael Goodge, *Independent*, 13 May 1995). The verbs *kick, rear, pop, jump* convey the same meaning.

light, light meter   see *bad light*.

lignum   heavy bails. Short for *lignum vitae*, the tree of life, a very hard and dense wood; sometimes wrongly called lignite, a type of brown coal.

limited-over game   is one which is a contest to see which team can score most runs in a number of overs, the bowling side usually having to restrict their bowlers to a certain number of overs each. The first was England v. Australia to replace a Test washed out by rain.

line   the *line* of the ball's trajectory between the wickets. 'Nash hit upon the perfect line ... keeping the ball mainly on the outside of off stump he made it hold its line' (Richard Hutton, *The Cricketer*, August 1994), i.e. it was not affected by the slope of the ground at Lord's.

The batsman has the same line to play at, so in the same match report: 'Fraser pinned him down with a spell ... which culminated in the young left-hander [Fleming of New Zealand] aiming fatally across the line ...' As Nyren says: 'To cross a ball is the worst of bad play' (1833).

line-up   chiefly used of the batting order, but also of the bowling. Refers to the order of batting.

live   of the ball, when it is in play, not *dead*.

lively   a *lively pitch* is one that has life in it to make the ball bounce, and/or deviate from seam or spin. As opposed to a dead pitch, which gives the bowler no help, or frustrates or negates bite or spin.

loam   clay with an admixture of sand and 'decomposing vegetable matter' (OED), which also gives the derivation from a root *lai*, to be sticky, which appears also in 'lime', coming from the L. *limus*, mud. A fairly heavy soil.

lob   the *ODEtym* derivation is through obsolete Dutch *lubbe*, 'hanging lip' (cf. lubberlips). The OED definition is too narrow as it specifies solely under-arm. It is in fact a slow, high ball, only usually delivered under-arm. 'The old-fashioned lobber who used to bowl on the leg-side with a twist from leg and have four or five fields on the leg side is gradually disappearing' (Lyttelton, BLC, 1888, 80).

In Winchester slang, also a *yorker* or *tice ball* (Lewis 150).

To *lob the wicketkeeper*, or the fielder at the other end, is to throw in over his head by mistake.

lobster   a practitioner of *lobs*. The last successful first-class *lobsters* were G.H.T. Simpson-Hayward of Worcestershire, who took 6 for 43, on matting, in his first Test in South Africa, on the 1909–10 tour, and came in from the off, from a vicious tweak between thumb and finger, and Digby Jephson of Surrey. Jephson came in from the leg, and had two short legs, two mid-ons, a long leg, long-on, and straight hit fielder on the boundary. T.J. Molony played three games for Surrey in 1921. His field had eight on the leg, four inner and four outer, and mid-off. He caused pandemonium with his high-pitched *leg-theory* lobs, Whysall trying a tennis smash which ended in the hands of Ducat at mid-off, and two wickets falling in the deep (sources: Frith, *Slow Men*, and Brodribb).

loft   to hit the ball in the air, often over the field, from the ON also meaning air, sky, upper room. A *lofted drive*, or to *loft the ball over the field*, means the ball is hit in the air deliberately, and it can signify the batsman is out doing so: 'Hardstaff had gone, lofting Toshack to the on' (Fingleton, *Don*, 99).

lollipop   a ball which is easy to hit, Geoffrey Boycott remarking 'a real lollipop . . . you don't want to bowl too many of those at West Indian batsmen' on the first day of the Old Trafford Test, 1995 (BBC TV).

lolly   the Australian or dialect for *lollipop*, but now more often an easy catch. See also *dolly*.

long field   out in the deep behind the bowler.

long handle   to take the *long handle* to the bowling is to hit out, all around the ground. That vigorous missionary C.T. Studd, whose Cambridge eleven defeated the 1882 Australians, had a bat handle made an inch longer to improve his hitting power. Bats can be bought with a long handle. When the bat was the shape of a crook it would have been far longer, so the expression may be of great antiquity.

long hit   invariably through the air and of great distance: the longest measured appears to be that of 175 yards, made by the Revd W. Fellows in 1856. The number of long hits made by C. I. L. Thornton – 168 yds. during practice at Brighton in 1871, 152 yards at Canterbury, and as a schoolboy over the old pavilion at Lord's – qualify him as one of the biggest hitters of all time (Altham, 145). The only man to have cleared the pavilion at Lord's was A.E. Trott, in 1899! Mike Llewellyn of Glamorgan came close to it, hitting the cast-iron insignium or its pedestal in the 1977 Gillette Cup Final. Brian Lara also has hit the top part of the pavilion towers. Keith Miller hit the roof in the Victory Test of 1946, and others who have done that are Gilbert Jessop, F.T. Mann, Kim Hughes, and Wasim Akram. More recently, the Australian Tim Moody is apparently the first to hit a ball over the Tavern, in the final of the Natwest Trophy of 1994. Alletson's innings is reputed to have contained a six which landed on the roof of the ice-rink which used to stand next to the Hove ground, about 160 yards. Arthur Wellard in India hit one over a pavilion some sixty feet high which stood some 120 yards from the pitch; the remarkable thing about this is it was a low hit, so should have carried further. Alfred Gover and N.W.D. Yardley, captain of Yorkshire and England, thought it was the longest hit they'd ever seen.

E.H. Budd hit a *volley* far enough for nine runs to be gathered, at Woolwich, and also hit a ball out of the old Lord's ground at Dorset Square, for which Thomas Lord had promised twenty guineas, 'But Lord was shabby and would not pay up,' wrote Budd. In 1992 the magazine *Cricket Lore* offered £2,500 to the first player to emulate Trott's feat by the end of the 1999 season.

long hop   *delivery* very short of a length. As it has already bounced, the batsman knows if it has turned or lifted, so can score off it. 'Long hops are the sin of bowlers for which there is no forgiveness' (J. Lillywhite, 9). First mention in Lewis is 1836.

long leg   grazes quietly by the fence at about 45 degrees behind the wicket. Fast bowlers often field there between overs. 'One day, when everybody was waiting to shoot the cricket scene, Stanley Baker [the actor] asked to field at long leg . . . the boys all tried to cart the bowling down the leg side just to get the actor running' (Michael Henderson's Winter Tour Diary, *The Cricketer*, April 1996).

long-nips   see *nips*.

long-off   a position deeper than mid-off. Probably shortened from *long-hit off*, a fielder in the game in Meredith's novel *Diana of the Crossways*, when Tom Redworth plays wearing flannel jacket and black trousers. Thomas Moult notes that George Meredith introduces cricket also in *Evan Harrington*, *The Ordeal of Richard Feverel* and *The Adventures of Harry Richmond*.

long-on   originally 'long field' which designated both sides, a deep *mid-on*. Also, obsolete, *extra long-on*, a fieldsman sometimes placed to the left of long-on, but deeper in the field. For a fast right-hand bowler on a sticky wicket, counsels Ranjitsinhji, 'extra long-on may be used instead of third man' (*Jubilee Book*, 102). It is a solitary place:

> Feeling sort of lonesome,
> Feeling sort of blue,
> Loafing in the long-field
> All day through . . .
>
> I've got those Long-On Blues,
>   Yes, umpire,
> I've got those Long-On Blues,
>   Yes, umpire . . .

Herbert Farjeon's song, with its reiterated chorus, says it all (Farjeon, 105).

long slip   obsolete, taken over by *fly-slip*. A deep slip position, rather fine.

long stop   the position behind the wicket-keeper, now seldom

used except in schoolboy matches or those on very poor
ground. First reference seems to be from 1767: 'I had almost
forgot – they deserve a large bumper – / Little George, the long
stop, and Tom Sueter, the Stumper' (Cotton, xi). The *long stop*
may have been the first to wear gloves, in the days when the
keeper was also the bowler at that end, because the 1880 *J.
Lillywhite's Cricketers' Annual* still advertises 'Long-Stop
Gloves'.

look out   old term for fielders, as was *watchers out:* 'Several
players were stationed to "look out" in different parts of the
field, and each fixed himself into the proper attitude by placing
one hand on each knee, and stooping very much as if he were
"making a back" for some beginner at leap-frog' (*Pickwick
Papers*, ch. vii).

loop   the arc of a slow delivery, but more specifically one
which, given some air, dips suddenly just before the batsman
with the effect of topspin and/or bowling into the wind. Both
the trajectory and the spin will cause the ball to bounce more
than normal, increasing the chance of a catch from a batsman
who thinks he is driving a half-volley. The effect is described
by Tony Lewis: 'The best wrist spinners get fast loop and the
ball dips and drifts before the bounce and turn' (*Sunday
Telegraph*, 4 December 1994).

loose   of either shot or ball, wayward, not demonstrating
proper application, or direction.

loosener   also formerly 'trial ball': a practice ball, not at the
wickets, by a bowler who has just come on to bowl. In the 19th
century this could be done down the pitch. Today, the relatively
innocuous deliveries with which some bowlers open.

lost ball   Law 14 in 1809: 'If *Lost Ball* be called, the striker
shall be allowed four; but, if more than four are run before *Lost
Ball* is called, then the striker to have all they have run.' By
1867, the runs had risen to six. Stories abound of balls hit into
the crooks of trees, alligator creeks, or, a particular end of
season peril, failure to retrieve under the baleful glare of a
rutting stag in Richmond Park.

lower, lower order   the batsmen from 8 to 11. No. 8 used to
be the place for the hitter. See *top order, middle order*.

M **adge**   always the fifth toast of the men of Hambleden, in the Bat and Ball Inn: To Madge. For long a
puzzlement. Why so fulsomely celebrated, this particular lady? Madge was, however, a particular of Woman, is
still in dialect and is still celebrated.

Magnus effect   see *Robins effect*.

Maharajah pair   a phrase suggested by Meyer-Homji to
describe the feat of A.J.S. Smith of Natal, who in 1972–3 scored
a duck in one innings and in the next was run out before he
faced a ball.

maiden   a *maiden* over is one from which no runs are obtained
by bat. Now always refers to an over, and included in the
analysis, but sometimes used in the past to refer to a single
delivery. In both there is another sense, the maiden over in for
example Test or county cricket being the first one bowled. First
mention appears to be in Pycroft, when he says 'In point of
style the old players did not play the steady game with maiden
overs as at present' (p. 58).

maker's name   to show (the bowler) the *maker's name* is to
bat defensively. Playing straight down the line, especially the
forward defensive shot, finished without *follow-through*, pre-
sents the bowler with it.

mamba   used by BBC Radio 4 commentary team on 15
December 1995 on the Durban Test to describe a *shooter*, or
a venomous ball, the green and the black mambas being
particularly poisonous and aggressive snakes. See also
mulligrubber.   .

manager   from Lewis we can see this word enjoyed some
currency as meaning *captain* in the mid-19th century, the last
mentions being in 1851. In 1996 Ray Illingworth had a full-
time managerial position with the England team.

mankadded   to be run out by the bowler pretending to release
the ball but running out the batsman when backing up. After
the famous Indian all-rounder Vinoo Mankad, who at Sydney
in 1947 ran out Australian opener Bill Brown, and again in the
same season. A warning should always be given by the bowler
and umpire to the batsman first.

mark, marker   the viewer can sometimes see the bowler press
a small white disc into the ground to mark the end of his run-
up. The words formerly had an entirely different meaning,
mark meaning to score runs (*get off the mark* meaning to start
scoring) and *marker* being a scorer: as Lewis points out from
The Covent-Garden Magazine of 1774: 'If one of these gentry
[sc. blacklegs] should be appointed marker, he will favour the

side that he wishes to win, and diminish or increase the notches
as suits his advantage' (283/2).

match-book   score-book.

matting   see *jute, coir.*

meat/y   the thick part of the blade. See also *middle.*

medium-pace   anything from about 50 m.p.h. in club cricket
to 70 at first-class level. The bowler of this type has a wide
variety at his command. Lewis has a close definition from the
1897 *Encyclopaedia of Sport* 1: 'The medium-paced bowler . . .
seldom bowls two consecutive balls of identical pace and length'
(252/1).

meet the ball   to go to *meet the ball* is to come forward, a
meaning practically the same since 1816, when Lambert's
Instructions and Rules of Cricket has: 'If the striker is in too great
haste to meet the ball . . . he is liable to miss' (28)

middle   in the *middle* the bowling looks more difficult: the
word refers to the area of the pitch. Also, *to middle a ball* is to
hit it with the meat of the bat. 'Bowling to Bradman? Easy. You
hit the middle of the bat every time' – A.E. Gover of Surrey
and England reminiscing.

middle order   refers to batsmen between 3 and 8 at widest
compass, usually 4–6. 'Once Hobbs's 2½ hour innings had
ended . . . the middle order was cut away by Gregory, Mac-
Donald, and Mailey' (Frith, *England v. Australia*, 122, of the
Third Test at Adelaide, 1921).

middle wicket   the old term for mid-wicket, but on the off
side; Nyren advises he 'should stand on the off-side not more
than eleven yards from the bowler's wicket or more than twenty-
two from the batsman's' (Lucas, 45). This makes him sound
like a short extra-cover.

midfield   the area of the field between the in- or close-fielders,
and the deep.

mid-off   the position on the bowler's left hand some five yards
away, but either in front of or behind him. Despite the
observation of W.G. Grace below, not an easy place to field as
the ball comes hard and fast. From *mid-wicket off,* through
middle off, to the present term, although there seems some
ambiguity about where the position actually was, as Fred Gale,
the Old Buffer, has them 'about equal distance from either
wicket, standing back some fifteen yards from the centre
between the wickets, opposite each other' – in other words,
where *mid-wicket* and *cover* are today.

mid-on   originally *middle-wicket-on,* and by abbreviation to its
present form. Not infrequently used to 'hide' an indifferent

fielder: 'the last refuge of mankind', according to Australian Premier Robert Menzies.

mid-wicket   originally on the off side, where *mid-off* fields now, up until at least 1891, when W.G. in his *Outdoor Games* says 'Mid-off is one of the easiest places in the field, a ball hit to mid-wicket having so seldom any spin on it' (Grace, 27).

military medium   description of bowling: a brisk canter to the wicket, an upright style, not much imagination, pretty good length and direction.

milk the bowling   play a relatively cautious game: 'Milk the bowling . . . get a couple of runs an over' – Michael Holding, former West Indies fast bowler, on how to play Shane Warne, World Cup, 4 March 1996.

mill the bowling   to wear the bowling down, according to the sole mention, which is found in Nyren: 'If you go in first, let two of your most safe and steady players be put in, that you may stand a chance of milling the bowling in the early part of the game' (Lucas, 118).

mince   to *mince* an attack means to punish it severely.

Minor Counties   such as Herefordshire, Norfolk, Stafford-shire, etc., are not *first-class* and have their own championship.

miscue   to fail to 'get hold of' a ball properly, often by hitting early: 'Kent could only wait patiently for mistakes. They came with Alan Fordham hitting across the line . . . and Kevin Curran miscued to square leg' (Geoffrey Dean, *Daily Telegraph*, 28 April 1995). From billiards.

mis-field   to fail to field cleanly: the old maxim is 'never run on a mis-field'. Alec Bedser might agree, run-out to end his 121 *stand* with Compton on a mis-field by Sam Loxton in the Third Test of 1948: 'You've done me!' he cried, as Loxton recovered quickly.

miss   is used in three contexts: dropping a catch; of a delivery, to *miss* the stumps; and plays a stroke and fails to make contact with the ball, he is said to have *played and missed*.   ·

mis-time, mis-timing, mis-timed   sometimes a ball will go fast off the bat, other times hardly at all, plumping with a dull and discordant metallic thud into the hands of the fielders: 'Morris . . . mistimed a cover-drive for Adams to take a diving catch' (Tony Pawson, *The Observer*, 12 June 1994).

mix them   Giffen advises in 1898: 'some bowlers forget that so soon as they begin to mix their bowling the batsman is more likely to make a mistake' (p. 232). Sir Leonard Hutton thought the fast-bowling all-rounder Keith Miller the most difficult bowler he ever faced because he never knew what was coming next.

molly-grabber   probably erroneous for *mulligrubber*.

move, movement   of a quickish bowler, referring to swing or swerve, or *movement* off the seam, when the seam hits the ground and causes the ball to deviate. 'Miller wasn't at his fastest that morning, but he moved the ball around beautifully in the conditions and was very accurate,' wrote Ian Johnson. 'By lunch on the first day at the MCG his figures were 9–8–5–3, Hutton, Compton and Edrich being his three victims' (*WCM*, October 1994).

mow   from the same Teutonic root that gives *mead* and *meadow*: of the pitch, but also a shot to leg – see *Stogumber mow*.

muck   a North Country word, probably of Scandinavian derivation as the earliest mentions are from the eastern parts of England. Related to ON *myki, mykr*, dung. In the cricketing context it denotes slow, high-flighted balls. See also *filth*.

mud   '"put it in de *mud*" is instruction to bowl a bouncer': West Indies slang, reported by Simon Hughes (*Daily Telegraph*, 28 August 1995).

mulligrubber   a ball which shoots on landing, a *shooter*. The rarer form is molly-grubber: Rundell quotes Peter Roebuck in *The Cricketer* November 1982: 'a dead pitch which from time to time produced a snorter or a shooter (Australians might prefer "rib-tickler" or "molly-grabber")'. The latter might be interpreted as 'testicle seizer', but as it shoots, the OED definition is apter: the mulligrubs is 'a state of depression of spirits, a fit of megrims or spleen', which might well define batsmen's feelings if bowled or lbw to such a ball. And *grub* or *grubber* is a shooter. Lord Harris with an England team in Australia is reported in *J. Lillywhite's Cricketers' Annual*: 'Emmett bowled with great accuracy and success, and with Mr Hornby's 'grubs' at the other end to stop the run-getting . . . we disposed of our opponents for 177.' That was in 1880, and in 1870 *Baily's Magazine* had reported rather disapprovingly that 'Never before did we see a species of underhand bowling, known to school-boys as "grubs", made use of in the crack match of the year' (Lewis).

N **elson** a score, either of individual or team, of 111, held by Australians to be unlucky for them. One of everything, but Nelson had only one of two items, one eye and one arm, being otherwise fully equipped, and unless Emma Hamilton is regarded as the other singular attribute, the term is a misnomer. It is, however, possible that the number refers to three of his great naval victories, perhaps Copenhagen, the Nile, and Trafalgar: thus giving won-won-won. In losing the 1954–5 Ashes series 3–1, Australia were twice dismissed for 111, as they were in the Headingley Test of 1981, when Botham made his famous 149★ and Bob Willis then took 8–34.

nets practice pitches, originally poles supporting netting.

neutral umpire see *independent umpire*.

new ball the game starts with a *new ball*, and there is usually one for each innings except in casual knock-up games, unless both captains agree not to have one. The new ball swings more and bounces more, so is more difficult to play. In first-class and some other categories of match, the new ball may be taken at various intervals (currently 85 overs in Tests in England; in the West Indies after 75 overs, the recommended 6-ball minimum). In 1948 the interval was only 55 overs, and Bradman was able to bowl Lindwall and Miller, both fast, then close up the game with Toshack and Johnston, waiting for the new ball. See also *swing*.

nibble to edge a ball. See also *feel for, fish, hang out, snick*.

nightwatchman if a wicket falls about twenty minutes or less before the close of play, a less adept batsman – the night watchman – is sent in to avoid the risk of a more valuable wicket than his falling – and sometimes to help the better batsman already at the other end. 'Gough shepherded Gooch through at Melbourne' (Second Test, 1994 – Sky TV commentary).

nip[1] 'a Stroke, or Nip . . . if the Ball be held before it touches the Ground . . . it's out . . . if a Ball is nipp'd up and he strikes it again wilfully, before it came to the Wicket, it's out' *Laws for the Strikers from the The Game at Cricket*, 1755.

nip[2] of the ball itself: either off the pitch, changing direction or speedily coming on to the bat.

nip[3] is an obsolete term for *point*, because that is where the nips flew; so *cover nips* is cover point, *long nips* extra cover. The term lasted until 1823 at Eton, but *nips* was more where cover is (Lewis).

nip-backer a ball which comes in to the batsman from off to leg, after pitching. See also *break-back*. '[M]uch bowling responsibility rested with Srinath, and three wickets in the top five, including Lamb, who was bowled by a *nip-backer*, was a respectable response' (David Hopps, *Guardian*, 11 August 1995).

no ball, to no-ball a bowler   first recorded separately from *byes* in 1830. Law 24 is one of the longest Laws, defining 11 different types of *no-ball*. Formerly also *noes*, the 1863 *Lilly-white's Scores* noting, '736 runs in this match, including 131 byes, wides, and noes'.

non-striker   the batsman who is not at that time facing the bowling.

not a man move   West Indian for a shot hit so hard that the fielders do not have time to react, written thus by C.L.R. James in *Beyond A Boundary*, but pronounced *notamanmove* by Tony Cosier on BBC Radio Test Match Special as Graham Thorpe cracked one through the covers, Oval Test, 23 August 1995.

notch   in the early days of cricket, *notches* were cut in sticks to record runs, and the phrase 'to notch up runs' is still in use. One of Lord Byron's letters records that he got '11 notches the first innings and 7 the second' against Eton. But as Tim Rice pointed out (*Daily Telegraph*, 8 June 1994), the score book has 7 and 2. Poetic licence, or did Byron nod?

not cricket, it's   the first recorded usage found is in the Revd James Pycroft's *Cricket Field*, where he refers to the a certain Harvey Fellows as bowling fast: 'we will not say that anything that hardest of hitters and thorough cricketer does is not cricket, but certainly it's anything but *play*.' Bowen (p.112) also foot-notes Pycroft describing the bowling of underhand sneaks as 'no cricket' in 1834.

Nottingham cut   a forward cut, both in the direction the ball takes and from having the left leg across; also called a 'front-foot cut'. Developed in the days of William Clark's All-England XI, apparently: 'the Nottingham forward cut with the left leg over ... more towards middle wicket' (Pycroft, 151: 'middle wicket' meaning an offside position when this was written in 1851). In 1866 mid-wicket was still also being referred to as on the off-side, and the shot as the *Nottingham drive*.

not out[1]   to be the batsman who has not been out at the end of the game or an interval.

not out[2]   umpire's response to an appeal by the fielding side which he adjudges unjustified by facts.

not out[3]   sign on basement lavatory at Lord's. David Steel of Northamptonshire and England, going in to bat from the dressing-room at Lord's in 1976, went on down past the Long Room, through which the batsman usually passes on his way to

the wicket, and down two further flights of stairs, finding himself
in this area.

nudge   to *nudge* and *nurdle* is to accumulate runs by grudging
little round-the-corner poke and shuffle strokes, e.g. nudging
the ball away for a single behind the wicket. See also *graft*.

nurdle   dates from at least 1955 at the Old Trafford ground,
when David Green, now with the *Daily Telegraph*, first joined
the ground staff and found it in use. It is a stroke which sends
the ball behind the wicket on the leg or off side, wilfully,
sometimes from a deliberate thick edge. David Lloyd of Lancs.
and England, possibly using it on BBC TV for the first time to
describe Jack Russell's methodology in his half-century at Old
Trafford against the West Indies in 1991, also describes it as
reaching parts of the ground other strokes can't reach.

nurdler   one who nurdles. Not given by OED, but origin may
be partly onomatopoeic. Not related to *nerd*, as in computer.

nutmeg   when John Emburey of England, Middlesex and
Northants was bowled, the ball passing between his legs, by
Austin of Lancs in the Benson and Hedges one-day final, 13
July 1996, commentating for Sky TV Bob Willis simply said
'*Nutmeg!*'

Obstructing the field   Law 37 states:
1. Either batsman, on appeal, shall be given out obstruct-ing the field, if he wilfully obstructs the opposite side by word or action. [There is, however, no known case of a batsman being given out for shouting 'Mine!' as a catch goes up and thus causing the fielder to miss the catch.]

2. Obstructing the ball from being caught. The striker on appeal shall be out should wilful obstruction by either batsman prevent a catch being made. This shall apply even though the striker causes the obstruction in lawfully guard-ing his wicket under the provisions of Law 34.
The most famous example of this in modern times happened at The Oval in August 1951, when Sir Len Hutton was batting against South Africa. He snicked a ball onto his pad and it started to rise in the air towards his shoulder. With a light-ning reaction, he knocked the ball aside with his bat as it was falling, as it did look as if it were going towards the stumps. But the South African wicket-keeper, Endean, was standing up and planning to catch the ball, an appeal was made and Dai Davies gave Hutton out. The speed of Sir Leonard's reaction was such that 'wilful' in this case must include reflex action.
   The batsman may also claim *obstruction* if a fielder or the bowler stops him from gaining his ground during a run.
occupation of the crease   the length of time the batsman stays in.
'oche   (pronounced 'ocki') in darts is the firing line. Thus slang for *pitch*; Mark Nicholas of Hampshire and the *Daily Telegraph* uses it describing the very late swing of Wasim Akram of Lancs and Pakistan: 'swung all over the 'oche and was to decimate the Lancashire innings . . .' (28 August 1995).
off, off-side   the side of the field that the batsman is facing: in road use (for driving on the left, as if the batsman was the driver) it would be the side furthest from the pavement.
off bat   obsolete for *point*. Winchester School term: the number of terms from the school may support the thesis of the early game arriving there from the Pilgrim's Way. In use until 1870, but by 1887 *point* was in use.
off-break   a ball spun from off to leg, by whatever method: thus a *chinaman* is also an *off-break*. *Off-spin* is the term for the method.
off-cutter   the faster bowler's *off-break*, done by cutting the fingers down the side of the ball, in a way similar to the off-

break action. Of relatively recent introduction, not being mentioned in Lewis.

off drive   anywhere on the offside, so can include *cover-drive*.

offer, offerings   the batsman can *offer* a chance, or like the fielding side be *offered the light*. *Offerings*, though, are served up by the bowler, the sense pejorative.

offie   a person who proffers off-breaks, cf. *leggie*.

off-spin, off-spinner   finger-spun (generally) *off-breaks*: the latter can mean the purveyor of same.

off-theory   the first apparent mention is from January 1883, when W.L. Murdoch is quoted (by Lewis) in *Longman's Magazine* (292): 'At the present time, when bowlers place their men on the off side and bowl on what I might term the "off-theory", batsmen should be very careful what they hit at.'

old enemy   in England, Australia, and vice versa. The first Tests were played against each other.

old-fashioned point   probably what we would call *silly point* today. See *point*.

on   as in driving, as if the batsman was driving a vehicle towards the bowler, the *on* side would be that nearest the kerb.

on-break   obsolete term for the opposite to an off-break. Now *leg-break*.

on drive   said to be the most difficult shot, the ball sent in the direction of mid-on. See entry under *V*.

one-day   a game which starts and should finish on the same day. May be held over to, or completed at, another time. The term implies limited-overs, at least in *first-class* cricket, although at a lower level a limit may not be needed. Also *one-dayer*.

one leg   the positioning of the bat, when the batsman takes guard, on the leg stump. It only covers one (the leg) stump.

one short   when a run is not completed because the batsman or his bat has not crossed the popping crease, the umpire bends his elbow to tap himself on the shoulder. Fergus McKendrick describes how he used to sit with his friend in the congregation, converting the mannerisms of ministers into cricket matches: 'Short runs were very rare, but we had one visiting preacher who kept hitching up his academic hood . . .' (p.12).

on-side   leg side. Probable derivation from the *onside* of a carriage, car – the side nearer the pavement. See *off, off-side*.

open   a bowler's *open action* means he is more chest-on to the batsman when he delivers the ball; this helps the right-handed *swing* bowler to in-swing.

opener   the two batsmen, 1 and 2 in the order, who open the innings. They are expected to stay there, quench the early fiery attack, cope with the unusual behaviour of the still-lacquered new ball, then soften it, taking some of its properties of swing and bounce off, and lay a foundation for the innings.

order   refers to the *batting order* (see *opener, middle-order, late-order*).

orthodox   said of a batsman who plays in the style of the coaching manuals, or of field placings for a bowler, e.g. 5 on the *off*, 4 on. the *leg*, for a left-hand spinner. Of the spinner himself, it means an ordinary type of finger-spinner.

out   Dr Gillmeister relates the terms to the medieval tournament, when those trying to force the passage were *dehors*, and those defending, say, the wicket gate, were *dedans*. See also *wicket*. A newspaper billboard in 1930 simply said 'HE'S OUT', referring to Bradman.

outcricket, outfield, outfielder this now means cricket played in the *outfield*.

outside, outside edge   Tim May of Australia, bowling off-spin and its associated arts from around the wicket to Graeme Hick in the Third Test in 1993, 'found the outside edge with one that went across his body' (BBC TV Commentary) and had Hick caught in the slips. Also the name of a popular ITV series about a village cricket team.

outswing/er   the ball that moves through the air away from the batsman, from leg to off. The late outswing of Ian Botham of Somerset, Worcestershire, Durham, and England, accounted for many of his Test victims. See also *swing*.

over[1]   the maximum number of balls bowled from one end by one bowler. It seems from *The Young Cricketer's Tutor* (Lucas 13, footnote) to have had six balls, then four, then six again, five sometimes, and sometimes eight in Australia. It is shortened from the umpire's old announcement 'The balls are over': thus Gale (who used 'The Old Buffer' among other *noms de plume*) in *New Sporting Magazine*, LX, 271: 'Some of the umpires of the present day corrupt the four words into *'Ver.'*

   The six sixes in an *over*, by Ravi Shastri in 1984, and by Sobers in 1968 for Nottingham off Malcolm Nash of Glamorgan are well known: but the two bowlers' record has been overtaken by Rob Jones, bowling for Durham University on 19 April 1995 against Surrey's David Ward in a pre-season 50-over friendly. With the help of two no-balls, each adding two runs, he also conceded 6, 6, 4, 4, 6, 6, 6, 6, off the bat for a grand total of 48, and was not asked to bowl again. The world record seems to be 62 by H. Morley off R. Grubb (four no-balls, nine sixes, and two fours) in a Queensland county match.

over²   to hit *over the ball*, or *over the field* have completely different meanings, thus Graham Thorpe got himself out (see *G.H.O.*) hitting over a ball from Shane Warne in the Brisbane Test of 1994, and in considering his batting *line-up* for the next Test, Michael Atherton said, 'We'll talk about Graham opening. But I think Alec hits it over the top still better,' Gooch being observed to dispatch Warne's googly over the inner field with little problem (John Thicknesse, *Evening Standard*, 12 December 1994).

overarm   the bowling action with the arm above the shoulder, legalised in 1864, which allowed developments such as *swing*, *bounce*, and of course *pace*. Synonymous with *overhand*, now obsolete, as: 'Bangkok . . . had only one bowler. He was named Smith and he mostly bowled tremendously fast full pitches with an ultra-overhand delivery' (Standing, 1, 178).

overpitch   the notion of the pitch of the ball came with the new *length-bowling* and is first seen in 1851, '[Fuller] Pilch . . . plays him [Clarke] back all day if he bowls short, and hits him hard all along the ground whenever he overpitches' (Pycroft, 177). An *overpitched* ball is easy to score off, as it does not have time to turn or lift, providing it is not a *yorker*.

over-rate   the number of overs bowled per hour or day: 90 a day or 15 (six-ball overs) an hour in Tests is the *required over-rate*. Legislated for when rates dropped, largely through a preponderance of fast bowling. 'The over-rate . . . was abysmal. In five hours only 54 eight-ball overs were sent down' (Ian Johnson on the England attack, led by Tyson and Statham, in the Melbourne Test of 1955, *WCM* October 1994).

overseas players   are cricketers who play in a country other than that of their birth, normally as professionals. In 1994 each county, including the Minor Counties, was allowed one player from outside the European Community. There were various residential qualifications for others born outside this area hoping to qualify, generally seven years.

overspin   see *top spin*. The word is used more in Australia than England.

over-the-crease play   playing without moving the feet, with the body staying literally over the popping crease.

over the top   to hit over the inner fielders, a trajectory as in the golfing 'approach shot'.

over the wicket   the side of the wicket the bowler bowls from with his bowling arm nearer the stumps, almost directly over the stumps. See *round the wicket*.

overthrow   from a hit by a batsman, the ball is gathered by a fielder and thrown to the stumps, not gathered, and goes on for *overthrows*. Waghorn has, from 1749, 'Five of Addington Club challenge any five in England for 50 guineas, to play bye-balls and overthrows' (p. 43). See *bye*.

Pace   pace bowlers are quick bowlers: the pace attack. 'Michael Atherton was beaten for pace more than anything,' said Charles Colville as Craig McDermott put one through the *gate* to bowl him for 88, Third Test, Sydney, 31 December 1994 (Sky TV). Also of a batting side or batsman: 'The point was that Gatting, throughout his 145 minutes at the crease, was "behind the pace" . . .' (Scyld Berry, *Daily Telegraph*, 16 November 1994).

paceman   one who bowls fast.

pacer   a fast ball: 'Bunce had to face Dan Newhall's strategic bowling as well as Charley's pacers' (*American Cricketer*, 1878).

pack   to *pack* the field is to put a number of fielders in one particular area: thus a *packed leg trap* would describe the *bodyline* field.

pad   the leg guard of the batsman. The Revd Pycroft has Daubeny inventing them in 1836: *Scores and Biographies* has it as the same Nixon who introduced cane handles to bats. In Hambledon days the bumps were seen to rise under the stockings, and occasionally blood. Now the shock-absorbing qualities of high density plastic, polyurethane, Velcro straps, detachable extra protection, are a far cry from the anti-bump treatment of two hundred years ago. See *pad-play*.

pad away   see *pad up*².

pad-bat catch   is out: see *bat-pad* above.

paddings   an early form of pad.

paddle   not unlike the *lap shot*. An inelegant shot, not unlike a duchess sweeping a Pekinese from her lap with both hands: 'Reeve . . . with the help of his trademark *paddled-sweep* . . .' (Charles Randall, *Daily Telegraph*, 13 August 1995, referring to Dermot Reeve's one-day play).

pad out   see *pad up*².

pad-play   of the batsman: to play the ball with his pads. The rules on lbw state that he cannot be out to a ball pitching outside the leg stump, but that he can be out to a ball pitching outside the off stump, and turning back so that it would hit the wicket but for the pad, if the batsman has not played a shot at it. This leads to mock shots being made, with the bat being shyly tucked behind the pads. When England, already bamboozled by the spin of Alf Valentine and Sonny Ramadhin, who had won them the Test at Lord's just before, played West Indies at Edgbaston in 1957, Peter May and Colin Cowdrey put on 411, still a record test-match stand for England. They were able to *pad* Ramadhin away with impunity if their pad was outside the off stump, under the 1948 lbw Law. That law read:

The Striker is out 'leg before wicket' – if with any part of his person except his hand, which is in a straight line between wicket and wicket, even though the point of impact be above the level of the bails, he intercepts a ball which has not first touched his hand or bat, and which in the opinion of the umpire, shall have or would have pitched in a straight line from the Bowler's wicket to the Striker's wicket, or shall have pitched on the off-side of the Striker's wicket, provided always that the ball would have hit the Striker's wicket.

Thus the ball had to be intercepted in line with the stumps for the Striker to be given out. Compare with the present Law 36 under *lbw*.

pad up[1]   to put pads on before batting or wicket-keeping.

pad up[2]   to use the pads as a line of defence against a delivery. 'Hutton (a Yorkshire Colt at the time) ... padded up to a good-length ball from Barnes pitching just outside the off stump. Barnes ... shouted down the wicket in a stern voice "If you do that again, I shall appeal!"' (Duckworth, 141).

pair   two *ducks* in two innings of the same match. 'This completed the first "pair" of his career, in his first Test as captain. He [Mark Taylor] is the first to make two ducks in a first Test as captain. He won't forget Karachi' (Michael Henderson, *The Times*, 1 October 1994). One hardly knows what this might be: *mandarin ducks*, perhaps? Also *pair of spectacles*, from 0 0 in the scorebook. 'It is believed [Lord Frederick Beauclerk] never made two noughts, or a pair of spectacles, in any match of note' (*Lillywhite's Scores*, 1862).

Paradox ball   Reginald Bosanquet's own name for the *googly*.

partner, partnership   said of either batsmen, bowlers, or a stand.

pavilion   a building of any size for players to change, store gear, take tea in, etc. The farthest *pavilion* was probably that of Combwich in Somerset, on the bank of the tidal River Parrett, which removed it to float off Burnham-on-Sea, but without anybody being in it at the time. Since then it has been moved to the other side of the ground. Possibly the first reference is the most infamous, as it destroyed many books and records, on its scale a loss like that of Alexandria's: 'fire broke out in the Pavilion at Lord's ...' (*The Times*, 30 June 1825).

peach   a *peach* of a ball means a beauty. See also *jaffa*.

pecking order   the batting order, a not particular happy derivation of the work of T.J. Schelderup-Ebbe, who in 1922 observed, 'A pattern of behaviour first observed in hens, later in other groups of social animals, in which those of high rank within the group are able to attack those of lower rank without provoking an attack in return' *(Zeitschrift für Psychologie, LXXXVIII,* 227: OED).

peculiars   obsolete for a peculiar type of bowling, the last mention in Lewis coming from 1876.

peg   any stump, e.g. *left peg, centre peg,* or a no-longer-used way of restoring the face of a bat when the grain has risen with use. A.E. Knight in *Complete Cricketer,* (1906, p. 48) has this to say: 'Pegging down the bat is simple, but destructive and ineffective' (Lewis). 'But Al Tolley removed his middle peg' comes from the *Nottingham Review,* 1868.

penalty runs   awarded to the batting side if the fieldsman wilfully stops it with anything other than his person: see *fiver.*

penetration   the bowling, *lacking penetration,* is failing to get through or take a wicket. 'The one common factor, however, was a lack of any *penetration* as the pair added 160' (Tony Pawson, *Observer,* 12 June 1994).

percher   a ball that 'perches' or hangs in the air, a high catch that seems to hesitate before it starts down. 'As big a percher as can ever have been missed in a match between England and Australia' (*The Times,* 23 June 1961: OED).

perhapser   an unintended stroke. 'Morris somewhat luckily got Bedser fine for 4 . . . It was what cricketers know as a "perhapser"' (Fingleton, *Ashes,* 247).

periscope   Stephen Lynch of *WCM* refers this to the 1969–70 Australia-South Africa series, when Doug Walters of Australia would duck a bouncer but leave the bat aloft, occasioning catches to the slips or keeper.

P.H.O. 'put himself out': before *declarations* were part of the game, the player would knock down his own wicket: whether a batsman would do it immediately or take a few runs first is not clear. The 1862 *Lillywhite* refers to a match in 1787 when 'G.Talbot, Esq., P H O 3'.

phantom seamer   Charles Colville and Derek Pringle mentioned Graham Gooch's *phantom outswinger* while commentating for Sky TV on the one-day international at Lords, May 1995, Pringle however remarking that Gooch had 7–4 as his best analysis. From Gk *phantazein,* to make visible. The meaning has moved away from that, as Gooch's deliveries did not swing.

pick, picked men   obsolete: chosen from outside, the idea being to balance the teams. OED gives: 'Sept. 28 was played at Egerton, a match at wicket . . . Egerton had two picked men on their side' from 1772 (Waghorn, 88), and 'The gentlemen of that place and one picked man' from 1773 (Waghorn, 98). See also *given men*.

pick   to *read* a *spinner*, to know what he's bowled; 'that was [Warne's] flipper . . . Aravinda da Silva didn't pick it out of the hand' (Richie Benaud for Sky TV at the World Cup final, Lahore, 17 March 1996).

pickpocket ball   as John Crawley attempted to play Shane Warne with his posterior, he 'fell to the famous pickpocket ball . . . that snapped behind his pads and tickled his leg peg' (Robert Craddock, *The Advertiser*, Adelaide, 25 January 1995).

pick the spot, pick out   Graeme Fowler, opener for Lancashire and England, advises the batsman to soften up the ball: 'pick out an advertising board or even better, a concrete wall, and hit the ball against that (Lara has mastered this)' (*Sunday Telegraph*, 11 June 1995).

pick-up, to pick up   of a bat, a good *pick-up* means that it comes up easily because of its balance. Of a fielder, the act of picking the ball off the ground. 'Nash . . . with a brilliant one-handed pick-up and return . . . was adjudged by the third umpire to have just beaten home White's attempt at a second run' (Richard Hutton, *The Cricketer*, August 1994).

pick-up shot   a shot which picks the ball up, similar to hitting it on the up, and takes it onto the leg side: 'Gough hit one of the best strokes of the afternoon, a skimming pick-up that still had 20 yards in it when it hit the square-leg fence 90 yards away' (John Thicknesse, *Evening Standard*, 12 January 1995).

Pilch's poke   named after Fuller Pilch, a Kentish batsman fl. in the Age before Grace. It may be associated with his defeat of the bowling of the large, eighteen-stone Alfred Mynn, or his being the first to combine forward and back play. *Pilch's poke* was more vigorous than its name suggests. The 'Old Buffer' said: 'If a "poke" means smothering a ball before it has time to rise and break, and placing it to the off or on with the greatest apparent ease, I shall much like to see it done again in these days . . .', and he goes on: 'he had a terrific hit between middle-off and cover, which gained him many a four and five runs . . . I rather fancy that Pilch's poke would puzzle some of the present bowlers' (*New Sporting Magazine*, LX, iii).

pinch-hitter   a term which has inserted itself from baseball. 'For openers, pinch-hitters, that is non-specialist batsmen promoted to take advantage of fielding restrictions . . . are, with one exception, "out". Unfortunately for England, the exception is Kaluwitharana, the brilliant Sri Lankan' (Simon Wilde, *The*

Times, 8 March 1996). However, when it came to the World Cup semi-finals on 9 March, he went cheaply while S. Jayasuriya made 82 scintillating runs.

pitch[1]   the strip of ground between the wickets which forms the arena for the contest between bowler and batsman. 'On the shiny pitch at Jamaica for the first Test, after Curtly's opening spell, there was a patch roughly six inches by six inches where every single delivery had pitched' (Michael Atherton, *Sunday Times*, 24 April 1994). Pitches of different soils play differently: see also *clay, loam*.

pitch[2]   where the ball hits the ground after leaving the bowler's hand: 'One of the main things in making an off-drive in any direction is to get well to the *pitch of the ball*' (Ranjitsinhji in 1897, *Jubilee Book of Cricket*, 167).

pitch-smacking   see also *gardening*. 'Australia was in no trouble though Bradman indulged hefty *pitch-smacking* after every ball' (Fingleton, *Don*, 136).

place   refers, apart from placing a stroke to avoid the field, to an old stroke, between square-leg and mid-on, used by A.C. Maclaren and Tom Hayward (Holland, *Cricket* 21).

platinum duck   term suggested by Meyer-Homji to describe being out on the first ball of a Test. Sunil Gavaskar did it three times (Arnold '74, Marshall '83–4, Imran Khan '86–7), nobody else even twice.

play!   is called by the umpire(s) to start a session or game, and has been for over quarter a millenium: Law 6 of 1744 and 1755 states: 'When both Umpires shall call Play 3 Times, 'tis at ye Peril of giving ye Game from them that refuse [to] Play.'

play at the pitch, of a slower bowler, means to come forward, playing as near to a half-volley as possible; it is also the bowler's aim to get the batsman to do that, to deceive him with flight and turn: 'Woolley succeeded in doing what Blythe very seldom did – he made the batsman play at the pitch of the ball' (Heffer, 83).

play forward, play back   to reach forward, or to step back, to play the ball. The first term was *to play out*, first practised by Fennex; another term was *running in* to hit (Pycroft, *Hambledon Club*, 1837 in Lucas, 135).

play yourself, himself, in   to get the eye in, the feel of the pitch.

play it off the pitch   a technique of playing slow bowling which seems only available to the very best: the ball is played, even off the front foot, as it comes off the pitch. Wally Hammond was most at home with this, rather than watching it out of the hand or spotting the rotation in the air: in *The Zen of Cricket*, Tony Francis quotes Sir Colin Cowdrey, not noticeably slow (the first man to hook the very nearly 100 m.p.h. Jeff Thompson): '[Hammond would] play it the moment it hit the ground which is quite staggering. I wanted it earlier than that because on an overcast day you had to work bloody hard to keep it out of your stumps. Wally didn't mind. Sir Don was the same. Their judgment was acute' (p.29).

played on   the batsman is recorded as bowled when the ball hits his wicket after it has hit his bat. 'He . . . played on a fast from Lang' (*Baily's Magazine*, August 1862, 83) seems to be one of the very early mentions.

plick-plock   on the back dust-jacket of Benny Green's *A History of Cricket:* 'Under the skies of Hambledon . . . the plick-plock of the bat against the ball first echoed on the English air.'

plim   the lush dampness of the grass on the pitch, making it a greentop: 'Minute by minute the grass sprang back to its true plim' (Arlott, in Batchelor, 41). From the intrans. verb to swell, fill out, but etymology unknown (OED).

plonk   'A good plonk,' said Tony Lewis, as Ealham of Kent and England got a good bit of *meat* onto the ball in the Lord's Test, 29 July 1996, BBC TV, and sent it away for two runs. 'I don't remember the word *plonk* coming up in the MCC Masterclass,' said David Gower.

plumb   to be plumb means *lbw* wihout a doubt. From L. for lead, *plumbum*, giving a plumb line i.e. in line wicket to wicket (and plumber). A *plumb wicket* means one that plays true, or one that does not accept spin.

pod   the blade of the bat, so-called for its shape. *Pod shaver* is either the instrument or the man who does the shaving: see under *bat*. 'The Bat should not be higher than twenty-one inches in the pod' (*Boy's Own Book*, 1828).

point   originally 'at the point of the bat', and a closer fielder than is normal today: Nyren speaks of him as if he were the closest, in adjuring the batsman: 'if . . . point . . . understand the game, he will get in close to the player while he is raising his bat; and will, in all probability, catch him out' (Lucas, 23).

poke   from the ME *poken*, a stroke made by a batsman, the general sense being that he pokes his bat at the ball as if at an undesirable object. See also *Cambridge poke, Nottingham poke, Pilch's poke, shuffle*.

poker, poking   as above. From 1836: 'A remarkably bad poking back player, with no hit in him at all' (*New Sporting Magazine*, October 1836, 360).

pomp   'in his pomp': first heard by John Arlott in Yorkshire discussing Fred Trueman. The *ODEtym* has 'ostentatious display', so can only apply to the ilk of Botham, Hammond, Dexter, perhaps Woolley and Colin Milburn, Dennis Lillee, Sir Richard Hadley, Michael Holding, whose character of playing is majestic.

pongo   for a bowler to get hit around: 'Unless bowlers can change their length and bowl reverse swing in places like Sydney they're going to get pongoed,' said Australia's Mike Whitney in *The Cricketer* (December 1994). The origin of the verb is obscure, but WWII slang for an untidy, shambling bloke was *pongo*, probably from the Angolan/Luandese for a large ape, gorilla, chimpanzee.

pop   see also *jump, kick, lifter*. Of a ball that rises unexpectedly, or, as here, the batsman's view: 'Mark Ramprakash popped an awkward bouncing delivery from Tom Moody to short leg' (David Foot, *Guardian*, 13 May 1995).

Poppy wicket   (1874 *Field* Magazine) is an obsolete term for such a wicket.

popping crease   the forward crease of the wicket, considered infinite in length, and now more commonly called the *batting crease*. 'the reason we hear sometimes of the blockhole was, not that the blockhole originally denoted guard, but because . . . there was cut a hole big enough to contain the ball, and . . . the hitter was made out in running a notch by the ball being popped into this hole (whence popping-crease) before the point of the bat could reach it' (Pycroft, in Lucas, 150). There is some doubt whether the hole was in the popping or wicket crease.

popty   obsolete, of unknown origin: 'A slow ball bowled underhand and pitched just out of the batsman's reach with a break to the off after pitching' (Lewis). Denison in *Sketches*, 1838: 'Dearman threw him in a slow under-hand "popty", which took down his "off" stump' (p.10).

post   to *post* runs on the board is simply to score.

posthumous swing   ball swings after it has bounced. Origin uncertain, but heard on Test Match Special on 6 August 1994.

pouch   to *pouch* a catch as the kangaroo pouches her joey, to make sure of holding it. 'Atherton didn't quite pouch it cleanly,' said Henry Blofeld of Michael Atherton, holding one in the Benson and Hedges Final (13 July 1996, BBC 2).

practice bowler   is a player who is kept on the staff of a club and is often overworked: 'Poor Errington or Harrington, who was so very poor he scarcely owned a name . . . made a precarious living on the Germanstown ground last year, subsisting on mushrooms, cast-off clothing, and occasional quarters, which cost him about five hundred balls apiece, for he was a good *practice bowler...*' (*American Cricketer*, 13 September 1877).

pro   short for *professional*, particularly referring to the *senior pro.*, the *old pro.*, put out to grass, coaching in schools, keeping a shop, etc. In the Lancashire Leagues he is more often referred to as 'the professional'. 'Just before the team left (Johnnesburg), Mr Abe Bailey presented each of the "pros." with a Kruger sovereign made up as a pendant for a watch-chain' (Warner, *Climes*, 232).

procession   when the batsmen follow each other in rapid succession: in 1852 the Lansdown Club put out West Gloucestershire for 6 runs in 9 overs: 'it was a most inglorious procession,' said W.G. Grace (*Cricket*, 1891, iii. 76).

prod   more cautious even than a *poke*, though it does not imply a cross bat: 'Boon, gripped by the demons of poor form, produced a tentative prod to be caught behind for the fourth successive time' (Robert Craddock, *The Advertiser*, on the Fifth Test in Perth, February 1995). The *post-war prod* was said by E.W. Swanton to be a response to the uncertain conditions in England after the war: 'prod' is not in Lewis.

professional   the noun means somebody who receives pay for playing. 'This movement [the touring Side of the All England Eleven] laid the foundation of the order called "professionals"' (Box, *Theory*, 98). Adjectivally, Screwtape advises Wormwood, on hearing that his patient has become a professional cricketer: 'Seek to distract him with jargon ... do not let him assess the real value of his innings ... let him think of it as "classy" or "swashbuckling". Best of all let him think of it as "professional". The use of this word is one of the really solid triumphs of our semantics department...' (Barnes, 119). The word goes back to at least 1751, when 'the Sheffield authorities engaged professional cricketers to amuse the populace, and so draw them from cock-fighting exhibitions' (Holmes, 10).

prop[1]   synonymous with *pop*: in the Leeds Test of 1948, 'Bradman remembered that Hassett's ball propped and he expected the same ... but it skidded through and miraculously found Bradman's bat not at home' (Fingleton, *Don*, 149). The derivation is probably Australian from horse racing (OED 1870), where a horse stops suddenly before a jump and the jockey clears it alone, 'to the great delight of some of the spectators and the horse' (Gerald Hammond, *Horse Racing, A Book of Words*, Carcanet, 1992).

prop[2]   in batting, to hold up an end: 'If I had my time over again, I would "prop and cop" instead of going for the big hits,' said the Yorkshire and Somerset pro Ellis Robinson to Alan Hill (*The Cricketer*, July 1995).

prune   the ball. See *purvey*.

pudding   'After heavy overnight rain the wicket played like a pudding – no-one could force their shots and the ball stood up rather than coming on to the bat' (Godfrey Evans on the Fifth Test at the Oval, 1948, *Cricket Lore*, II. iii. 20). See *sticky*.

puddle   still extant, the first mention being Pycroft quoting Beldham: 'These men played puddling about their crease . . . I like to see a player upright and well forward . . .' (*Cricket Field*, 51).

pull, pull shot, pull stroke   the ball is hit off the back foot between mid-on and square leg. The master of the shot was Sir Donald Bradman, who had to develop it when as a young boy he was playing against grown men on matting and, being short anyway, found the ball getting up too high to cope with. The Don describes two kinds of *pull*. In the first,

> the back foot is taken back and across, toes pointing down the pitch . . . pull it hard to mid-wicket rolling the wrists over to keep the ball on the ground . . . finish facing square leg. Secondly, put the right foot straight back . . . pull your body away from the line of flight as the left foot is swung round to leg . . . tremendous power . . . sometimes I found myself behind the leg stump with my left leg. (Bradman, 60-1)

Sir Donald is sometimes seen with a dropped left shoulder in this shot, a further aid in keeping the ball down. It can be a highly productive shot. Formerly, the pull was the *pull-drive*, off the front foot, as D.J. Knight says: 'Bear in mind that the difference between a hook and a pull is that in the former the ball is a long hop, in the latter it is a half-volley' (BLC, 1920, 37).

pull-drive   a drive off the front foot, which is not quite to the pitch of the ball, allowing the bat to hit *across the line*, thus taking the ball from, say, outside the off stump and hitting it past mid-on. Not wholly distinguishable from the *cow-shot*: 'Harvey sauntered out in a sun-hat . . . Later, he pull-drove Tufnell for six . . .' (Scyld Berry, *Sunday Telegraph*, 11 December 1994).

punch   a forcing stroke, more often than not from the back foot: 'there have been no better strokes all match than those punched by [Alec Stewart in the Bridgetown Test] through extra cover off the back foot' (*Guardian*, 13 April 1994).

purvey with the original sense to see or foresee (cf. Fr. *pourvu que . . .)* and from the Latin *providere*, to provide, the word has come to mean to bowl: 'Liaqat Ali was the man who was going to purvey the first *prune* of my Test career . . . short . . . placid Edgbaston Test wicket . . . just hit it' – for four (*The David Gower Story*, Parkfield Publishing video, 1989).

push '[W.G. Grace] introduced what was then a novel stroke . . . viz., the push to leg with a straight bat off the straight ball' (Harris, 58).

push through in batting: play down the line of the ball for a shot worth perhaps a single. In bowling: *push the ball through* is for a spinner to bowl a flatter line, denying the batsman time to get to the pitch and drive, but unless on a very responsive pitch (*pudding* or *sticky)* also denying himself much turn, as the ball has less time to grip.

put down can be used of a dropped catch, or the wicket being broken, which is the usage in the 1744 Laws. Another archaism is the meaning of the batsman dropping the ball dead at his feet.

put in for a side to be *put in* means that they have lost the toss and been made to bat – invariably because it is a good bowling wicket.

pyjamas slang for the coloured strip used in some forms of cricket, often with numbers on the back, sometimes under floodlights. *The Pajama Game*, with its American spelling of the word, was a long-running West End musical of the 1950s, thus the sobriquet 'pyjama game'. From the Urdu *pae jamah*, loose trousers tied around the waist, from Persian *pae* or *pay* (the root *ped-*, *pes-*, can be seen), plus *jamah:* foot clothing. Thus the expression symbolizes the descent to the bazaar.

Q **uack** this term seems unique to a South London team who use it as 'he's quacked again', or refer to batsmen as 'incorrigible quackers', i.e. they make ducks.

uick, quickie, quicks as in fast, but also *a quickie* or *the West Indies quicks* refers to fast bowlers. 'Mark Taylor ... really hasn't got much out of his quickies' (Ian Chappell for Sky TV, World Cup semi-final, 14 March 1996).

quick one a sudden faster ball from a bowler: 'Your quick one is essentially a shock ball ... it must always be straight at the stumps and well pitched up' (Marriott, 74). V. Kumble, the India and Northants leg-spinner, has a fast ball around 60 m.p.h.

quilt see *ball*. Also, obsolescent verb for hitting the ball hard: 'Mr. Lyttelton had an early taste of the lobs: these he quilted awfully' (*Baily's Magazine*, November 1882, 39).

R a way of recording *runouts* giving credit to the fielder: 'Small 3 c by Lumpey 4 r by Simmons' (Waghorn's *Cricket Scores*, 1773). As this is the last mention given by Lewis, it seems that the custom died out.

rabbit one who is inept with the bat, and soon sent back to the *hutch*. See also *ferret*.

rambler always red or similar, meaning the ball: 'The Huns' skipper tossed the crimson rambler to Himmelweit to open the bowling' (Tinniswood, 76).

ramrod obsolete: 'Ramrod, Raymonder, names given to a ball bowled all along the ground' (R.B. Mansfield, *School-Life at Winchester College*, 1870, 228); 'It [a quick underhand ball] must be very straight so as to ensure a L.B.W., and provided it pitches half-way – for "ramrods" are *not* cricket proper – the more irregular the pitch the better' (*Baily's Magazine*, February 1880, 93) – OED.

read to *read* a bowler means to know, or have a good idea, of what is coming at you. Bowling can be read out of the hand (from the action of wrist and finger), in the air by spotting the rotation, though even in the light of the Caribbean it is difficult, or off the pitch. 'The Western Province guys are learning to read him ... The batsman can't take liberties if he's not sure what the next ball is going to do' (Jacques Kallis, *South African Cricket Action*, 18 January 1996).

rebel *rebel tours* are those organised privately, not under the aegis of governing bodies of the game from which the players come. Examples are the West Indies tour to South Africa in 1983, and that captained by M.W. Gatting of Middlesex and England in 1992, also to South Africa.

Red Stripe Cup the *first-class* West Indian inter-island trophy.

red-mist shot is how Richie Benaud (BBC TV) described Carl Hooper's lofted, footless shot to the hands of mid-off in the Second Test at Lord's, on Sunday 25 June 1995.

referee an arbitrator between two parties, introduced in 1991. ICC referees uphold the Code of Conduct, which states that Captains are responsible for ensuring that play is conducted within the spirit of the game as well as within the Laws. Other heads of the Code cover conduct unbecoming, dissent, intimidation of the umpire, *sledging*, offensive gestures, drugs, comment on any hearing, and comment detrimental to the game in general. A referee may decide the winner of a tie, on wickets lost, and if a game is cut short for any reason such as rain, the number of overs to be bowled. Referees are entitled to fine players up to 75 per cent of their match fee for poor conduct.

replacement ball   when a ball has been damaged in the course of play – for whatever reason – it may be replaced by one of similar wear. It has been suggested that if tampering has gone on, the replacement ball shall be in worse condition.

result   how the game ends – a win for one side or the other, or a draw or tie: *no result.*

result wicket   a wicket which, usually as the result of preparation but sometimes by weather, ensures the match is not drawn.

retired, retired hurt   if a batsman *retires* of his own free will, he may not come back, and his innings is complete for the purpose of averages; the batsman may not resume later. This is not the case with *retired hurt*, where the batsman may resume and is regarded as not out. Also with a slightly archaic sense of retiring the batsman by getting him out, as in William Clarke's *Practical Cricket Hints* (1851): 'Perhaps . . . you will have caused him to retire [by driving him onto his wicket].' Some players are noted as 'retired dead', e.g the Revd Tom Killick.

return   'Tom Taylor . . . had such a rapid return, (for no sooner was it in his hand, than with the quickness of thought it was returned to the top of the wicket)' (Nyren in Lucas, 54).

return catch   as in *c&b.*

return crease   the bowling crease has two lines extending backwards from it, and the bowler has to land his feet inside these marks, which are 8'8" apart. This stops him bowling from too great an angle.

reverse pull   as the *pull shot*, but the bat is crossed over so that the batsman hits to his off side with a type of leg side shot: accurately described by John Thicknesse: 'He [Gough] also produced the day's most audacious shot, a reverse pull off Robertson that any left-hander would have relished as it sped to the third man boundary' (*Evening Standard*, 21 January 1995). Also termed *reverse slog.*

reverse sweep   a sweep shot in which the bat is brought through in the opposite arc to normal, so the ball is swept to the third man area rather than long leg: most famously causing the downfall of Mike Gatting and Ian Botham.

reverse swing   see *swing.*

rib-roaster   from pugilism: 'Newhall's bowling rose dangerously high, and it was difficult to avoid his rib-roasters' (Fitzgerald, 256), *rib-tickler* is synonymous.

rick   to make the ball turn. Archaic, Hampshire dialect.

rifle   to hit the ball as a shot from a rifle: 'Hussein rifles away to first slip' (Christopher Martin-Jenkins, Test Match Special, First Test, June 1996).

rill   a delicate late cut, played very close to the stumps (Barnes, 74 fn.).

ring   in some limited-over or one-day matches a certain number of fielders, usually six, sometimes fewer, must be within a circle, often forty yards from the crease, the aim being to stop defensive field placings with all the fielders on the boundary: 'in order to make full use of the fielding restrictions which allow only two fielders outside the inner ring during the first 50 overs . . . Hudson and Snell opened with a real flourish' (Mark Nicolas, *Daily Telegraph*, 12 January 1996).

rip   Sri Lanka had four wickets in hand and needed 36 from 15 overs. The ball was tossed to Shane Warne whose (bowling) average was then 338. 'Hearing Greg Matthews's plea to "spin it hard", Warne took 3/0 in 13 balls . . . He won it giving it a *rip* and tossing it up, said Matthews later' (*The Advertiser*, Adelaide, 25 January 1995). Ripping the fingers across the ball makes it spin hard.

Robins effect   a rotating ball will tend to drift away from its direction of spin: in other words, a leg spinner with top-spin on it, particularly one who spins the ball savagely, will drift towards the leg side from the off before bouncing. The effect is said to occur because the rotation of the ball means that one side, in this case the side of the ball on the leg side of the seam, which is angled at about 45 degrees to a line drawn between the wickets, is moving through the air faster (the speed of the ball through the air plus the forward component of the spin), while the other is moving slower (the speed of the ball minus the backward component of the spin). Bernoulli's theorem states that the higher the speed of a liquid the less pressure it exerts, so the pressure is lower in this case on the leg side of the ball, and it curves to leg. The effect may be enhanced by having the smoother side of the ball on the off side, so that the boundary layer breaks away sooner than on the leg side, increasing the pressure on the offside of the ball, although no wind-tunnel tests to demonstrate this appear to have been done yet, maybe because of the complexity in the movement of the ball. The *Robins effect* is usually referred to as the *Magnus effect*, but Dr Brian Wilkins at Victoria University of Wellington, New Zealand, points out that the first research was done in England by Benjamin Robins, whose *New Principles of Gunnery* of 1742 dealt with the mysterious fact that musket balls swung off

course for no apparent reason. He thought this might be
because the balls spun, although they came from an unrifled
barrel. So he bent the barrels slightly, increasing the pressure
on one side of the ball, which made the balls spin, and found
they swerved left if the barrel was bent right, and vice versa.
Isaac Newton in 1672 had already noted how the flight of a
tennis ball was affected by spin, but Robins was a hundred
years before Herr Magnus, who 'has no real claim to association
with ball games, since he failed in his test with spheres and
obtained his results from rotating cylinders. Robins will be
accorded his due honour throughout this book,' says Dr Wilkins
in *The Bowler's Art*. But it is important, even at this stage, to
distinguish clearly between *swing* (which comes from seam and
differential pressures), and the two terms, *swerve* and *spin-
swerve*, which are synonymous here, and are used to indicate
movement through the air caused by rotation.

rollers   heavy or light, are used to smooth out the pitch, and
can be used at the request of the captain of the batting side, for
no more than seven minutes before the start of each innings,
other than the first innings of the match, and before the start of
each day's play. 'The friends of Surrey hoped to see Hobbs and
Hayward hit while the wicket still felt the results of the heavy
roller . . .' (*Daily Telegraph*, 23 August 1911). On the last day
of the Headingley Test in 1948, England's captain N.W.D.
Yardley batted for two overs only: but this gave him the use of
the roller before sending Australia in to try to make just over
400 to win. He may have hoped for later effects, such as the
dry pitch breaking up more easily, but the Australians got the
runs, the success of Compton's chinamen and googlies under-
lining the absence of the brisk world-class wrist-spinner Doug
Wright of Kent. Sometimes the heavy roller would break up a
damp pitch, thus defeating its own object. John Wisden (see
under the *Little Wonder*), voyaging to America, where he took
six in six, surveyed the heaving Atlantic, and said 'What this
pitch needs is ten minutes of the heavy roller!' This was in
1859, on the first true tour abroad.

rough   the patch of roughened pitch, made by the bowler
running through after he has delivered the ball. This can make
problems for the batsman, particularly if left-handed, if the
marks are on a line and length where a bowler from the other
end, especially turning from leg to off, may pitch a good ball.
'Now that he [Richard Illingworth] has dispensed with the
wretched stock policy of bowling over the wicket and into the
rough, he has begun to discover himself as a considerable

cricketer' (Mark Nicholas, *Daily Telegraph*, 15 December 1995).

roundarm   a bowling action in which the arm is brought in from the side; the halfway mark between underarm and the full overarm of today. It is said that John Willes's sister Christina had to raise her arm because of her voluminous skirts while giving him a little batting practice. Willes, seeing the difficulty this *action* caused him, practised it himself. This led to the report in the *Morning Post* of 1807 that 'The straight-arm bowling, introduced by John Willes Esq., was generally practised in this game, and proved a great obstacle against getting runs in comparison to what might have been got by straightforward bowling.' Trying it in a match for Kent v. MCC in 1822, Willes was no-balled by Noah Mann. He is said to have thrown down the ball in disgust, and galloped away. Willes was the first bowler known by Nyren to have revived the 'throwing' style (probably meaning round-arm), after a council of the Hambledon Club had esteemed it foul play. Mr Knight of Alton was also supposed to have come to the same discovery at about this time, and also by playing against his two sisters 'in wintery weather, in a barn' (*American Cricketer*, 24 January 1878).

The story about Christina gains some much-needed credence because the bustle was fashionable both before 1807 and after the svelte draperies of Empire style. It was a sausage-shaped appurtenance under the skirt and tied at the front, so the dress flared from the waist. An attempt to ban round-arm had failed in 1816: Tom Walker of Hambledon had already been warned in the 1780s for bowling in this style. Round-arm was legalised in 1835. But it seems to have been in wide use shortly before. Miss Mary Russell Mitford wrote, in 1830, *Our Village*, which includes the famous account of the village cricket match, but also, at about this time, she produced *Lost and Won*, in which Paul Holton makes two ducks, drops three sitters, and is dismissed from the presence of Lettie. He disappears for three years, until Lettie's father announces that her village will have the services of a player 'who practices the new Sussex bowling', which he does to good effect: 'My dear Lettie!' . . . he becomes the first real victim of roundarm.

Extraordinary figures were realised by Alfred Shaw, who took round-arm up early, and bowled 24,700 (four-ball) overs conceding only 24,107 runs for 2,051 wickets – an average of under a run an over and 11.75 a wicket.

round the corner   for a bowler to come from an acute angle to the wicket, often left-handers appearing from behind the umpire. For a batsman, a glide, nurdle, nudge, a tuck away, a tickle *round the corner*.

round the wicket   to bowl with the wicket on the other side of the body to the bowling arm. The opposite to *over the wicket*, bowling round gives a different angle to the ball, and thus the turn or swing. It also does not travel in a wicket-to-wicket line, so can make lbw decisions more difficult to obtain. 'Outside the Wicket. When the bowler delivers the ball with the wicket at his left side' (Selkirk, 32).

rubber   generally a Test series, but can be any other. 'A more attacking disposition on England's' part ... and the rubber might have been popped safely in the bag' (E.W. Swanton, *Report*, 12). Probably from OG and Du., *robber*, applying to bowls, perhaps, related to the meaning of an obstacle in that pastime, as in 'rub of the green'. First mention seems to be in 1895, when Pentelow reports 'Shaw's team thus winning the rubber in fine style' (*England v. Australia*, 76). Also the *grip* of the bat (not USA or Canada).

run   a *run* is scored by the batsmen exchanging ends or being awarded runs through the ball being hit to the boundary, or a wide or no-ball being bowled, or by a fielder fielding the ball with his hat or cap; see *fiver*.

run the ball away   of pace bowlers, to move from leg to off either by swing and its continuation of direction after pitching, or off the seam. Fingleton tells of Maurice Tate's methods: 'He rolled his two fingers over the ball towards the batsman ... so that the ball was delivered with what we might call a leg-break roll ... I think Jackson, of Derbyshire, was the only one we met, apart from Bedser, who ran the ball away. Tate's methods might repay study' (*Don*, 53).

run in   to *run in* the bat means to slide it in front of the batsman along the ground to avoid being *run out*. The original meaning was to run out to the pitch of the ball; the sense has inverted. See also *charge, chassé*.

run-getter   phrase with same meaning as in 1855 when *Lilly-white's Guide to Cricketers* says, 'a pretty sure run-getter' (p. 99): a batsman who usually makes runs.

runner[1]   to be a good *runner* between the wickets means to turn to profit all the available runs, quick singles, turning those into twos, twos into threes, etc.

runner[2]   the substitute allowed for an injured batsman. The Law is complex. Haygarth records the aptly-named Rumball, 'who had a man to run for him, hit a leg ball hard, which struck the man who was running for him in the small of the back, and he was caught by the wicket-keeper!' (I, xxi).

running   *running* between the wickets to score runs can cause much chaos, John Boots being 'killed at Newick by running against another man in crossing the wicket' (*Sussex Notes and Queries*, Padwick 891). See *steal, catch*. In *Playing for England*, Jack Hobbs tells of two runners 'who tried to make their signals very secret indeed. Their plan was : "When I say No, you run; when I say Yes, don't." And they always succeeded in running themselves out.' Whether a panic call of 'Get back!' resulted in a headlong rush for the far crease is not recorded. See also *call*.

running ground   the accident to poor Boots above may have been caused by the Law 4 of 1744 and 1755, which finishes: 'When the ball is hit up either of the Strikers may hinder the catch in his running Ground', which seems to mean the pitch.

run out   Law 38: 'if a bail or bails have been dislodged, a run-out may be effected by pulling up a stump with the ball in the same hand' (see *appeal*).

Denis Compton's call for a run has been likened to a first call at bridge, and the sequence of events as 'Yes! No! Wait! Damn!' If only one could have seen him at work with that 'study for Phidias', the 'glorious and unrivalled Silver Billy' Beldham, who played from 1787 to 1821, 'never could keep his bat, his eyes, or his legs still, and he was generally run out . . .' (Nyren, in Lucas, 128).

Hubert Doggart OBE, President of the Cricket Society, puts a word in from Sir Leonard Hutton in the Society's *Journal*, referring to the Delphic style of some of his utterances: 'Procrastination, that's the secret of many a run-out in Test Matches.'

run rate, required rate, runs per over (r.p.o)   the number of runs that have to be scored in each over to achieve a result, by the side batting last.

run-saving field   to stop the batsman scoring fast, usually with *outfielders*.

run through   either to continue running past the crease with the impetus of the speed when runs are taken quickly, or see *go through*.

run-up   the approach to the wicket of a bowler who intends to deliver a ball. *Run-ups* are highly individual matters: the acceleration and balance of Larwood was that of a top sprinter; Sarfraz Nawaz of Pakistan was described by John Arlott as akin to Groucho Marx pursuing a pretty waitress. Bill O'Reilly's run was that of an inventor who had just had the idea for an autogiro, or perhaps thought he was one. More recently, Mervyn Hughes of Australia might resemble a Sergeant-Major of Pomeranian Grenadiers running towards the English trenches, pausing for a few tripping steps over the barbed wire, and then on to hurl his fizzing bomb at the foe. While in India, Alf Gover's run took him into the pavilion, to the later sound of primitive plumbing. His ordinary run-up was described 'rather as if he were exchanging insults at extreme range with the flighty conductor of an omnibus that had the legs of him by half a mile per hour' (Robertson-Glasgow, 105).

run up!   exhortation to batsman or -men to run faster between the wickets. See also *tich*.

rush   to *rush* the bowling, or 'give it the rush', *c*. 1780: to run or jump down the pitch to the high, underarm lobs that were then being used, to hit them on the half-volley. Still in use.

Rutherford   'It was the summer that the lazy cut to second slip became known as "the Rutherford" after the man who replaced Crowe as captain' (Hamish McDonall, *Evening Standard*, 28 April 1994, writing about the New Zealand tourists).

S **alix**   L. for 'willow', the adjective being *salicaceous*.

andshoe ball, sandshoe crusher 'He'll use the searing yorker, the sandshoe ball,' said Richie Benaud (BBC TV) at the Fifth Test at Trent Bridge, 1995.

save   either of a fielder, stationed to *save* runs, or to *save the follow-on*, so the other side have to bat again.

scalper   bouncer. This usage refers specifically to Ray Lindwall nearly doing just that to Denis Compton in 1948, in the Third Test, when he made 145* despite being gashed by Lindwall : 'The England players ... accepted that the scalper was a legitimate weapon and longed for the day when some English fast bowler would come along to redress the balance' (Barker).

scarify   the pitch is sometimes very closely mown to get a better surface, remove the top spine of the grass, and rid it of the watergrass. The *scarifier* is a small vehicle which does this. A scarificator is also a surgical instrument fitted with a series of small retractable blades for making multiple simultaneous incisions in the skin. The derivation leads right back to the Greek, through the verb 'to scratch an outline', to *skariphos*, a stilus or pencil (OED).

scone   *to be sconed* is to be struck by a rising ball, or scalped, as Allan Border explains in his autobiography: 'Dennis sconed me with a bouncer ... it was my fault really. I ducked into the ball' (p.102). When after an attempted hook he returned to the dressing room, he found his cap was full of blood. See also *crusted*.

score   runs made by team or individual. Originally synonymous with *notch* and *tally*, and the number 20. This shows the idea of cutting: 'Awakened Eccho speaks the innings o'er,/ And forty notches deep indent the Score' – J. Love (J. Dance), *Cricket – An Heroick Poem* (1744), iii.60.

scoreboard   the first 'telegraph' *scoreboard* came into Lord's in 1846. Today, the amount of information on them needs more than a quick glance to take in.

scorebook   the standard *scorebook* has been unchanged for many years, but the 'Fergie' method is used by broadcasters today. The page is divided into columns vertically, one for each batsman and for the bowling ends. This allows the action to be more closely analysed; it can be seen, for example, which batsman faced which ball.

scorecard   next to the *plick-plock* of reed on leather, the raucous crowcry of 'Scorecard! Scorecard!' or 'Card of the match!', implying amazing and disastrous events, springs to memory from days at Lord's. Fred Lillywhite was the first to bring scorecards to the crowds at Lord's, with his portable printing press of 1848. Thomas Pratt of Sevenoaks, however, sold his decorated scorecards (the surround is called the Pratt Box) of the Gentlemen Cricketers engaged in matches on the Vine at Sevenoaks, in 1776.

scorer   not unnaturally, the man who keeps the score. From *notch* the habit of cutting a stick will be remembered, and *scoring* it has the same meaning. Roman numerals, of course, are easy to cut into material. On tours, the scorers occasionally doubled as baggage masters. In 18th-century prints they appear to sit in front of square leg and just before him. Also the Almighty:

> And when the last Great Scorer comes,
> To write against your name,
> He'll ask not if you won or lost
> But how you played the game. – Grantland Rice.

scout   old term for fielder and fielding. Lewis also has it as 'a boy employed on a cricket ground to pick up and return the balls to the bowlers during practice.' But the word was used by Neville Cardus in 1924: 'great gaps between the leg-side scouts' (*Days*, 49).

scratch   Altham says from the same basic root as 'crease', and it may go back to OG *kratz*. It was used as late as 1767 in one of the Hambledon songs: 'Stand firm to your Scratch, let your bat be upright!' *Scratch forward* or *scratch around* means to bat uncertainly, runlessly.   ·

screw   19th-century term for *spin*.

scuttle   *to be scuttled* is to be removed by a ball which keeps low, scuttles along the ground, by transference from the sinking of a ship by opening the scuttles or hatchways. From OF *escoutille*, hatchway.

scythe   Mike Gatting, a notable player of slow bowling, 'would step down the pitch first ball and plant Derek Underwood into the pavilion, or step back and scythe him past cover' (Simon Hughes, *Sunday Telegraph*, 23 October 1994). But it is more often understood as a leg-side hit. See *Stogumber mow*.

seam   that part of the ball where the two halves join. The ball can *seam away* from the batsman or *seam into him*. Pedantically it should refer only to the stitching which is, after all the part which makes the ball move *off the seam*. For obvious reasons, *seamers* are not called stitchers. International bowlers can *hit the seam*, so the ball moves either way after bouncing, fairly often: 'The outstanding bowler in the match, Ambrose was the only one to land the ball on the seam with regularity' – Richard Hutton (*The Cricketer*, October 1995) reporting the Sixth Test at the Oval, where Ambrose's figures were 5–96 and 2–35.

seamer   a bowler who tries to use the seam to make the ball move off the ground or in the air.

seam-up   the ball is held with the seam vertical to achieve the results above. Most common type of bowling.

seamy, seaming   wicket which helps bowlers who rely on movement off the seam.

season   the time of year in which the game is played: mid-April to the end of September in England, November to March in Australia.

second class   Minor Counties, which includes the second XIs of major counties.

second stop   obsolete term for *long-stop*, first seen in Lewis as 1773, and last recorded mention of inferior men letting *byes* through being in Denison's *Cricketer's Companion* of 1847 (p.xv).

seek out, seekers-out   18th century on: to field, the fielders. 'A game may be won by a very bad batsman, owing to the inability of the wicket-man, or the inattention of the seekers-out' – M. Angelo, *Juvenile Sports* (1776).

sell a match   a not-infrequent practice when large amounts were wagered on the outcome: 'Silver Billy' Beldham, one of the great players of the late 18th–early 19th centuries, known for his sense of fair play, says: 'just under the pavilion sat men ready, with money down, to give and take the current odds: these were by far the best men to bet with; because, if they lost, it was all in the way of business; they paid their money and they did not grumble. Still, they had all kinds of tricks to make their betting safe.' They would, for example, said William Ward, who bought Lord's from Thomas Lord, 'keep a player out of the way by a false report that his wife was dead. Then these men would come down to the Green Man and Still, and drink with me, and always said, that those who backed us, or "the snobs", as they called them, sold the matches ... but don't believe it. That any gentleman in my day ever put himself into the power of these blacklegs, by selling matches, I can't credit.' And he relates that he was once playing with a member of the nobility who told him he had bet against himself, but he and Silver Billy put on the runs 'though every run seemed to me like a guinea out of his Lordship's pocket'. But E.H. Budd found differently: 'In 1817, we went with [squire] Osbaldeston to play twenty-two of Nottingham ... In common with others

I lost my money, and was greatly disappointed at the termination. One paid player was accused of selling, and never employed after' (Lucas, 227). *The Covent Garden Magazine* in 1774 noted, 'if one of these gentry should be appointed marker, he will favour the side that he wishes to win, and diminish or increase the notches as suits his advantage.' Marker is an obsolete term for *scorer*.

The OED entry under *snob* gives 'blackleg' as one of its possible synonyms, and turning to that, one finds 'a turf swindler, a sharper generally', referenced to 1771, about the right time. Ward's words can be interpreted with both meanings, but it seems most likely that 'those who backed us' refers to the opposing team or members thereof, who would find it easier to back themselves to lose than win.

semibreve   the standard unit of measurement in music, and written as a zero on its side, thus an archaic term for a *duck*. From the Latin *brevis*, short, brief. The word is culled by Lewis from *Surrey Cricket* of 1902 by Lord Alverstone and C.W. Alcock: 'It took Lillywhite forty minutes to make his "semibreve".' The pun is obvious.

semi-circle   area delineated on the ground in some *one-dayers* within which a certain number of fielders must be stationed. See *over the top*.

send back   a batsman *sends back* his partner, refusing a run, the shout of 'No!' having priority over all others. Also a bowler *sends back* a bat by dismissing him.

session   one of the periods of a day's play – morning, afternoon or evening.

set¹   when a batsman has been in for some time and looks confident, he is said to be *set*, not implying immobility. In use from 1865, when *F. Lillywhite's Guide to Cricketers* (126) has 'Splendid hitter all round, and very dangerous if once set.'

set²   a team is *set* a total to win. This seems to have started with a obsolete expression: 'The innings closed ... for 218 runs, leaving Oxford a "set" of 212' (*The Times*, 4 July 1870).

set out his stall   Jack Bailey of *The Times* describes Malcolm Maynard of Glamorgan and England having a look at the pitch, playing a few shots, getting *set:* 'Maynard's first century of the season was a sharp reminder of how good a player he can be. He set out his stall more carefully than he sometimes does, taking 82 balls to reach his half-century' (10 June 1995). Or as Keating puts it in *Gents and Players* (145), 'Revd J.H. Aitchison, who set out his stall at the wicket like a Presbyterian Boycott ...'

shamateur   one who plays for no direct financial reward but is nevertheless in fee of emolument – often not inconsiderable. It is sometimes thought that W.G. Grace was the first *shamateur* as he had his *locum tenens* paid for by Gloucestershire when he played for them and as an amateur he was allowed expenses. This seems a mite harsh, although he did take fees before qualifying as a doctor. And after, he followed the practice of the time by treating many poor patients free. So although he took fees earlier, and then when playing for U.S.E. XI (United South of England Eleven, written in those prudish times as U.S.E.E.), it's difficult to classify him as an outright shamateur, although his fees were high: £50 for Gentlemen v. Players, for example, about £2000 today. But then, the gate money could go from sixpence to a shilling if he played. On the 1891–2 tour to Australia, he had £3000 expenses, say £120,000 today, paid locums, and free passage for his wife and children. MCC had bought him the practice with a **testimonial** fund. Of course, one does not know how wide the definition of 'expenses' was, nor whether he returned in pocket.

His brother G.F. was barred from playing for the Gentlemen v. the Players on the grounds that 'no gentleman should make any profit from playing cricket.'

shape   to get into position to play a shot. 'To shape at a ball'.

sharp   the obsolete form of *fine*: 'In very fast [bowling] the point is placed behind the wicket . . . and the slips set sharp' (Box, *English Game*, 460). Now a bowler is said to be *sharp* or *nippy*.

Sheffield Shield   the *first-class* domestic championship of Australia, founded by Lord Sheffield, who brought out the 12th English team in 1892–3, and left £150 to the Australian Cricket Council.

Shell Trophy and Cup   the New Zealand *first-class* trophies, succeeding the Plunket Shield, first presented in 1906 by Lord Plunket, the Governor-General.

shin-bone, ox   scraping with this was an alternative method of *knocking-in* a cricket bat (Bradman, 100). In years gone by, the bat was hardened after drying and pressing by an application of powdered bone.

shine   'West Indies got off to a terrible start when Manoj Prabhakar, who was taking the shine off the ball before the intoduction of the spinners, dismissed Phil Simmons and Brian Lara in the first over of the innings' (*The Times*, 22 November 1994).

shirtfront   a bland, flat and innocuous playing surface.

shock bowler   a bowler fast enough and aggressive enough to shock the batsman. 'Hogg, our only "shock" bowler was in bed with a chest complaint, so our opening attack was Porter and Dymock' (Border, 94). See also *gun bowler*.

shoot/er   a ball bowled which on hitting the ground. does not rise but skids along it (see also *mulligrubber*). 'Harris always chose a ground where his ball would *rise*. Lumpy endeavoured to gain the advantage of a declivity where the ball would *shoot*' (Revd John Mitford, *Gentleman's Magazine*, 1833). See *mamba*. To *shoot out* a side is to bowl them out quickly.

short   a fielding position closer than normal: thus *short extra* is in the same line from the batsman but nearer to him; see below, and *silly*. A *short ball* is one short of a length.

short leg   a fielding position, close to the batsman on the leg side; can be in front of or behind the bat. 'Atherton's very aware of his two short legs hovering' (Trevor Bailey, Test Match Special, 7 April 1994).

short-pitched   a ball which is short of a length. This has a special meaning associated with intimidation, Law 42 starting with the sentence: 'the bowling of fast short-pitched balls is unfair if, in the opinion of the umpire at the bowler's end, it constitutes an attempt to intimidate the striker.'

short run   has two meanings, firstly a successfully completed run where time is short, and also *one short*, meaning one run, or the run, has not been completed. 'Beldham was one of the best judges of a short run I ever knew,' said Nyren, which contrasts oddly with his remark under *run out*.

short stop   another name for *short-slip*, last used in *The Australasian* (6 January 1912): 'Hobbs . . . was caught at short-stop by Carter' (Lewis).

shot   the action performed by the batsman in hitting the ball. The original root was OG or OE *sk-*, *sc-* , which may explain 'scooter'.

shoulder   of the bat. Also to *shoulder arms*, when the bat is placed as in rifle drill on the shoulder and no shot attempted. But the ball can then *come back* and hit the stumps: 'last weekend's heroes, Greenfield and Moores, perished tamely, shouldering arms and flashing respectively' (Nick Stewart, *Sunday Times*, 28 May 1995).

shout   a loud appeal, 'That's a good shout' – Ray Illingworth commentating in the Headingley Test 1993 as Gooch padded up to Warne, implying that it was a close decision (BBC TV).

shuffle, shuffle across   of the batsman, moving from leg to off as the ball comes to him: 'He couldn't play cricket . . . he would shuffle and poke' is how Mrs Ramsay thinks of her unsatisfactory guest Charles Tansley (Virginia Woolf, *To the Lighthouse*, 1928). Notable shufflers have been Javed Miandad of Pakistan, and, especially in Australia in 1994–5, Graham Gooch. The word also occurs in Nyren in another sense, when he stigmatises Yalden (see *catch*) as a despoiler of Arcadia: 'His word was not always to be depended on when he had another man out – he would now and again shuffle, and resort to trick' (in Lucas, 61).

shutters to put them up is to play defensively, to shut the bowler out, maybe with the end of the day's play in mind.

side cricket is played between two *sides*, or teams, of eleven players each, unless otherwise stated. Law 1 of 1744 says that the winner of the toss may 'order which side shall go in first'. *To let the side down* is to fail in performance or behaviour in such a way that one's team is disadvantaged. This has passed into the language so that 'side' can mean any grouping: house at school, race, class, nation. Cf. *not cricket*.

side-on cricket is a *side-on* game, both in bowling and batting. 'He lost the side-on action and, therefore, the outswing' (Imran Khan on Botham, *Sunday Times*, 9 October 1994).

sight the ball to see the ball, or to get used to the particular conditions of play.

sightboard *sight-screen*, archaic.

sighter a delivery used to get one's sight in. Thus a batsman in his benefit might have an easy ball to 'get off the mark', or might *leave* a ball outside the stumps.

sight-screen a screen erected behind the bowler's arm so that the ball may be seen early and clear. May be slatted or solid, and was always white. Compton favoured, however, a duck-egg blue screen, and experiments seemed to show that at least an off-white made for better visibility. A black screen is used in day-night games with a white ball.

The development is given in Thomas Moult's *Bat and Ball*:
In the early nineteenth century a sightscreen was often used; but it was a strip of white canvas stretched on poles five feet high, and this, while it keeps the stupid spectators from standing in the eye of the ball, provides a white background for each wicket. This is good also in a Park, where the deep shade of trees increases the confessed uncertainty of the game. Some such plan is much wanted on all public grounds, where the sixpenny freeholders stand and hug their portly corporations, and, by standing in the line of the wicket, give

the ball all the shades of green coat, light waistcoat, and drab smalls.

silly   a fielding position very close to the bat. The two entries below are the most common, but it can be applied to any place, except for slip and gully. *Silly* started off, and still survives in the North and Scotland, as 'sely, seely', deserving of pity, 'poor'. By 1500 it had come to mean helpless, defenceless, and when Shakespeare wrote *Timon of Athens* it had its present meaning of 'ridiculous'.

silly mid-off   mid-off, but brought close to the bat: Keating tells the famous story of Brian Close being brought in to captain England for the last Test in 1966 and asked how to contain a rampaging Sobers: "Sure, I'll stand at silly silly mid-off and catch him first ball off Snow, you see." Sobers c Close b Snow 0.

silly mid-on   is one of the few places in the field we know to have been effectively created by one man, Spofforth's bowling partner Boyle, who stood only six or seven yards from the bat. 'It was practically never seen in England until the Australians introduced it in 1878,' says R.H. Lyttelton in the Badminton Library's *Cricket* of 1888. The Australians toured England in 1878 but didn't play any Tests. And the great all-rounder George Giffen wrote in *With Bat and Ball* (1898) that 'Boyle . . . created a new position, "short mid-on" or "silly mid-on" as it is colloquially known, a place where few men have the pluck to stand these days when the wickets are so true.' *Silly point, short leg* (sometimes just *silly leg*), *silly mid-off* or *on, cover* (but *short extra-cover*), *silly midwicket* can be used.

single   one run.

single wicket   now almost extinct; described by Nyren at the end of *Young Cricketer's Tutor:*

The parties . . . vary in number . . . from one to six a side. The distance between the wickets is twenty-two yards. At the bowler's wicket, two stumps are placed with a bail upon them; and this the striker, when running, must come to, and strike off, and return to his own wicket. This is counted one run. If the bail should be off, the batter must strike the stump out of the ground. When the party consists of fewer than four on each side, if the striker leave his ground to hit the ball, he will not be permitted to reckon a notch . . . When the parties consist of fewer than five on each side, the custom of the game is, to make bounds on either side of the wicket; which bounds are to be laid down parallel with it, as well as with each other: they must likewise extend twenty-two yards from the wicket. The man who is in, must strike the ball before these limits, or boundary lines; and it must be returned in the same direction by those who are seeking out ... the ball is dead when once it has been behind the wicket ... Single Wicket with more than four on each side is subject to the same rules as when the game at double wicket, with the full complement of men, is played.

The old game could be flexible: an innkeeper, Silas Quarterman, once bet himself and his dog against a one-armed man and his ten-year-old son. It was noticed that the dog took double the time to field, as he had to return the ball by mouth. 'Bets were doubled on the one-armed man's favour, and he won the battle' (*Cricketer's Note Book*, by 'an Old Cricketer').

sit   to *sit* upon the splice: to block, stonewall, score slowly. A delivery may also *sit up*, meaning to *pop*, but generally of slower bowling. To *sit upon the handle* means to fail to back up.

sitter   'Among recent neologisms of the cricket field is "sitter". A "sitter" is a catch which falls absolutely into the hands and cannot, except by a genius for such things, be "buttered"' (*Tit-Bits*, 25 June 1898).

six   for some time, the ball had to be hit out of the ground for a *six* to be scored. Now it is a shot which clears the boundary without bouncing. Jim Smith of Middlesex once hit nine in a row, in a second-class match in 1935.

skid   the ball *skids* low off the pitch.

skimmer   has two uses, the first seeming only for underhand bowling as when the old professional William Clarke says in *Practical Hints on Cricket*, (1851) that a *skimming* bowler is 'seldom any use on level or soft grounds'. Today a skimming hit or throw travels low, level, and fast.

skittle   usually of a side, to be *shot out*.

slant   see *angle*.

sledging   the oaf's parlette: the verbal harassment and insult of a batsman by the bowler, wicket-keeper or fielders. Would be more unsettling but for the pitiful level of repartee. 'It might be more acceptable if it was more witty, but most of it is very basic stuff' (Gower, 31). No instance of wit in *sledging* has yet been recorded: the zenith is that once in the West Indies Alec Stewart, while batting, was apparently apprised of the fact that but for his father he would not be there.

The word arose, according to Ian Chappell in *The Cutting Edge* (154), when Grahame Corling of NSW and Australia described a party's failure as 'It's all f ... up,' in front of a waitress. He was told he was as subtle as a sledgehammer. Percy Sledge, a singer, had just had a big hit. Corling was nicknamed

'Percy', and the term 'sledging' or 'a sledge' was originally anybody who made a faux pas in front of a woman.

slice   to hit the ball either with an angled bat or with a thick edge. 'Watched by his parents on their wedding anniversary Smith sliced his first ball from Donald over the slips . . .' (C. Martin-Jenkins, *Daily Telegraph*, 16 December 1995).

slinger   a fast or medium bowler who delivers with a round-arm action. Notable was Bill Edrich, reputedly as fast as anyone in England for a few years – and a few overs – just after 1945.

slip   the fielder(s) in an off-side arc by the wicket keeper; first slip is the *finest*. Also used as a verb, and as a shot, in America: 'Marsh . . . slipped a ball into Gibbons's hands' and 'Moeran's contribution being . . . marked by three 3s – drives and a slip' (*American Cricketer*, 1878). An example of the word lasting over there longer than in England is Pycroft talking of Beldham, who flourished *c*. 1800: 'Nearly every ball was cut or slipped away by Beldham' (*Cricket Field*, 69). First printed mention is 1816, in the 6th edition of Lambert's *Cricketer's Guide*: 'In *backing up*, he [point] should take care to give the man at the slip sufficient room' (p.41). Thus seems to imply first of all a purposeful shot, which would have been very difficult with the old hockey-stick type of bat.

slip-bait   'the ball just short of a length yet compelling a stroke which great body-swing causes to lift steeply before the batsman can withdraw his bat – the true *slip-bait*.' – Arlott of Reg Perks, (*Worcs CCC Yearbook*, 1947).

slipper   term for the surface of a pitch: 'rub a ball over the surface of a pitch, while pressing down fairly hard on it; a simple test which separates the "slippers" from the "grippers"' (Wilkins, 75). See also *gripper*. Also obsolete term for a slip fieldsman, which has made a come-back: Michael Holding reporting for Sky TV on the Antigua Test in 1994 as Lara made his 375: 'it's the good slippers who are dropping the catches,' as Hick *grassed* Arthurton.

slip-up   neologism by Scyld Berry, failure to take a catch in the slips: 'In Barbados, Hick has appeared to get over his slip-ups, taking three catches' (*Sunday Telegraph*, 17 April 1994).

slobber   etymologically related to 'slabber', 'slaver', cf. *lob*. Obsolete for not fielding the ball cleanly. Last reference appears to be 1867, when in Selkirk's *Guide to the Cricket Ground* the advice is 'Run for the least slobbering.' (p.122). N.B. This has been replaced by 'never run on a misfield.' But it may have started as in part deliberate: 'Try also, "slobbering" a ball, to see how many arts of recovering it there are afterwards' (Pycroft, *Cricket Field*, 187), so see also *fox*.

slog   usually as a verb, to hit the ball hard and inelegantly, but also the hard hitting batsman who plays incorrect strokes, tries to hit good balls over the ropes, and so on. 'Pakistan were always ahead on run-rate, but without Wasim [Akram] coming in at No 6 they could not rely on the slog overs to achieve the target' (Emma Levine reporting the World Cup from Bangalore, 10 March 1996, *Sunday Times*).

slot   the ball is in the *slot* when it is there to be hit, as for example a *full toss*.

slow   of a pitch, without devil or pace off, but *slows* are the deliveries of a slow bowler.

smear   'Hegg ... persistently stepped away to leg to smear the ball through the offside' (Alan Lee, *The Times*, 14 August 1996). An inelegant shot as the bat seems to *smear* itself across the ball.

smell the ball   'Moxon batted here much as Geoffrey Boycott, his one-time opening partner would have done ... he "smelt" the ball' (Ivo Tennant, *The Times*, 15 June 1996), i.e. he got his head right over it.

smell the leather   'if Craig McDermott sees that big front foot [of Angus Fraser] coming down the pitch, he might just invite him to smell the leather' (Bob Willis on Sky TV, 31 December 1994), i.e. *bounce* him.

smother   to play well forward, handle angled forward as well, so the ball has no time to turn or lift.

snaffle   to make a catch, difficult either because of the speed with which the ball travels or the distance away from the fielder. 'Lamb ... fell to an outstanding catch at second slip by Byas, who did remarkably well to snaffle a forcing shot off Milburn' (Andy Roberts, *Sunday Times*, 28 May 1995). OED has 'to seize, to acquire by means or machinations not strictly lawful, purloin.'

snap, snatch   of a catch, to grab at it. *Snap* is now obsolete except in the sense of a catch which comes so quickly it can only be taken by reflex.

sneak/sneaker   a ball bowled along the ground. See *mulligrub, shooter*.

sneezer   'When in the next Test at Lord's, McDonald bowled [Hendren] for 0 with a "snorter", or what George Giffen once called a "sneezer", some critics murmured long and loudly' (P.F. Warner, *Morning Post*, 11 March 1929; Lewis). See *snorter*.

snick   the ball contacts the edge of the bat and flies in the direction of the slips, wicket-keeper, or even **gully**; Lewis perhaps overdefines *leg snick* as one passing between bat and legs. See also *dog shot, Chinese cut, Surrey cut*, etc. From 1868, the *Nottingham Review*: 'The latter snicked the ball finely in the slips for three.'

snob[1]   the humble journeyman cobbler turned ball-maker, as in ball-snob (see *ball*).

snob[2]   a manipulator of betting (see *sell a match*).

snob[3]   a game of cricket played with a soft ball and a thick stick in lieu of a bat (of obscure origin). Now obsolete. 'There is a sport known at some schools as "stump-cricket", "snob-cricket", or ... "Dex", which is a degenerate shape of the game' (A. Long, 1888: OED). One possible line of etymology for the first and third above is through the Scandinavian, Swedish dialect *snopp*, a boy.

snorter   a delivery with much *anti-batsman behaviour*, possibly derived from proximity to the nostril. Either very fast and with much movement, accurate, implying bounce. See *sneezer*.

soft hands   a batsman is said to have *soft hands* if he lets the ball strike a bat so that it does not rebound off and give a catch; the hands are relaxed rather than loose, and can recoil with the impetus of the ball. Especially when playing forward to spin, to smother it, or back to a rising fast ball. 'Atherton played with soft hands and mostly off the back foot, as he did in Sydney four years ago and Peter Kirsten did so effectively in Adelaide last year' (Peter Roebuck, *Sunday Times*, 23 October 1994).

sostenuto, sosteneuter   as used by Tom Emmett means a ball that pitches on the leg stump and hits the off. The probable derivation is given by Mr W. A. Marshall in *The Times* (13 June 1919), as being the past participle of the Italian *sostenere*, to maintain, sustain, to hold up, with the past participle *sostenuto* having the same sense in music. Quite why this should apply to this ball is unclear; Emmett himself, when challenged, merely answering 'What else would you call it?' But he bowled W. G. with it first ball.

spectacles, pair of   a *duck* in each innings.

Spedegue   deep in the New Forest the slender, bespectacled, and asthmatic young schoolteacher Mr Spedegue stretched a rope between two trees, over fifty feet up, and marked out a pitch directly underneath. He practised bowling the ball over the rope to hit the stumps full toss. By one of those coincidences that rightly belong to fiction, a former England captain, and one who still had the selectors' ear, was passing by and idly watched and then enquired the purpose of the exercise and whether he could have a bat with his walking-stick. The ball, bowled with a leg-spin swerve, and descending with more speed than expected (the stated geometry, and the 32' per sec. per sec. acceleration producing a terminal velocity of some 40 m.p.h., almost vertically onto the wicket), gave him more problems than he expected. So after some trials Mr Spedegue was put in the England team against the marauding Australians, the *Ashes* being in the balance. The unknown rapidly dismissed the Australian captain, and finished with an *analysis* of 7–31. He repeated his triumph in the second inings, and England retained the Ashes. But the strain upon his frail physique was such that he never played again, under doctor's orders. Nevertheless, we owe Sir Arthur Conan Doyle the story, the word, still in use, and the geometry, which he got right. Not to be confused with the *beamer* directed at the batsman's head, which is outlawed. Also known as *Spedegue's dropper*.

The origin of the Spedegue is related by A.A. Thomson in *Odd Men In* (43), when A.P. Lucas, the writer who played for Essex and England, bowled one at Sir Arthur. Trying to slash it past point, he broke his bat knocking two of this stumps over, 'the ball descended mockingly on the remaining stump and knocked it sideways.'

spell   the length of time a bowler bowls for as in 'a *spell* from the Stretford end', but also a meaning almost oxymoronic as when a bowler is *spelled* he is rested, or replaced: this possibly comes from the word which in German means 'to play' – *spielen*.

spike   metal *spikes* in shoes or boots to obtain better grip. 'I spiked my right foot with my left so that both feet were almost locked ... All I could do was to fall forward and as I did so I waved my bat, middled the ball and it went for a four ... that was the kind of luck I had all through the 1947 season' (Compton, *Innings*, 35). Probably introduced around 1800; the screw-in type, of various lengths, are mentioned by Grace in 1888 in the Badminton *Cricket*. See also *sprig*.

spin   the rotation of the ball around any axis. Originally the more common word was *twist*: speaking of Lamborn, 'the Little Farmer', Nyren says that 'not like the generality of right-handed bowlers ... his ball would twist from off to leg.' This would be soon after 1776, when Nyren first, at twelve years of age, came upon the Hambledon scene. He records that all the bowling was fast then, which may have precluded much spinning. *Spin* as a word may be related to the verb 'span', which has an archaic sense of winding up the wheel-lock of a pistol or musket, or screwing tight with a spanner. This would explain 'twist', as referring to the wrist, as the first term used. *Against the spin* or *with the spin:* hitting against the spin is in a sense an erroneous term. This is because when a leg-break lands, its direction of spin is reversed, so the next time it bounces it will turn the other way, which can be easily verified. Thus *sweeping* a leg-spinner is in fact hitting *with* the newly-imparted spin, while the reverse sweep in the same situation is more dangerous than sometimes realised.

spinner a bowler who spins the ball or a ball that spins. It appears to have started with the latter, as in 1895 the *Westminster Gazette* has 'The bowler got an undeniable spinner past the bat . . .' (2 March). Lewis evidently did not find a use for today's usual term, which applies to the bowler who spins. See Boxall and *twist*.

splice the part of the handle that goes down into the bat. Sitting on it means to play defensively.

spoon 'Ward startled everyone by spooning a fluffed pull off Emburey to mid-wicket' (John Sheppard, *The Observer*, 12 June 1994). This simply means he hit it up in the air, the bat finishing as if offering a spoon. See also *sitter*. First mention in Lewis is from Box (1877, p.461): 'In derision, it is called "spoon victuals" especially at Cambridge.' Sometimes it is deliberate: 'his very effective scoop, the high point of his reputation as a batsman . . . In essence, the blade of the bat was placed horizontal on the pitch and lifted briskly as the ball came into line with it, rather as one tosses a pancake' – Singleton describing the 'old England bowler' Tom Mitchell, batting in the 1930s, in a letter to *The Times* (20 August 1975, reprinted Williams, 277).

sporting especially of a declaration, which gives the other side a chance to win. Gary Sobers in the 1968 Trinidad Test gave England 165 minutes to score 215, against the likes of himself, Hall and Lance Gibbs, and England made the runs with three minutes to spare. Sir Garfield was rather unpopular in the West Indies. Also of a pitch.

sprig the studs or spikes in the shoe or boot: 'On Monday, though, we turned up to play and found that the cracks had closed and that if you scratched the surface of the wicket with your sprigs it was moist underneath' (Ian Johnson, Australia's captain, on the supposed watering incident in Melbourne in 1954, *WCM*, October 1994). Same as *spike*.

squad   the nucleus of players from which the team is drawn, or the team itself. Particularly applies to the sixteen or seventeen players selected for overseas tours.

square   either the closer-mown part of the ground in the middle where the wickets are pitched, or as defining direction, at right angles to a line drawn from wicket to wicket. Thus *square leg, square-leg umpire, square cutter* – a batsman who is proficient in making the *square cut* as is Robin Smith of Hampshire and England. Also *square drive,* a drive off either front or back foot which goes squarish of the wicket. 'He struck a square-driven four off the back foot, then performed an involuntary skip of delight' (Alan Lee, *The Times,* 13 April 1994, reporting on Alec Stewart's 2nd century in Barbados v. West Indies match at Bridgetown). A batsman can be *turned square* when he has to play the ball from a square-on rather than a side-on stance, by the movement of the ball in the air or off the pitch.

squat   of a ball, to hit the ground and skid along, *shoot.*

squirt   two meanings: to *squirt* the ball is half deflection, half dab, travelling behind the wicket: see also *nurdle.* A bowler can also *squirt* the ball: 'Gloucester's roly-poly off-spinner, Bomber Wells, kept squirting the thing through the cleric's guard but never hitting the wicket. "Been on your prayer-mat all night, Vicar?" enquired he of the Rev. David Sheppard . . .' (Keating, 144).

stance   the position taken by a batsman when facing bowling. It is usually side-on, but the *two-eyed stance,* as used by Peter Willey of Leicestershire, Durham, and England, has the head and body swivelled to face the bowler. J.D.Carr of Middlesex has taken this to extremes (1994), pointing his feet to mid-wicket. He also lifts his bat with a movement of his wrists alone, keeping his arms almost straight.

stand   when two batsman remain together at the wicket, scoring an amount of runs, they are said to be in a *stand.* At Leeds and the Oval, in 1934, Bradman and Ponsford, who had been dropped in the preceding 'Bodyline' series, were in stands of 388 and 451 respectively. To *break a stand* is to dismiss one of the partners. For first mention see *dead stand.* Also of an umpire, to stand in a match, though whether this applies to the mainly seated third umpire is not clear: 'Smith sat in the first Test' does not sound right.

stand out   obsolete term for fielding, first recorded in the Laws of 1798: 'if a striker is hurt, some person may be allowed to stand out for him, but not go in.'

stand up[1]   of a wicket-keeper, to stand just behind the wicket, which is usual to slow bowling, but: 'at 46 [Rod Marsh] took a fine catch off Graham Gooch's inside edge when standing up at Lilac Hill . . .' (Scyld Berry on the Australian Cricket Academy's director at the start of the 1994–5 tour, *Sunday Telegraph*). In the same way, Godfrey Evans *stood up* to Alec Bedser bowling medium-fast.

stand up²   of a bowler: 'Tufnell . . . is not at his best . . . he did not stand up in the crease and get his arm up high' (Scyld Berry, *Daily Telegraph*, 16 November 1994).

steal   to take a quick run, or runs.

> And I look through my tears on a soundless-clapping host
> As the run-stealers flicker to and fro,
> To and fro:——
> O my Hornby and my Barlow long ago!
> – Francis Thompson, 'At Lord's'

Hobbs and Sandham were also expert at it, few noticing the almost imperceptible finger signal between the two.

steeple, steepler, steepling catch   to make a shot that goes high into the air, and the shot itself.

steer   'To anything short on the offside [Kepler Wessels] plays his well-grooved steer. In other hands, this stroke could prove a weakness . . . But Wessels has soft hands, and exemplary control' (Slater, *Cricket Lore*, II.i.35). The shot runs the ball behind the wicket.

stick   there are a variety of meanings, some contradictory. The first is simply a stump or stumps. The second, or *sticker*, is obsolete for a *stonewaller*. Haygarth, the historian of *Scores and Biographies*, was 'always a great stick', but 'did not stick so long as to cause matches to be drawn' (*Lillywhite's Scores*, 1863, p.242: Lewis). A contradictory use, to *give it stick*, is to hit the ball hard, adopt aggressive batting.

stick up   Lewis does not quote this as obsolete usage in 1934, but his last example is 1904, in Warner's *Recovering the Ashes* (p.70): 'Rhodes stuck up all the batsmen, with the exception of Trumper', i.e. forced them on to the defensive.

stick it up 'im, he don't like it is recorded by Peter Roebuck as echoing across the grounds of England from Mike Gatting, when he detected a batsman who was scared of fast bowling and who might be susceptible to a *rising ball* (*Sunday Times*, 17 September 1995). Reputedly from the television series *Dad's Army*, when Corporal Jones boasted of his campaign in the Sudan.

sticky, sticky dog, sticky wicket after a rainfall, a pitch is soft, even muddy. The ball does unpredictable things, or rather did, since now pitches are covered. D.R. Jardine in *The Best Innings I Ever Played*, which was on a *sticky* at Melbourne in the Third Test of 1928–9, explains that while on a sticky in England the ball turns quickly, there is a certain uniformity of pace and height, it is not so in Australia: 'In the course of a single over it would not be unusual for one ball to shoot, two to turn like greased lightning, and three to lift shoulder high . . . of my own efforts with the bat the less said the better.' Jardine in fact got 33 – worth at least 120, said Herbert Sutcliffe, who chose the same place for his best innings: 135 made in 6½ hours. George Hele (*Bodyline Umpire*) explains the savagery of the Melbourne crusty by the fact that only the Australian sun is hot enough to bake the pitch hard above the soft, rain-soaked, sub-soil, making a treacherous surface which the ball breaks through.

On a sticky, 'there are one or two "musts". One is to make the batsman play at every ball . . . Another is to pitch the ball a little further up than usual. It is a crime to drop the ball short on a wet wicket' (Bradman, 92). On the *sticky dog* of Brisbane in 1950, after Australia had scored 228 in good conditions on the first day, the rain came down. England declared at 68 for 7 the next day, Hutton 8* from number 6; the first ball from Ray Lindwall dug in and soared over Reg Simpson's head, as John Woodcock remembered in *The Times*: 'The fast bowlers were ineffective, Bill Johnston first doing the damage, then Bedser and Bailey for England. Australia declared at 32 for 7, leaving England 193 to win. Hutton, kept back to 8 in the order, for the pitch to improve or somebody else to bat long enough for it to do so, was 62*, but England totalled only 122 to lose by 70 runs. Since then pitches have been covered for almost all Tests.' (See *Brumbrella*.) Why *dog* is unclear, but possibly from the meaning of a 'mechanical device for gripping or holding' (OED), as it is first described as 'A wet wicket, dried to the consistency of glue by the rays of the sun' (*Country Life*, July 1925).

stitching   around the ball are six lines of stitched flax, which hold the two halves together. The flax comes from one factory in Northern Ireland, and is of nine strands, as no other twine will withstand the wear. The Latin for the plant is *linum usitatissimum* meaning the most common flax: thus *linen*, meaning a cloth woven from flax. The plant has another use, for after its blue flowering has passed, the seeds are used for *linseed oil*, which is used to harden the face of the bat.

See also *swing*.

stock ball   the type of delivery that a bowler bowls most frequently. 'With pace came two deliveries; his stock ball, the away-swinger, and a skidding, well-directed bouncer ... after much practice and hard work on the nets the inswinging yorker was added to his repertoire' – Paul Allott on Darren Gough of Yorkshire and England (*The Cricketer*, August 1994).

stock bowler   is one who does most of, or bears the brunt, of the bowling. Often a medium-pacer, but also as Sky TV commentator Charles Colville said, 'Atherton used Tufnell [slow-medium left arm] as a stock bowler' (Brisbane Test, 1994).

Stogumber mow   'Of course batting wasn't so good then ... lots of players used the Stogumber mow, a sort of scything stroke ...', commented an 84-year-old veteran of Kilve Cricket Club, on the opposite side of the Quantock Hills to Stogumber (BBC Radio 2, 2 October 1994). Village rivalry might be thought to render the remark suspect, but the *mow* is still correctly played by the club today: the hands are wide apart, the batsman bends his left leg into the correct position for the two-handed scythe, and the ball goes over mid-wicket. It reaped match figures of 0–102 off Vic Marks of Somerset and England at the match to mark the official re-opening of Stogumber C.C., J.C. White's old club, in May 1995.

stonewall   to protect one's wicket at all costs, to score slowly, using one's bat as a stone wall. 'Mead, you've been in five hours and you've just stonewalled,' said Walter Robins to Phil Mead of Hampshire and England, when in that time he had made 218* v. Middlesex. His captain, Lionel, Lord Tennyson, once sent him a telegram from the pavilion at Lord's while he was batting: 'Mead – get on or get out – signed Tennyson' (Ball & Hopps, 27). According to Arlott, in those better-ordered days Mead did receive telegrams on the field, but they recounted results and prices.

   Tennyson's grandfather Alfred, the poet laureate, finished one of his shorter poems

>   Break, break, break
>   At the foot of thy crags, O Sea!
>   But the tender grace of a day that is dead
>   Will never come back to me.

This inspired *Punch* to write, after W.H. Scotton of Notts and England had produced extreme tedium in an innings at Lord's:

>   Block, block, block,
>   At the foot of thy wickets, ah, do!
>   But one hour of Grace or Walter Read
>   Were worth a week of you!

stool-ball   may well be one of the forms of ur-cricket, part of the natural tendency to play or hit a projectile with a stick, splitting off and developing particularly in the West Country. Still flourishing in Hampshire, played by ladies' teams across Southern England. The 'wicket' is about four feet from the ground so the ball does not bounce. (See etymology of *cricket* at the start of this book.)

stop   not only of a fielder *stopping* the ball, but also of the ball itself *popping*, or *sitting up*: Lewis quotes Jack Hobbs: 'Then the ball commenced to "pop", in cricket parlance – to stop and look at them – and Grimmett had the two brilliant batsmen in difficulties' (*Test Match Surprise*, 211).

stop behind   *long stop*, when that position was important. The Laws of 1830–45 state that 'no substitute shall be allowed to bowl, keep wicket, stand at the point or middle wicket, or stop behind to a fast bowler, unless by the consent of the opposite party.'

stop-nets   old term for nets.

straight   to play *straight* is to play with a straight bat. To 'bowl straight' is self-explanatory, but in batting ('He played straight and could hit the ball with enormous power' – Imran Khan on Botham, *Sunday Times*, 9 October 1994), it has an extended meaning. To *go through life with a straight bat* has come to mean the adherence to a moral code of honest decency, while to *play it straight* means to face a question or situation without being disingenuous. *To bowl straight* is to ask a question straight-forwardly, without angle or implied aspersions.

straight-arm   i.e. not throwing the ball (see *throwing*). See also *round-arm*, or *over-arm* bowling. 'The straight-arm bowling, introduced by John Willes, Esq.,' declares Box (1868); at this time, *straight-arm* seems to have meant what we today would call round-arm. This quotation, combined with Nyren's description of the great fast bowler David Harris, makes one think that the supercession of the original bowling along the ground by length bowling (but still underhand) gave rise to a style that was throwing, but legal if it was underarm, a style which might resemble the underarm flick of fielders such as Viv Richards today: 'drawing back his right foot, [Harris] started off with his left. His mode of delivering the ball was very singular. He would bring it from under the arm with a twist and nearly as high as his armpit, and with this action push it, as it were, from him. How it was that the balls acquired the velocity that they did by this mode of delivery I could never comprehend' (Lucas, 75). Nyren also says that those who had only seen the new-fangled round-arm style could not understand the speed achieved by such as Harris. The argument about speed and the skimming effect is reinforced by his next sentence: the balls 'were very little beholden to the ground when pitched; it was but a touch and up again ... they would grind his fingers against the bat ... many a time have I seen blood drawn from a batter'.

straight drive   usually off the front foot, a drive played almost straight down the pitch or over the bowler's head: the most satisfying for the batsman.

streaky   a shot poorly played by a batsman, with a consequent risk of dismissal: 'Early on, [Vic] Richardson made one streaky shot, which did not quite carry to the slips ...' (Richardson finished with 83; Jardine, 157). Probably in the sense that the shot *streaks* off the edge of the bat, and still current today.

strike   to be *on strike* is to be at the wicket-keeper's end, facing the bowling; or to hit the ball: 'youre father was at Mr Payne and plaid at cricket and came home please anuf for he *struck* the best ball on the game and wished he had not annything to do he could play at cricket all his life' – letter from Mary Turner to her son, 2 September 1739 (MCC Library).

strike bowler   a bowler whose main purpose is to take wickets quickly, usually an opening bowler; see also *gun bowler*.

striker   of the ball. E.R. Dexter of Sussex and England is said to have been 'a magnificent striker of the ball', hitting it hard and cleanly.   .

strike rate   the frequency with which a bowler claims a wicket. Pace bowlers get wickets more quickly than slow bowlers. Thus *The Observer*, assessing the fast bowling attack England took to Australia in 1994, compares the balls/wkt ratio of Larwood in 1931–2 (40.06) with Frank Tyson's in 1954–5 (43.14) and John Snow's in 1970–1 (58.22). It is worth noting that Larwood's wickets in the series came twice as quickly for less than half the cost of his 31 in his previous 10 Tests against Australia, but in the second innings of the first Test, when he seldom bowled short to a leg-side field, he had figures of 5–28, his best for the series.

F.S. Trueman's *strike rate* of 49.4 in all Tests is the lowest for an English fast bowler. The only lower strike rates belong to Malcolm Marshall (46.77), and to Waqar Younis of Pakistan, with a mere 36.13. Spinners, however, have a higher strike rate, Shane Warne leading the field with 65.55: but then he only concedes about two runs an over.

Also, but more rarely, used of batting, as by Ian Chappell on

Sky TV: 'Healy had a hundred at Old Trafford in something like 138 balls, a very good strike rate.'

strip   synonym for pitch: 'The fact that I took the first two wickets . . . was an indication that their spinners were going to love that bare Bombay strip' (Border, 34).

stroke   a shot.

strokeplay   an array of scoring shots: 'Graham Thorpe had picked up his theme, revealing a bracing breadth of strokeplay' (Michael Henderson on Thorpe partnering Stewart in Barbados, *The Times*, 13 April 1994).

stroke sheet   shows where every scoring shot in an innings goes, the ground being represented by a circle. Thus a habitual pattern can be seen.

studs   in the bottom of some cricket shoes to increase hold: 'Two studs fell out' (Angus Fraser, *Independent on Sunday*, 17 April 1994).

stuff   slow bowling. 'All the players . . . ridicule slow bowling as "stuff" . . . but what have they done against it when in?' (Denison, 1846). See also *filth, muck, tosh*.

stump   the early form of cricket had two *stumps*, two feet apart, and one long bail, about a foot off the ground. *At stumps* means at close of play.

stumped   the *wickie* or *stumper* whips off the bails when the batsman is not grounded behind his crease.

submarine   'The experimental opening partnership of Richardson and Oakman did not come off, since the latter, as he is apt to do, allowed himself to be submarined by a yorker' (Swanton, *Report*, 67).

substitute, sub   a fielder taking the place of one of the fielding side who is injured. Various rules apply to what he may or may not do, such as bowl or keep wicket: Law 2 is long and complex. See *stop-behind*. *Bell's Life*, 5 August 1827: 'received as a substitute.'

sundries   Australian term for *extras*: no-balls, wides, byes, leg-byes, which are entered separately in the score book, and with the exception of wides not debited to the bowler. From the OE singular *syndrig*, separate, private, special, exceptional.

sway   method of avoiding bouncers: see also *ducker*. Robin Smith of Hampshire and England, known for his courage and skill in playing fast bowling, is a *swayer*, the ball passing his body. This allows him to keep his eye on the ball. If duckers start too early, they cannot do this and risk the ball not getting up far enough to pass over their heads.

sweater   when the bowler takes his *sweater* he has finished his *spell*.

sweep   the foot is advanced down the pitch, toe pointing towards the ball: the stroke is effected by sinking down almost on the right knee and sweeping the ball right round in the direction of long leg. Denis Compton was acknowledged as 'King of the Sweep' (he was once lbw trying to *sweep* Keith Miller), and advice is often given that the shot is one of the ways to combat Shane Warne, Dave Crowe writing, 'Warne exploited the folly of front-leg sweeping when he bowled the captain round his legs' (*The Cricketer*, January 1994). This is only part of the story, as the front leg must be behind the line of the ball so that if the bat misses, the pad is there as a second line of defence – a problem with the late *swerve*, or *curve*, of Warne's savagely spun leg-break. See also *free hit*. Formerly called the *George Parr sweep* after the Notts batsman, the first mention from Lewis is 1888. See also *reverse sweep*.

sweeper   a fielder who covers the cover (usually) or midwicket area of the boundary to *sweep up* the strokes that penetrate the inner field.

sweet spot   the area of the bat from which the ball flies with greatest impetus, some inches up from the toe: 'The alarming bounce generated originally by Garner ... forced batsmen to learn new shots ... and ask for the sweet spot of their bats to be located higher up' (Simon Hughes, *Daily Telegraph*, 28 August 1995). David Collyer researched the engineering aspects of the bat at the Bolton Institute of Higher Education and found the size and bounciness of the spot varied from bat to bat: his sample found more bounce on a smaller area on one, less bounce on a larger area on another. C. Grant and P. Thethi (p.669) found 'hitting the ball at the correct point known as the *sweet spot* will dispatch the ball with great speed for remarkably little effort.' They also found that under certain conditions the faster the ball, the higher on the bat the optimum point of impact (see Hughes above), and that energy absorbed by vibrations in the bat can be a significant factor in its performance. A more rigid handle might lessen the vibrations of the impact and increase the speed of the ball off the bat.

swerve   to some extent interchangeable with *swing*, but used here, and generally, to denote movement in the air due to the spin on the ball rather than seam and turbulence. 'In 1901 George Hirst discovered the secret of "swerve", and became the best bowler in England on fast wickets' (BLC, 1920, 67). Hirst got the ball to swerve by spin, thus the term spin-swerve.

Dr Wilkins's work in the wind tunnel provided a surprising increase of **Robins** force with a new four-piece ball, spun around a horizontal seam, at a spin rate of 12.5 a second, over 54 m.p.h., just within the range of even a slow-medium bowler, especially with the wind against him. With the seam vertical, some of the results were even more startling. Spin rate was important throughout. Batsmen playing a spinner who gives a real tweak to the ball, such as Shane Warne, might pick up a quick clue that a savage *leggie* is on the way if it drifts out to leg in the air, as the direction of spin swerve – in this case – is opposite to the direction of turn.

In the same way, Alec Bedser says that the ball he bowled Bradman with at Adelaide in 1947 – the best ball he ever received, said the Don – was spun, not cut. Like his normal inswinger, it started on the off stump, swung to the leg stump, then came rapidly off the pitch to take the off stump. All this in the speed range 60–70 m.p.h.

The hard practice leading to this kind of devastation is described by S.F. Barnes. At around the turn of the century he asked M.A. Noble for advice, and was told

> it was possible to put two poles down the wicket, one ten or eleven yards from the bowling crease and another five or six yards from the batsman and to bowl a ball outside the first pole and make it swing to the off side of the other pole and then nip back and hit the wicket. That's how I learned to spin a ball to make it swing. It is also possible to bowl in between these two poles, pitch the ball outside the leg stump and hit the wicket. I spent hours trying all this out in the nets. (Bedlam and Fry, 232)

swing   the lateral movement of the ball in the air, from leg to off or vice versa. Normal *swing* and reverse swing are caused only by the boundary layer separating at different distances on each side from the front of the ball during flight through the air, causing pressure differentials on different sides of the ball. It should not be confused with *swerve, curl* or *curve*, generally used of a spun ball (at least here) and referring to the **Robins** or Magnus *effect*.

As the ball moves through the air, some of the air sticks to it in a very thin layer. There is no relative motion between the surface of the ball and the air, but a short distance away the air is travelling past at the speed of the airstream. The thickness of the air in which its speed changes from zero to that of the airstream is known as the boundary layer. The jump is not quantum but more or less continuous. The boundary layer does not remain 'attached' to the ball all the way round; it breaks away or separates, from the ball at some point. But if it can be made to break away from one side before the other, the pressure difference on the ball will make it swing to one side. Now the boundary layer can come in two states, laminar (smooth-flowing) or turbulent. By chance, the laminar boundary layer is about the same thickness as the seam, or rather thinner, the difference being roughly between 1mm. and 0.5mm. The seam is thus about the right height to trip the laminar boundary layer into turbulence. Dr R.D. Mehta of NASA's Ames Research Centre, who opened the bowling with Imran Khan some twenty years ago for the Royal Grammar School, Worcester, says that as the turbulent layer is more energetic, it is able to remain attached to the ball's surface for a longer distance. Here we must bring in Bernoulli's Theorem, which states that the faster the airflow (or the flow of any liquid) the lower the pressure – and the airflow is at its fastest at the apex of the ball. 'The main point to note is that once the boundary layer separates, the pressure is more or less constant further downstream, maintaining the value achieved just prior to separation. So with the laminar boundary layer, which separates before reaching the apex location, the pressure is *relatively high* compared to that on the turbulent side where the minimum pressure has been achieved since the layer was still attached at the apex' (Mehta, letter to author). That shows us, taken with the downstream pressure remaining constant at the value just before separation, i.e. high, that the pressure is greater where the laminar boundary has broken away sooner. As a consequence the side force will push the ball towards the side with the turbulent separation.

So the bowler's problem is how to get the boundary layer into a turbulent state on one side of the ball.

If the seam is held across the direction of motion, the boundary layer becomes turbulent on one side of the ball only, the side that the seam is angled towards, so that the seam is angled towards the slips for an outswinger or to fine or long leg for an inswinger. As the roughness of the ball also helps to create the turbulent layer, that side of the ball is held on the slips side for an outswinger, on the leg side for an inswinger.

A number of other factors can also contribute to swing: wind conditions and turbulence, dampening of one side of the ball, and back spin. In a major series of wind tunnel tests, Dr Wilkins found that the higher the speed (and this of course includes wind speed and direction) the greater the swing force. Swing was produced at angles up to and above 30 degrees, although different angles of seam and speeds produced different results.

Dr Andrew Lewis from the University of Hertfordshire found that a wide angle of the seam, up to about 40 degrees, produced strong swing over a wide range of speeds (*The Cricketer*, May 1993). 'Swing may manifest itself above 25 m.p.h., peaking about 80, and dropping off slightly towards 90. The effect is increased if one side of the ball (the one with least die-stamping) is kept polished and the other allowed to deteriorate.' (See also *ball-tampering*.)

Mehta found that 'Except for the ball that had been used for 40 overs . . . the normalized side force is seen to increase with flowspeed up to about 30 m/s (70 m.p.h.)' (*Annual Review of Fluid Mechanics*, 1985).

The other aspects of swing bowling are those of humidity, reverse swing, and late swing. Humid conditions do seem to affect the way the ball behaves in the air. Match results tend to support the theory that humidity helps swing, possibly late swing: in 1995, Mark Ilott of Essex and England took 9–19 (including a hat-trick of lbws) in the first innings of Northamptonshire, and Paul Taylor replied for Northants with match figures of 9–68: the late swing was put down to heavy cloud over a pitch which was still drying out from the rain of the previous week.

There may be other, as yet unrecognised, causes for this. Wind tunnels can never do more than approximate the life of the cricket ball, which is being hurled onto a damp ground, perhaps picking up moisture in both leather and stitching, bashed by a hard bat and rasped by the keeper's gloves. Mehta avers he is 'a strong believer in the effect, having played in England for several years where there was never a shortage of damp weather, particularly on weekends!' Wilkins claims that his tests show humidity has no effect and Mehta confirms that there has been no conclusive evidence for the positive effects of humidity amongst all the wind tunnel tests that have been conducted by the various researchers. But Mr E. Palfrey wonders if the levels of relative humidity achieved were lower than those of Professor A. V. Stephens (see below), and points out the seam does swell in damp conditions.

When the quarter-ball, as used in first-class cricket and Tests, and most competitive cricket, is bowled at over 75 m.p.h., another phenomenon may appear: first the swing disappears and is then replaced *c.* 85 m.p.h. by *reverse swing* as practised by a large number of bowlers, notably Wasim Akram and

Waqar Younis of Pakistan, whose late in-swinging yorker demolished the lower English batting line-up in 1992. Imran Khan had some years earlier told Dr Mehta that his in-swinger sometimes swung out. It did so, as Dr Mehta pointed out in his article in the *New Scientist* (21 August 1993), because the aerodynamics are completely changed. The boundary layer becomes turbulent relatively early (before reaching the seam) and the main seam acts like a ramp, thickening the turbulent boundary layer which then separates relatively early. This creates a side force pushing the ball in the 'wrong' direction, away from the direction the seam is pointing in.

But although this could only be done at speeds few bowlers could reach, bowlers in Pakistan were finding that a ball scuffed on one side by contact with the hard pitches there would reverse swing at lower speeds. The scuffed edge helps to induce early transition of the laminar boundary layer to a turbulent state. Apart from natural wear and accident, the quarter seam may have been raised by picking, which is illegal (the referee Bob Cowper of Australia, who inspected the ball used by the two Pakistanis after they had had spectacular success in a particular Test, found no evidence of this and suggested their success was because they were very good bowlers indeed). Sarfraz Nawaz of Pakistan is generally credited with being the ancestor of reverse swing, it was thought by saturating a worn ball on one side with sweat and spittle so that an imbalance in weight was created. But swing is produced only by differential pressures, and Dr Wilkins points out that wet leather is rougher, has a softer surface, and is naturally more difficult to polish.

But he notes that wetting the leather produces surface irregularities as well as making it more receptive to damage: also 'above each of the totally hidden stitches there now appeared a pronounced little ridge which remained even after the outside of the leather had dried.' Possibly this is because the stitching underneath the quarter seam swells; the appearance of these little bumps is well known. Thus the rough forward face, rather than the weight imbalance, is probably responsible for reverse swing on a ball with one side saturated with moisture.

As in normal swing, the ideal ball has one rough side and one kept smooth through constant polishing. 'This ball can then be used to produce conventional or reverse swing (with the same grip or bowling action) depending on which side is facing forward' (Dr Mehta, correspondence with author).

Wilkins also produced some surprising results by smearing wet soil over the seam so that it showed a rounded profile.

Although at seam angles under 10 degrees swing force dropped
by 30–50 per cent, at 15–35 degrees it increased by 20 per
cent, a very valuable pointer: apart from any other consider-
ations it shows a worn ball will still swing. Even minute
protuberances affect swing: in his 1955 paper written while at
the Dept of Aeronautics, University of Sydney, Professor
Stephens found that lateral forces were affected by a strip of
sellotape only 3/1000″ thick placed across a two-piece ball
where the secondary seam usually is. He also found that a
cricket ball bowled at just above 120 ft per second with a
quarter seam across the line of flight, on the leg for an
outswinger, and the seam angled at 20 degrees, experienced a
sharp discontinuity, with a lateral force suddenly appearing,
which he thought was the cause of late swing. But the sharp
discontinuity is not observed in tests on spinning cricket balls.

The most deadly form of swing is *late swing*, which does not
give the batsman time to react. Dr Wilkins reproduces a path of
a swinging ball bowled by Australian left-hander Gary Gilmore,
showing the parabolic path of swing. And in his 1985 paper Dr
Mehta concluded, after extensive wind-tunnel tests: 'The
assumption of constant side force seems to be valid for spinning
baseballs and cricket balls; it results in a deflection that is
proportional to the square of the elapsed time, and hence in a
parabolic flight path.' Late swing, however difficult to achieve,
can be seen as having a fairly simple cause.

switch-hitting   to bat left-handed if right-handed and vice
versa (from baseball). Mushtaq Mohammad seems to be the
only player to have done this in the Test arena, in the Karachi
Stadium against England in 1973. In 1930 George Hunt of
Somerset found the fast left-armer Bill Voce's inswingers so
painful to play that he switched to a left-handed stance when
facing him. See also *reverse pull*.

Tail, tailender   usually held to be the last three or four batsmen, though a long tail might include number 7 as well, and a particularly inept side be said to be all tail. The tail is often engaged in a desperate *wag*: 'The two last men of an eleven are twins: they hold one life between them; so that he who dies extinguishes the other . . . in defending your own you fight for your comrade's existence. You are assured that the dread of shame, if not emulation, is making him equally wary and alert' (Meredith, *Evan Harrington*).

talent money   money paid to a player for good batting or bowling: 'Formerly the talent money of a sovereign for fifty runs and the ridiculous custom of giving the same sum for six wickets was the rough and ready rule' (Lord Hawke in Holmes, 5).

tally   *ODEtym* has it from the L. *tallia, talia*, cutting, rod, stick (cf. mod. Italian *tagliare*, to cut), and OF *taille* (or *tailleur*, tailor), through to a rod of wood cut with with notches, originally recording payments, here runs scored, wickets taken, catches caught, over any specified period of time: 'He has played more big-time cricket than anyone: 156 Tests and 273 One-Day internationals; his tally of 11,174 runs is an all-time record' (Ken Piesse, *The Cricketer*, July 1994, on Allan Border). *Tallywag* is the scoreboard, with a possible derivation from 'Telegraph'.

tap   refers to two kinds of batting: to *tap the ball around* is to hit it easily to different parts of the ground, while to give the *bowling tap* is to use the long handle, hit the ball hard – sometimes the two meanings converge.

telegraph, telegraph board   score board. In 1846 introduced into Lord's, with the score, last man's score, and wickets down. The tyro cricket-watcher can be mightily confused by the array of marching figures, flashing lights, and intermittent lights.

Test, Test Match   originally written without capitals, in the first mention of 1861–2, when an English side toured Australia, and played Victoria, Tasmania, and a combined New South Wales and Victoria side. This was a commercial venture, got up by Messrs Spiers and Pond, and Surrey players formed the nucleus of the side. The matches then were tests of relative strengths, as they are today.

testimonial   akin to a *benefit* but rather than the receipts from a single match, the sums gathered at given matches.

thick-edge, thick edge   the ball is hit with more of the bat than a *snick*, diverting towards the third slip-gully area.

thick stumps   what the batsman defends. See *thin stumps*.

thigh-pad   protection for the batsman, worn on the forward thigh and often also on the inner thigh of the back leg, above the ordinary pads.

think out   a bowler does this to a batsman when he studies his style, and slips him a delivery to which he is susceptible, perhaps leading up to it by tempting him with a similar but innocuous delivery.

thin edge   just a touch of the bat on the ball, so it usually goes to the 'keeper.

thin stumps   what a bowler who has shaved the stumps or just missed an lbw appeal is said to be bowling at, as in, 'Thin stumps today, I'm afraid' (Battersea Park umpire, 1994).

third man   a fielding position near the boundary, at about 45 degrees to the pitch.

third umpire   the first Test to use a third umpire to decide from video replays, particularly of stumpings and run-outs, was England v. Australia at Lord's in 1993. The first decision was Healy's stumping of Robin Smith off the bowling of Tim May, and was made by Chris Balderstone. The third umpire, and before that the television replay, has in general confirmed the extreme acuteness of judgement of Test umpires. Sometimes called the television umpire.

thrash, thresh   (rare) 'the immaculate Burtt wheeling away, Compton and company thrashing him into the covers' – Reg Hayter (*Cricket Lore*, II.iii). 'Joseph Caddle was even to the most unpracticed eye more essentially a thresher than a cricketer' (Robertson-Glasgow, *Crusoe*, 78).

throat ball   a ball that comes off at the batsman's throat, so often a skidding *bouncer* at that level. Because it comes on quickly and the batsman may duck into it, much feared. *Throat theory* is the type of attack depending on it, as in *leg theory*.

throw   the return of the ball from the fielder to the pitch, either wicket-keeper or bowler. The longest throw recorded is still that of Robert Percival on the Durham Sands racecourse in 1882: 140 yards and 2 feet.

throw-in: 'Before 1930 it was frequently the case that a fieldsman would break the wicket with a throw-in, but this is not often seen now' (Hammond, *Secret History*, 51). And Altham adds a reason, that the gradual introduction of boundaries 'dating from the [18]60s, had an adverse effect on deep fielding, and especially on throwing, to which the simultaneous urbanisation of the countryside also contributed' (p. 120).

Brian Lara scored a direct hit from side-on in the Oval one-day match of 1995 from sixty-five yards, and another from

lesser distance in the same game. And in the Tied Test, West
Indies v. Australia, December 1960, Joe Solomon of W.I. twice
hit the stumps direct, once to dismiss Alan Davidson on 80,
from square leg, and then hitting the only visible stump to tie
the match, running out Meckiff. Curiously, Ian Meckiff was the
last person to be involved in a

throwing controversy   before Sri Lanka's Muralithan in Australia 1995–6. This is when a bowler throws a ball with a bent
elbow rather than a straight arm, which can be completely
unintentional. Meckiff's suspect action led him to be *no-balled*
continually against South Africa in 1963. In 1995, Henry
Olonga of Zimbabwe, the first black to represent his country,
was also no-balled for throwing, but was suffering from a side-
strain. Often, it was the faster ball that was thought to be
thrown: even in the case of slower bowlers like Tony Lock, who
immediately abandoned his faster ball when he was incontrov-
ertibly shown to be throwing it, *c.* 1955.

There was a whole phase between 1955 and 1963, between
Lock and Meckiff, when numbers of other bowlers were
thought to be possibly suspect: Peter Loader, Surrey and
England, West Indies' Charlie Griffith, Griffin of South Africa.
In 1960 *The Cricketer* magazine took a firm stand, with Robin
Marlar writing 'all over the world, I believe, there is a tie-up
between throwing and bouncing . . . a whole bevy of dubious
bowlers capable of delivering the ultimate weapon, the bouncer,
have arrived on the scene.' And E.W. Swanton, quoting Bradman on the subject, said 'The winning or losing of the Ashes is
a small matter compared with "the greatest catastrophe in
cricket history"' and said he thought a moratorium of games
against Australia would be preferable.

With some *pacemen* there was a question of unusually
flexible limbs. Derbyshire's Harold Rhodes pointed out in 1966
that 'If they re-write the Laws and say that double-jointed
people must not be allowed to play the first-class game, well,
fair enough.' (Sources: Swanton, *Barclay's*, Ball & Hopps 157.)

throw it up   misleading, as it is not an invitation to start
chucking. More exact would be 'give it some air'. *Bowl up* is
occasionally used as exhortation to get on with it or put a bit
more into it. See also *toss it up*. Sometimes the reason is to
hasten a declaration by bowling *filth*.

throw out   to run a batsman out by a direct hit on the stumps.

tice, tice ball   obsolete, but a ball which would *entice* the
batsman into thinking it was a half-volley: in 1871 it was

described as something between a half-volley and a *yorker*, but
in 1888 as a yorker pure (Lewis).

tich, tick   not Tich Freeman, but 'Go hard! – Tich and turn!
tich and turn!' was Hambledon for 'Run up!' Rowland Bowen
points out that in the American game of Wicket, *tick* was the
same as *tich*, meaning touch: 'The striker shall tick his bat down
over the tick marks to have a cross count . . .' a cross meaning a
run, and to be *ticked out* was to be run out. May come from the
old method of notching a run, when the umpire had to be
touched with the bat, and often carried his own for this purpose.

tickle   'So when John Carr *tickled* Dominic Cork down the leg
side . . .' he was caught by the 'keeper. The batsman may *tickle*
the bowler, in which case he may score, or may be dismissed,
and this may be voluntary; but if he *gets a tickle*, it is a
dangerously light application of bat to ball.

tie   the game has been completed and both sides have amassed
the same score. A possible origin is that of having the two tally-
sticks tied together while the game was in progress. They were
then cut apart. Not a *draw*[1], which is an unfinished game.

timber, timbers, timber-yard   an obsolete colloquial term
for the wicket. Thus in 1866 'Capt. Crawley' advises: 'If you
attempt a drive and miss it, you will probably find what the
cricketers call "a row in your timber yard"' (Pardon, 26).

timed out   a new batsman is out if he wilfully takes more than
two minutes to come in. An appeal must be made, however,
and the timing starts from that appeal.

timing   some batsmen have a mysterious ability to hit the ball
hard with apparently little effort, unanalysable, a talent amount-
ing to genius. With a slow sweep of the bat like Gower, the left
hand hardly seeming to grasp the handle, the elegance of Greg
Chappell, perhaps above all, Frank Woolley. Not quite the
same as the *timing* of the wristy punch of Bradman, who, as
observed by the umpire George Hele, made the bat do all the
work. But for these geniuses the effort is no more than 'taking
the top off a bottle of stout . . . noise like a trout taking a fly . . .'
(Tom Stoppard, *The Real Thing*). See *touch*.

tins   rectangular metal pieces each with a single white number
painted on a black ground, set on the score-board or *telegraph*
to show the score, etc. during a match. 'Poor old Surrey in the
soup again! . . . The mouldy eight runs on the tins were only
hoisted there by a mighty effort' (D.L.A. Jephson, 1903:
Lewis). In 1994 Jeff Dujon, formerly of West Indies, commentating on a slow scoreboard: 'The runs aren't on the tins yet'

(BBC Radio 4). Refers as well to the beer cans filled with stones which are then rattled.

tip-and-run   hitting gently and running, as: 'Using the long handle when tip-and-run might have been wiser, Arthurton and Drakes were both caught in the deep' (Alex Fortune, *Sunday Times*, 18 April 1995). Also, a variant of the game itself when on hitting a ball the batsmen must run, usually played in schools or to fill in spare time.

toe, toe-end   the bottom of the bat, often jarring to the hand when a ball hit there, productive of *bump-balls* and mis-hits: 'from a ball Stewart did well to reach, never mind toe-end to square cover' (Martin Johnson, *The Independent*, 23 June 1995).

ton   a century. Relates not to the British weight of 2240 lb., or the American 2000 lb., but to the maritime measure of 100 cubic feet for registered tonnage. Originating from the same word as *tun*, a wine cask, the original estimations being how much space such a cask would take up.

tonk   partly onomatopoeic from the sound of a good thwack of bat on ball: 'Tonker Taylor lets rip with morning 100' (Barry Fairall, *The Independent*, 12 May 1995).

top-edge   the batsman justs gets the *top edge* of his bat to a ball, and as he doesn't connect properly is often caught. Naturally, this happens with a cross-batted shot: 'Mal Love top-edged a pull' (Geoffrey Dean, *Daily Telegraph*, 28 April 1995).

top-hand   the upper hand on the bat, the left for right-hand batsmen, the right for left. Supposed to be the power hand, making shots, but 'his "top hand" play is definitely not from the MCC coaching book', said Roger Twose of Brian Lara (Keating, *Spectator*, 20 August 1994). Sir Donald had his left hand further round behind the handle than usual, but changed his grip from time to time, according to the conditions and the bowling. In the Master Class section of *The Cricketer* (October 1992) Alec Stewart explains: 'Now that my top hand is dominant I play much straighter.'

top order   the first batsmen in the order, down to 5 or 6.

topsawyer   opening batsman. Jack MacBryan, 'being chosen from a field of openers that included Jack Hobbs, Herbert Sutcliffe, George Gunn, Jack (A.C.) Russell, Andrew Sandham, and Chales Hallows, all of them rightaway professional topsaw-yers' (Robertson-Glasgow, *Crusoe*, 27). The meaning is the sawyer who works the upper handle of a pit-saw, so someone holding a superior position, so 'a first-rate hand at something' (1823, OED).

top-scorer   one who makes the highest score, usually in an innings.

top-spin, toppie   spin imparted in a forward direction to the ball. This makes it hurry on to the batsman, bouncing high as well if the pitch is suitable. In combination with side-spin, a formidable weapon: Bradman in *The Art of Cricket* and Mailey in *10 for 66 And All That* are in agreement that *top-spin* will cause a ball to drop eighteen inches or two feet shorter. It can, of course, be combined with side-spin. The top-spinner is a formidable adjunct to the leg-break: the *action* is rather the same, so it may find the batsman's pads or stumps. 'The old devil knows he can get me out. He bowls that leg-break to me a couple of times, then he bowls me that top-spinner with the same action which goes straight on and I can't spot it, so it's only a matter of time before he bowls me neck and crop' – Dave Nourse to Herb Taylor, South Africa Third Test, 1914 (Duckworth, 122).

'Shane Warne has two top-spinners – one he shows to the batsman on purpose, and one more difficult to pick.' – Richie Benaud, commentating on the Lord's Test (BBC TV, England v. Australia, 1993).

tosh   origin unknown, see also *muck, filth:* high-tossed, frequently leg-spinning bowling. Thought of as being easy, but as this is part of the spinner's web, the definition is only sometimes correct. D.L.A. Jephson records *tosh* as being applied to leg-spin bowling in 1921. But the admirable *Tit-Bits* seems to have had an eye for this sort of thing, reporting on 25 June 1898, 'Among the recent neologisms of the cricket field is "tosh", which means bowling of contemptible easiness.'

toss   originally a *full toss:* 'Harris would make the best bowler in England if he did not toss' said old Nyren of the young David Harris, referring thus to *c.* 1780 (*The Hambledon Men*). The other meaning is *to toss the ball up*, meaning to give it air and keep a full length. *The toss* is the flipping of a coin to determine choice of innings.

touch   a *touch* bat plays by instinct, however fine his technique: he finds his touch instantly, flicks the ball around, seems just as likely to last three overs or make 150, and does not bat by the rules. Examples might be Grahame Thorpe, David Gower, Tom Graveney, all of England.

track   the pitch, or more precisely that part of it which lies within the pitch area and is the narrower line where the balls actually pitch and are played at. Thus *fast track* means a pitch where the ball 'comes on' to the bat.

trap ball   'That was a trap ball,' said Tony Lewis, commentating for BBC TV as Mervyn Hughes bowled a short wide one which got up to shoulder height, and which Graeme Hick hit straight to cover in the air, and was caught, at Old Trafford in the first Test of 1993.

trealer   very rare. Never seen today, not in OED, and only mentioned once in Lewis, from A.E. Knight in *The Complete Cricketer* of 1906: 'Trealer. – A ball bowled as in the game of "bowls", all along the ground.'

trickle   see *rill*.

trimmer   exceptionally well-bowled ball which removes the bail or bails, hitting the top of the stumps: 'the Derbyshire all-rounder produced the ball of the day, and of the series, bowling Hooper with a trimmer that swung away, pitched around off and middle, and hit the off stump' (Richard Hutton, *The Cricketer*, July 1995). The word has a long pedigree, first noted by Lewis from 1832, when in *P. Egan's Book of Sports* (349/1) Dick Driver sent down a trimmer and Bob Bowler had his leg bail removed.

trull, troll, trowl   19th-century terms for bowling, *troll* from Mary Mitford in *Our Village* (1826): 'Jack Hatch, who had trolled . . .'; *trull* from 1851 (see also *aim*), and *trowl* from the *Australasian* (12 January 1867): 'Greater favourites . . . never . . . trowled the ball.' *Troller* is found in 1827, referring to an underhand bowler. OED shows both a Fr. derivation *trôler* to run about, ramble, and G. *trollen,* to roll.

trundle, trundler   from OE *trendel* circle, ring, etc., with a dialect form of wheel, or of a (partly cleaned) bundle of sticks, which together give an impression of the modern meaning: a stock bowler, not blessed with any great gifts, much as the word implies: he trundles in to bowl, in a way which is best suited to a medium-pacer. But at the turn of the century and before the word seems to imply excellence: 'The veracious *Wisden* gives a terrifying account of the trundler who wrought all the mischief for the Dominion, Laing, a very fast bowler with a high action, one of the best balls he sends down being a yorker on the leg side' – Standing (p. 127) describing Canada v. the USA in 1896.

tuck, tuck away   'Wessels then tucks Ambrose out of his hip-pocket to fine leg' (Slater, II, 34). More elegant and purposeful than *round the corner, nudge, nurdle*.

tuck in   'Lara now appeared, and at once tucked into the bowling' (Peter Roebuck, *Sunday Times*, 13 August 1995, Trent Bridge Test). In this sense the word first appears in

England in 1857, and *tucker* as victuals in Australia is given as 1858 by the OED.

tuck up   of a batsman: from couture, to fold or pleat drapery. Used when a ball comes in to the batsman, either by *line* or *break*, so he folds in half in his efforts to put bat to ball.

turn   the lateral movement of the ball off the pitch. A *turner* or *turning pitch* is thus one receptive to turn; *playing for the turn* means to make a stroke presuming the ball will deviate: 'van Ryneveld was soon bowled by Laker ... played for the turn and the ball came straight through' (Swanton, *Report*, 31).

turned him inside-out   of a bowler, to bring the right-handed batsman into a position where his right shoulder leads, i.e. wrong foot forward. But a batsman can do it himself: 'Three quarters of an hour and 101 runs divided Middlesex from victory, when Compton, turning himself inside out to force a ball wide of the leg stump over cover-point, failed to clear the fieldsman's head' – E.W. Swanton on Middlesex v. Kent 1947 (Heffer, 148).

tweaker   synonym for *spinner*, one who gives the ball a *tweak* when it leaves his hand.

twelfth man   the reserve player for a cricket XI. Often takes out drinks. 'Some of the twelfth men are lazy buggers. While I'm running around, they just go to sleep and do sod-all' (Angus Fraser, *Independent on Sunday*, 17 April 1994).

twist   the early term for *spin*: 'we *believe* that Boxall was the first who by a turn of the wrist gave his balls a twist to the wicket.' So said the Revd John Mitford, *Gentleman's Magazine* (July and September 1833), reviewing *The Young Cricketer's Tutor*. Boxall is elusive, going unmentioned in Nyren's work, and in Altham's and Bowen's. Even H. P-T. does not have him. *Scores and Biographies*, however, has Boxall appearing for the Colts of Surrey v. Colts of Hants in 1789; as 'Colonel the Hon. Lennox' was a player, the term does not seem to refer to teenagers. In 1791 he was twice chosen for England v. Kent, and in 1790, or 1800, or 1803, he wrote the first known manual, *Rules and Instructions for playing the Game of Cricket,* and this includes: 'For a bowler to twist the ball: Let the bowler hold the ball with the seam across ... but so as the tips of the fingers may just reach over the seam.' Disappointingly, he does not describe grips, inviting the bowler to watch the ball in the air to see which way it will turn. He is in all probability the father of spin.

The art was almost certainly around by then, to judge by Nyren's reference to Lamborn, 'the Little Farmer' as the tenth knight of the Hambledon round table. He bowled off-breaks, right-handed and underarm, 'not like the generality of right-handed bowlers, but just the reverse way: that is ... his ball would twist from off to leg.' So leg-breaks were already a part of the scene when this was written, an almost inevitable development.

two-eyed   a batsman's squarish stance which brings both eyes into play.

two-leg   the guard given by the umpire when the batsman puts his bat in a line which goes between middle and leg stumps.

two-man's land   '[Shane Warne] ... troubles batsmen retreating onto the back foot or dithering in what Ken Barrington once called "two-man's land"' (Peter Roebuck, *Sunday Times*, 23 October 1994). See also *over-the-crease*.

two-paced   West Indian batsman Jimmy Adams, not out after a steadily defensive innings on the second day of the Lord's Test 1995, said: 'The pitch was a bit two-paced', meaning variable bounce and speed off (BBC TV). 'The first palpable evidence of the two-paced nature of the pitch. The tall Cronje has to hurry the bat down as the ball keeps a fraction low' (Slater, *Cricket Lore*, II. 36).

U**mbrella** has two meanings, the first quoted by David Frith in *The Slow Men*: 'Captains regarded [Derek] Underwood as an "umbrella bowler"; i.e. you carried him around in case of rain.' *Umbrella field* seems to have two meanings: one is with the majority of the fielders spread on leg and off side behind the batsman, e.g. for a fast bowler, or simply around the boundary. It comes from the L *umbra*, shade, and was originally a parasol, or an African or Oriental symbol of dignity (OED). See also *Brumbrella*.

umpire from OF *noumpere*, meaning non+peer, i.e. a third person called in to decide between two (*ODEtym*). Thus by misdivision into 'an umpire'. Players have bad luck, *umpires* make mistakes, although one, Alec Skelding, was also literally dogged by misfortune. It happened in 1948, and all started when Sidney Barnes, the Australian opener, was dissatisfied by Skelding's lbw decision against him at Leicester, and remarked that he should have a stick and a dog to go with his white coat. When, soon after, Skelding *stood* in the Australia v. Surrey game, a small brown and white terrier duly bounded happily on the ground. Naturally, it was finally caught by Barnes, probably the only player in England with a volitional aura strong enough to create such a situation (and who had again been lbw in this game, but for 168). Naturally, he presented it to Skelding. Naturally, Skelding had a phobia about dogs, and removed the bails and marched smartly off the field. Fortunately, neither C.G. Jung nor Arthur Koestler were aware of the story.

Some umpires were at the start of the game manifestly unwilling to give out amateur players of standing and renown. W.G. Grace once averred that the crowd had come to see him play and was not given out in consequence. Today, it is unlikely the Bangkok incident will be repeated: 'at that moment the umpire – *our* umpire – had his back turned to the field of play, and was engaged in frantically signalling the bartender to bring him a cocktail' (Standing, 1, 178).

'Each Umpire is the sole Judge of all Nips and Catches; Inns and Outs; good or bad runs, at his own wicket, and his determination shall be absolute; and he shall not be changed for another umpire without the Consent of both sides' (Laws, 1855). But the umpires may not be the final court on the field: D.J. Insole and Maurice Turnbull both recalled batsmen, and W.A. Hadlee, father of Sir Richard, invited Cyril Washbrook to continue his innings after an lbw decision with which he disagreed, in the first Test of 1950–1 (Brodribb, 108).

Katherine Whitehorn in *The Observer* has the last word,

however: 'Why are the umpires, the only two people on a cricket field who aren't going to get grass stains on their knees, the only ones allowed to wear dark trousers?'

unbeaten   when a batsman is not out, at close of play, or innings.

uncapped   see *capped*.

under-arm, under-hand   the first method of bowling was *under-arm* along the ground, superseded by length bowling, also under-arm, but which appears to have been sometimes with a bent arm, for Daft's *Kings of Cricket* describes Old Clarke, originator of the 'All England' matches: 'instead of delivering the ball from the height of, or between, the hips, he at the last moment bent back his elbow, bringing the ball almost under his right armpit, and delivered the ball, thus, from as great a height as it was possible to obtain and still to be under-hand.' See *straight arm*.

undercut   as backspin, but usually doing it with the forefinger in the finger-spinner's position but the palm of the hand turned to the sky so the finger cuts the ball backwards.

underedge, under-edge   'Kent's relief was evident when Lamb under-edged a cut on to his stumps' (Geoffrey Dean, *Daily Telegraph*, 28 April 1995). Lamb had threshed 54 in 58 balls, Northants v. Kent.

under-leg stroke   was demonstrated surprisingly recently in Ranjitsinjhi's *Jubilee Book* by W.L. Murdoch of Australia and Sussex. The leading leg is lifted, rather in the Groucho Marx style, or as the first pace of a solemn and stately temple dance, and the ball is hit through the aperture thus made, in the direction of square leg. It is related to an equally curious shot, the *draw*.

underpitch, underpitched   to bowl short of a length.

unfair play   conduct within the laws but not the spirit of the game. The 1755 Laws state that the umpires are 'the sole Judges of all Outs and Inns: of all fair or unfair Play; of all frivolous delays; of all Hurts, whether real or pretended'. An example of this might be appealing for a catch when the ball has hit the ground. W.G. once ran three with the ball lodged in his shirt. When stopped (although we are not told how), he refused to take the ball out himself, for fear of being out *handling the ball*.

uncertainty   the *corridor* or line of uncertainty is on or around the off stump, so that the batsman is *uncertain* whether it is safe to play or leave alone. The intention of bowling to the *patio* of uncertainty, thus bringing length into the equation, is credited to K. Andrews, quondam Worcestershire 2nds.

unplayable   can be said of the pitch, bowler, or delivery.

unsight   the line of sight of player or umpire is blocked: if a batsman, it can be because of a movement behind the bowler. An unusual case occurred in 1956, at the Old Trafford Test when Laker took 19–90, when Australian captain Ian Johnson complained that sawdust for the bowlers' footholds, whipped up by the wind, was impairing his vision (Mosey, *Laker*, 28).

up   'Most West indians have trouble with leg-spinners because they like to hit on the up without getting to the pitch of the ball. That's imprudent' (Francis, p. 42). To *pitch up* means to bowl a *full length*. To catch a ball *on the up* means the ball has not bounced before being caught, or as in the first example above.

upper-cut   from 1865: '[He] has . . . made some good scores this year, his "upper cut" being particularly effective' (*Lilly-white's Guide*, 128). The ball flies over the slips-gully area, infuriating fast bowlers.

uppish, upstroke   a stroke that puts the ball in the air.

utility player   who can do a bit of everything, see also *bits-and-pieces player*.

V A drive played through the V which is formed by the batsman at the base and mid-on and mid-off at the end of the two arms.

Tall and not an obviously natural mover – though he won a Soccer blue at Cambridge as an inside-forward – he stroked the ball from off the front foot and the back foot, and because he played so straight he favoured the 'V' between wide mid-off and wide mid-on. He was a classic on-driver, the shot he liked best – timed easily and effortlessly, the ball sped past mid-on's right hand to the boundary. (Hubert Doggart on Peter May, *Journal of The Cricket Society*, Spring 1993).

Wag when the tail scores unexpected runs, it *wags*, and it wagged longest when Arthur Kippax of New South Wales, supreme stylist, was joined by Hal Hooker at no. 11 in the Sheffield Shield match against Victoria in the 1930s. They took the score from 113 for 9 to 420, the world record for the tenth wicket.

waft means to wave the hand, thus a wave of the bat, not a firm stroke: can be either off or legside. See also *hanging out to dry*.

walk to voluntarily dismiss oneself, usually if a faint snick is caught behind the wicket. David Gower was a practitioner. 'Ferreira sportingly walked on looping a silent bat-and-pad chance to Bruce French' (Doug Ibbotson, *Daily Telegraph Century of County Cricket*, on Notts v. Warwicks 25–8 August 1984). Thus *walker*, one who *walks*.

warn, warning given by an umpire for persistent unfair play, including intimidatory bowling, or for the bowler running on the pitch, making a *rough* patch, or given by bowler to batsman for backing up too far before the ball is bowled.

watchers-out an old name for fielders. 'Little Tom Clement is visiting at Petersfield, where he plays much at cricket: his grandmother bowls: and his great-grandmother watches out!!!' Gilbert White, author of *A Natural History of Selborne*, writing in 1768.

web refers purely to the spinner, and his real or imagined cunning. Thus Terry Alderman for the ABC in the Fourth Test at Adelaide: 'Shane Warne will now try to spin his web.' And Derek Pringle refers to 'A WEB OF ENGLAND'S MAKING', headline in *The Independent*, 4 December 1994.

welly of obscure origin, possibly attributable to welly-throwing or welly-whanging competitions of the 1960s. 'Solanki, hitherto the epitome of common sense, decided it was time for some welly and located extra-cover' means he decided to hit out and was caught (Rob Steen, *Sunday Times*, 10 September 1995).

whale a sopper-upping machine, or a super sopper-upper, used to soak up water from a pitch. Durham CCC's was stolen in 1995, though why nobody knows.

wheel said either of a field, Bradman setting a *wheel* (or *umbrella*) for Compton at Adelaide in 1948 to stop boundaries and even encourage him to run two at the end of an over, so that his partner Godfrey Evans would have to face the next over; or of the circular arm action of the bowler. *Wheeling away* implies a long spell from a slow bowler: 'As the afternoon wore on ... and Richard Illingworth wheeled away, gradually the home batsmen scraped and saved the last 37 runs to avert the follow-on' (Scyld Berry, *Sunday Telegraph*, 10 December 1995).

whip, whipped   movement of the bat is fast and wristy: 'Lara was quickly into his stride, playing that famous whipped shot off his legs ...' as Peter Deeley reported from the Kingston Test, Australia vs West Indies 1995 series. *Whip-hook*: 'When seventy-seven in 140 minutes ... Boycott whip-hooked Connolly, and Gleeson held the catch' (Whitington, 316).

whippy   springy, backbone-bending action of a bowler. See also *inswinger*.

wicket   refers, or should refer, only to the stumps and the bails and the events that befall them. Thus 'I wonder what the wicket will do', suggesting the stumps may suddenly march in file down the *pitch* or start leap-frogging each other, is strictly nonsense, and deprecated by the editors of both *WCM* and *The Cricketer*. However, OED has as examples 'the wicket did not seem to play particularly well' (1881), and 'the English eleven commenced batting on a perfect wicket.' And there is no phrase *sticky pitch*, but *sticky wicket*, or *dog*.

Originally about two feet wide by one foot high in the days of under-arm bowling and the popping crease, the size was changed to 22″ by 6″ in 1779–80, when the third stump was added.

The etymology of the word is given in the introduction, and the earliest description of the wicket seems to agree: John Nyren, author of *The Young Cricketer's Tutor* (1833) and son of Richard Nyren, one of the Hambledon greats, had been given a small manuscript 'by an old cricketer', which stated that about 150 years before (thus around 1683), the pitch was the same length, but the wicket one foot high by two wide. Nyren thought that was an error, but it is probably correct: the low wide wicket, with or without popping-hole, seems to be still in use when the first Laws in 1744 ordain: 'The Bail hanging on one Stump, though the Ball hit the Wicket, it's Not Out.' This must mean, at the least, that the wicket was then wider than long.

The hole seems to be in the wicket crease itself: 'Between the stumps a hole was cut in the ground, large enough to contain the ball and the butt-end of the bat. To run a notch, the striker was required to put the bat into this hole,' and the wicket-keeper had to pop the ball in there first to run him out. Obviously, this needed a wide wicket. It also led to so many hand injuries that the rule changed, perhaps first to tapping the umpire's bat where he stood at silly leg slip, then to running the bat in as today, with the popping crease now an ell's distance in front of the stumps: the name has been retained. Curiously, the custom of the umpire taking a bat with him, for no apparent reason, survived until the 1950s, at least in preparatory schools. This is also remarked by Frank Tyson in *Terms of the Game* in junior cricket. That there was now a wicket with bail across it is beyond any doubt from Littleton's *Latine Dictionary* of 1678, which defines *vibia* as 'A pole or stick laid across on forks, like the Cricket-bar at ball-play.'

The third stump had been tried before; the *Hampshire Gazette* of September 1776 saying 'Another match of cricket will be played on Broad-Halfpenny Down, at Hambleden, 5 of a side [the common number then], where they are to have three stumps instead of two, in order to shorten the game.' And three stumps were used in the Kent vs. Hambledon game at Sevenoaks Vine in 1777. The Vine has had cricket on it for at least 250 years, and was presented to the town by the third Duke of Dorset in 1773. The philanthropy of the Duke extended to his attempting to import the game to France, he having had to interrupt his cricketing to become the ambassador in Paris. The task of getting the team across the Channel was entrusted to the licensed victualler Yalden of catching fame above. But at Dover they were met by the Duke. The French Revolution had broken out. Had they set out a week earlier, what might not have happened to the course of history?

The wicket was gradually enlarged, to 24″ by 7″ in 1798, then to 26″ by 7″ in 1819, according to Haygarth's *Scores and Biographies*. Then another inch all round was added around 1820, and two bails became common (see also under *bail*). 'Before 1820 the title of MCC to control the terms of important cricket was not admitted,' as H. P.-T. puts it. In 1797 the Earl of Winchelsea had four stumps instead of three, and another two inches on the wicket, which made bowling out easier, and the game shorter (*Hampshire Chronicle*, 15 July 1797). This may have had something to do with the new straight bats with shoulders, because in 1773 *Kentish Cricketers* has the lines 'Unlike the modern way/Of blocking every ball at play'. Finally, in 1931, perhaps as a result of the high scores on perfect *pitches* in 1930, another inch was added to both height and width, to 28½″ × 9″, the present size.

The result of a match can be expressed in terms of wickets left standing, or to spare, when the batting side overhauls the target total: 'The Wellesburn match was played out with great success yesterday, the School winning by three wickets' (Hughes, *Tom Brown's School Days*, II.viii, 1857).

The batting side makes *stands* for each wicket: 'Hobbs and Rhodes carried their partnership to 323 in 268 minutes . . . the stand – not chanceless – remains an England–Australia *first-wicket record*' (Frith, *England v. Australia*, 113).

Wickets fall when they are taken by the fielding side, and the innings of a side is completed when ten of the batting side are out or retired, unless a declaration has been made.

Wickets are captured by a bowler: 'Shane Warne captured four wickets in six balls, three of them stumped, to bowl Australia to a 23-run victory over South Africa' (*The Times*, 19 October 1994). They may also have a *haul*, or *tally*, whether over an innings, a season, or a career.

wicket-keeper the fielder behind the striker's stumps, who takes the ball from the bowler's delivery. Denoted by a dagger on the scoreboard. Originally it was 'the duty of the bowler to be the wicket-keeper at his own wicket, during the intervals of his own bowling. He will have many balls to stop in the field, and many a struggle will ensue between him and the batsman, one to get the run, and the other to save it' (Nyren in Lucas, 20). Wearing gloves and pads, 'J. M'Carthy Blackham had practically all his front teeth knocked out, being one of the first to stand up to the stumps' (Standing, 128).

The highest record innings without byes is Hampshire's 672 at Taunton in 1899, and the Revd Wickham kept wicket for that. Gordon Strong in *The Cricketer* of 1983 records that Wickham would wear a Harlequin cap, black-topped pads, grey flannels, and a black cummerbund. Godfrey Evans sealed his presence in the England side in the 1946/7 series when in Australia's total of 659 at Sydney in 1947 he did not concede a single bye.

wicket-keeper-batsman considered as an all-rounder, a player who would hold his own in a side for either. Pre-eminent would be Leslie Ames of England and Kent, who did the wicket-keeper's double of 1000 runs and 100 wickets in a season three times. He also scored a hundred hundreds. The unortho-dox determination of Jack Russell, Gloucestershire and England, made him the most successful batsman in the England team touring South Africa 1995–6.

wicket-keepers' union reference to loquacity of the breed: 'he wouldn't be a member of the wicket-keepers' union if he didn't have something to say' – Ian Chappell of Steve Rhodes, as Steve Waugh missed cutting Phil Tufnell, 2nd Test at Sydney 1994 (Sky TV).

wicket maiden   an over in which the bowler takes a wicket and no runs are marked down to the bowler, including no-balls and wides. When Paul Adams of South Africa had Mike Watkinson of Lancashire and England lbw with a *chinaman* in the final Test at Capetown on 4 January 1996, his over read OOOWOO: it was only a single *wicket maiden* as Graham Thorpe had been run out off the first ball.

wickie   slang for wicket-keeper, rather pejorative: 'the little race of Wickies' (Barnes, 43).

wide   a ball which passes out of the batsman's reach, first recorded as such in 1827. Some *wides* are wider than others, depending on the type of game, one-day cricket giving less margin for error. Batsmen can be out to a wide as follows: hit wicket, run out, handled the ball, obstructing the field, or stumped, this last being an occasional weapon of the slow bowler: 'Udal pushed the ball cleverly down the leg side and Rhodes completed the stumping, given out by umpire Ken Palmer at square leg and wide by Mervyn Kitchen at the bowler's end' (*The Cricketer*, October 1994).

willow   from the Teutonic, the English form *wilwe* present in the 14th century. The tree, a dicotyledon very closely related to the poplar, has over 150 varieties world-wide. The bark has been chewed for centuries, one of its constituents being an ingredient of aspirin. One of the types of willow is called the creak willow as the branches break underfoot with a dry crack: a possible, but rather unlikely, derivation of or contribution to the word cricket itself. The only tree that has the ability to be made into a cricket bat is one variety, *Salix caerulea*: *caerulea* having a Latin meaning riverine as well as cerulean, it simply means 'river willow'. Its lightness and resilience make it almost ideal: no other wood has been found suitable. See *bat*.

windmill   most often applied to bowlers who take a preparatory swing or swings of the arm in the strides before delivery: 'A change in bowling was tried, Wardill going on with his "windmills"' (Bettesworth, 124). See also *cartwheel*.

winkle   'You get two guys stuck in, and it takes some time to winkle or wheedle them out ...' Geoff Boycott, BBC TV commentating on the First Test at Old Trafford, 1993. He means that by hard thought or low cunning, the batsmen would be deceived or tempted into error, perhaps by guilefully flighting an over, or by the adept positioning of a fielder for a catch.

Wisden's   even by itself is understood as the Almanac, akin to the reputation once enjoyed by *The Times*, a publication of record. Founded by John Wisden in 1864 and developed, via some incongruous byways, into the annual we know today. See *Wonder*.

wobble   a ball that has an eccentric movement, or a corkscrew effect, along its horizontal axis, as its goes towards the batsman. (See also *swing*.) Also one of the grades of the wax applied to the twine of the ball.

Wonder, the Little   John Wisden, the fast bowler and founder of the Almanac, which he edited 1865–85. On his Sussex debut in 1846, at nineteen, he stood 5′ 4″ and weighed 7 stone.

work   *work the ball around* means to send it to different parts of the field. Mid-19th-century usage was the same as *break*, *turn*.

workhorse   a stock bowler, used to bowling long periods at a time. Dick Pollard of Lancashire was called the 'chain horse', an animal used for pulling barges and opening lock gates, he 'worried Bradman as much as any bowler England produced . . . Dick Pollard was a magnificent trier . . .' (Hammond, *Secret History*, 60). Tom Richardson was called 'the carthorse' for the same reason.

wrist-spin   spin of any kind imparted with the wrist rather than the fingers, e.g. right-hand bowler's *leg-break*, or the *googly*.

wrist, wristy, wristwork   'The strength that sends a ball to the boundary comes not from the weight of the bat but from timing and good wrists' (Hammond, *Secret History*, 51). The story is told that Walter Lindrum, the great Australian billiards champion, refused to play Sir Donald Bradman because of the strength of his wrists.

wrong'un   Australian term for *googly*.

Y **ips**   'Research by James Watson at the Chelsea School of Physical Education in London suggests that a number of yips sufferers find they can bowl perfectly well until they are being watched by others' (*The Third Man*, September 1995, 10). Also used in golf, and of obscure origin, it denotes the inability to perform on the occasion.

yorker, to york   a delivery that *yorks* the batsman. It lands on the popping crease, or even further up, at the base of the stumps. The batsman cannot get his bat down in time, often thinking it is a half-volley or full toss while disaster zooms in. Notable exponents have been Jeff Thomson with his 'sandshoe crusher', Curtly Ambrose with height, Waqar Younis with late in-swing. The *yorker* starting on the leg-stump, and moving late to uproot the off, was practised by F.S. Trueman. The origin seems obscure: it emerges at the end of the 19th century, and must come at the earliest from the general adoption of over-arm bowling. In October 1870 *Baily's Magazine* refers to a Surrey bowler as 'fast and straight, and not infrequently delivers that useful kind of ball known as a Yorker.' A.G. Steel 'can find no derivation . . . but we are told that it came from Yorkshire-men, who were fonder of bowling this ball than any other' (BLC, 1888, 133).

Z **at** colloquial pronunciation of the cricket appeal 'How's that?' 'Not a bad record ... for a game that consists chiefly of standing about ... and shouting "Zat?" at intervals' (*Humorist*, 27 January 1934: OED).

References

Place of publication is London, unless otherwise stated.

Altham, H. S. (1962 edn) *A History of Cricket*, George Allen & Unwin.

Arlott, John (1989) *The Essential John Arlott*, Willow Books.

Armstrong, Warwick (1922) *The Art of Cricket*, Methuen & Co.

Alverstone, Lord and Alcock, C. W. (eds) (1904) *Surrey Cricket, Its History and Associations*, Longmans & Co.

Badminton Library of Sports and Pastimes: *Cricket* (1888–), essays by several authors

Baily's Monthly Magazine of Sports and Pastimes (1860–88), then as *Baily's Magazine . . .* (1869–1926)

Ball, Peter and Hopps, David (eds) *The Book of Cricket Quotations*, Stanley Paul.

Barnes, Simon, (1989) *A la Recherche du Cricket Perdu*, Macmillan.

Batchelor, Denzil (ed.) (1967) *Best Cricket Stories*, Faber & Faber.

Beldam, G. and Fry, C. B. (1906) *Great Bowlers and Fielders*, Macmillan & Co.

Bell's Life in London and Sporting Chronicle (1822–86)

Benaud, Richie (1984) *On Reflection*, Collins.

Bleackley, H. (1901) *Tales of the Stumps*, Ward, Lock & Co.

Border, Allan (1986) *An Autobiography*, North Ryde: Methuen.

Bowen, Roland (1970) *Cricket: A History of its Growth and Development throughout the World*, Eyre & Spottiswoode.

Bowes, Bill (1978) *In Celebration of Cricket*, Granada.

Box, C. (1868) *The Theory and Practice of Cricket*, F. Warne & Co.

Box, C. (1877) *The English Game of Cricket*, The Field.

Boycott, Geoff (1990) *Boycott on Cricket*, Partridge Press.

Bradman, Sir Donald (1958) *The Art of Cricket*, Hodder & Stoughton.

Brodribb, Gerald (1953) *The Next Man In*, The Sportsman's Book Club.

Cardus, Sir Neville (1924) *Days in the Sun*, Grant Richards.

Cardus, Sir Neville (1949) *The Essential Neville Cardus*, Jonathan Cape.

Cardus, Sir Neville (1977 edn) *Cardus on Cricket*, Souvenir Press.

Cardus, Sir Neville and Arlott, John (1969) *The Noblest Game*, Harrap.

Chappell, Ian (1992) *The Cutting Edge*, Western Australia: Swan Publications.

Clarke, [William] (1851) *Practical Hints [on the game of cricket]*.

Collyer, David (1993) 'An Engineering Study of the Cricket Bat', Bolton Institute of Higher Education.

Compton, D. C. S. (1980) *Cricketers Past and Present*, Cassell.

Compton, D. C. S. (1988) *End of an Innings*, Pavilion Books.

Cricket Lore (November 1991–), Cricket Lore Publishing Ltd.

Cricketer, The (1921–), now *The Cricketer International*.

Denison, W. (1846) *Cricket, Sketches of the Players*, Simpkin, Marshall & Co.

Denison, W. (1846, 1847) *The Cricketers' Companion*.

Dickens, Charles (1837) *The Posthumous Papers of the Pickwick Club*.

Duckworth, Leslie (1968) *S. F. Barnes – Master Bowler*, The Sportsman's Book Club.

Farjeon, Herbert (1969) *Herbert Farjeon's Cricket Bag*, Pelham Books.

Fender, P. G. H. (1994) 'The Art and Craft of Fielding', in Moult.

Fingleton, Jack (1949) *Brightly Fades the Don*, Pavilion Library.

Fingleton, Jack (1972) *Fingleton on Cricket*, Collins.

Fitzgerald, R. A. (1873) *Wickets in the West; or, the Twelve in America*.

Francis, Tony (1992) *The Zen of Cricket*, Stanley Paul.

Frith, David (1984) *England vs Australia*, Willow Books.

Frith, David (1984) *The Slow Men*, George Allen & Unwin.

Gale, Fred (1885) *The Life of the Hon. Robert Grimston*, Longmans & Co.

Gale, Fred (1887) *Game of Cricket*, Sonnenschein & Co.

Giffen, George (1898), *With Bat and Ball*, Ward, Lock & Co.

Gower, David with Martin Johnson (1992) *The Autobiography*, Willow Books.

Grace, W. G. (1891) *Outdoor Games*.

Grace, W. G. (1899) *"W.G." Cricketing Reminiscences and Personal Recollections*, J. Bowden.

Grant, C. and Thethi, P. (1994) 'Impact mechanics of the bat and ball', in *Proceedings of the 10th International Conference on Experimental Mechanics*, Lisbon, 18–22 July.

Green, Benny (1988) *A History of Cricket*, Guild Publishing.

H.P.–T. (1994) *Early English Cricket, Six Pamphlets* [1st edn 1922–9], Willow Press.

Hammond, Walter (1950) *Cricketers' School*, Stanley Paul & Co.

Hammond, Walter (1952) *Cricket's Secret History*, Stanley Paul & Co.

Harris, G. R. C. (Baron Harris) (1921) *A Few Short Runs*, John Murray.

Harris, G. R. C. (Baron Harris) and F. S. Ashley-Cooper, (1914) *Lord's and the MCC*, London & Counties Press Association.

Haygarth, A. *Scores and Biographies*, vols 5 and 6 of *F. Lillywhite's Cricket Scores and Biographies of celebrated cricketers from 1746* (1862–), Longmans.

Heffer, Simon (ed.) (1990) *The Daily Telegraph Century of County Cricket The Hundred best Matches*, Sidgwick & Jackson.

Hele, George (1974) *Bodyline Umpire*, Adelaide: Rigby.

Heller, Hume and Dror (1984) *The Private Lives of English Words*, Routledge & Kegan Paul.

Hobbs, Jack (1912) *Recovering the Ashes*, Sir Isaac Pitman & Sons.

Hobbs, Jack (1931) *Playing for England*, Victor Gollancz.

Holland, F. C. (1904) *Cricket*, All England Series.

Holmes, R. S. (1904) *The History of Yorkshire County Cricket*.

James, C. L. R. (1969) *Beyond a Boundary*, Stanley Paul.

Jardine, Douglas (1933) *In Quest of the Ashes*, Hutchinson & Co.

Jessop, Gilbert (1925) *Cricket and How to Play It*, G. G. Harrap & Co.

Keating, Frank (1986) *Gents and Players*, Robson Books.

Knight, A. E. (1906) *Complete Cricketer*, Methuen & Co.

Larwood, Harold, with Kevin Perkins (1965) *The Larwood Story*, W. H. Allen.

Lawrence, B. (1988) *100 Great West Indian Test Cricketers*, Hansib Publications.

Lewis, W. J. (1934) *The Language of Cricket*, Oxford University Press.

Lilley, A. A. (1912), *Twenty-Four Years' Cricket*, Mills & Boon.

Lillywhite, F. (1865) *F. Lillywhite's Guide to Cricketers*.

Lillywhite, John (1867) *Cricketers' Companion*.

Lucas, E. V. (ed.) (1952 edn) *The Hambledon Men*, 'Being a new edition of John Nyren's "Young Cricketer's Tutor", together with a collection of other matter drawn from various sources all bearing on the great batsmen and bowlers before round-arm came in', The Sportsman's Book Club.

Lyttelton, R. H. (1901) *Out-door Games*, Haddon Hall Library.

McKendrick, Fergus (1983) *Pulpit Cricket and Other Stories*
    Willow Books.
Maclaren, Archie (1924) *Cricket Old and New*, Longmans & Co.
Marriott, C. S. (1968) *The Complete Leg-Break Bowler*, Eyre &
    Spottiswoode.
Marshall, John (1959) *Sussex Cricket*, Heinemann.
Meher-Homji, Kersi (1993) *Out for a DUCK*, NSW: Kangaroo
    Press.
Meher-Homji, Kersi (1996) *Hat-Tricks*, NSW: Kangaroo Press.
Mehta, Rabi (1985) 'The Aerodynamics of Sports Balls', *Annual
    Review of Fluid Mechanics*, vol. 17, pp. 151–89.
Mehta, Rabi & Wood, David (7 August 1980) 'Aerodynamics of
    the cricket ball', *New Scientist*, vol. 87, pp. 442–7.
Meredith, Anthony (1987) *The Demon and the Lobster: Charles
    Kortrig*, Kingswood Press.
Meredith, George (1860) *Evan Harrington*.
Mitford, Revd John (September 1833) *Gentleman's Magazine*.
Moor, E. (1823) *Suffolk Words and Phrases*, Woodbridge: J.
    Loder.
Mosey, Don (1989) *Laker*, Queen Anne Press.
Mosey, Don (1991) *Fred Then and Now*, Mandarin.
Moult, Thomas (ed.) (1994) *Bat and Ball: Book of Cricket*,
    Magna Books (first edn 1935).
Munns, Joy (1994) *Beyond Reasonable Doubt . . . the birthplace of
    the Ashes*, Melbourne.
Nyren, John (1833) *Young Cricketer's Tutor*, reprinted in Lucas.
Nyren, John (1833) *The Cricketers of My Time*, reprinted in
    Lucas.
Oslear, Don, with Don Mosey (1988) *The Wisden Book of
    Cricket Laws*, Stanley Paul.
Padwick, Eric W. (1984 edn) *A Bibliography of Cricket*, The
    Library Association in association with McKenzie Bookseller
    on behalf of the Cricket Society.
Pardon, G. F. (1860) *Cricket, Its Theory and Practice*, London &
    Edinburgh: K. Chambers.
Payn, James (1888) *The Mystery of Mirdbridge*, Chatto &
    Windus.
Pentelow, J. N. (1895) *England v. Australia*, Arrowsmith's Bristol
    Library.
Playfair Cricket Annual (1962).
Potter, Stephen (1947) *Gamesmanship*, Rupert Hart-Davis.
Pycroft, Revd James (1851) *Cricket Field*.
Rait Kerr, Col. R. S. (1950) *The Laws of Cricket: Their Growth
    and History*, Longmans Green & Co.

Ranjitsinhji, K. S. (1897) *Jubilee Book of Cricket*, Edinburgh & London: W. Blackwood & Sons.

Ranjitsinhji, K. S. (1898, 3rd edn) *With Stoddart's Team in Australia*, J. Bowden.

Raven, Simon (1982) *Shadows on the Grass*, Blond & Brigs.

Robertson-Glasgow, R. C. (1943) *Cricket Prints*, T. Werner Laurie.

Robertson-Glasgow, R. C. (1985) *Crusoe on Cricket*, Pavilion Library.

Roebuck, Peter (1987) *Ashes to Ashes: the 1986-n87 Test Series*, Kingswood Press.

Ross, Alan (ed.) (1960) *Cricketer's Companion*, Eyre Methuen.

Selkirk, G. H. (1867) *Guide to the Cricket Ground*, London & Cambridge.

Shawcroft, John (1986) *Derbyshire Bowlers*, Derbyshire: J. Hall & Sons.

Simons, John *History of Cricket in Hampshire 1760–1914*, Hampshire County Council.

Standing, Percy Cross (1902) *Cricket*, London & Edinburgh: T. C. & E. C. Jack.

Swanton, E. W. (1951) *Elusive Victory*, Hodder & Stoughton.

Swanton, E. H. (1957) *Report from South Africa, with P. B. H. May's M. C. C. Team 1956–57*, Robert Hale.

Swanton, E. W., with Michael Melford (1966) *Barclay's World of Cricket*, Michael Joseph.

Taylor, A. D. (1903) *Annals of Lord's and History of the MCC*, Simpkin, Marshall & Co.

Thomson, A. A. (1958) *Odd Men In*, Museum Press.

Tinniswood, Peter (1985) *The Punch Book of Cricket*, Granada Publishing.

Trueman, F. S. with Peter Grosvenor (1990) *Fred Trueman's Cricket Masterpieces*, Sidgwick & Jackson.

Tyson, Frank (1990) *Terms of the Game*, Australia: Houghton Mifflin.

Verity, Hedley (1994) 'The Best Bowling I Have Ever Done', in Moult.

Waghorn, H. T. (1899) *Cricket Scores, Notes &c. from 1730 to 1773*, London & Edinburgh: W. Blackwood & Sons.

Warner, P. F. (1900) *Cricket in Many Climes*, W. Heinemann.

Warner, P. F. (1904) *How We Recovered the Ashes*, Chapman & Hall.

Whitington, R. S. (1974) *Book of Australian Test Matches*, Melbourne: Wren Publishing.

Wilde, Simon (1994) *Letting Rip*, Gollancz/Witherby.

Wilkins, Brian (1991) *The Bowler's Art*, A. & C. Black.

Williams, Marcus (ed.) (1983) *The Way to Lord's: Cricketing Letters to 'The Times'*, Willow Books.

Wilson, F. B. (1922) *Sporting Pie*, Chapman and Hall.

Wisden Cricket Monthly

Wodehouse, P. G. (1903) *Tales of St Austin's*, A. & C. Black.

Wodehouse, P. G. (1988) *The Parrot and Other Poems*, Hutchinson.

Wykehamist, A (1843) *Practical Hints on Cricket*.